THE GHOSTS OF
HERO STREET

THE GHOSTS OF
HERO STREET

How One Small Mexican-American Community
Gave So Much in World War II and Korea

Carlos Harrison

BERKLEY CALIBER, NEW YORK

THE BERKLEY PUBLISHING GROUP
Published by the Penguin Group
Penguin Group (USA) LLC
375 Hudson Street, New York, New York 10014

USA • Canada • UK • Ireland • Australia • New Zealand • India • South Africa • China

penguin.com

A Penguin Random House Company

This book is an original publication of The Berkley Publishing Group.

THE GHOSTS OF HERO STREET

ISBN: 978-0-425-26253-5

An application to register this book for cataloging has been submitted to the Library of Congress.

First edition: May 2014

PRINTED IN THE UNITED STATES OF AMERICA

10 9 8 7 6 5 4 3 2 1

Interior text design by Tiffany Estreicher

CONTENTS

THE GHOSTS OF
HERO STREET

CHAPTER ONE

HERO STREET, U.S.A.

On the brilliant, crisp morning of Memorial Day, 1968, a crowd gathered at the foot of Billy Goat Hill. They shuffled expectantly, craning to see the Los Amigos Marching Band parade into view in their dazzling orange satin shirts and flat-brimmed bolero hats. The sun glinted off line after line of bobbing horns as the band strutted up the street. Cameras flashed and children clapped. Then smiles flickered through the crowd like the twinkling of stars, as they recognized the song the band played and the words echoed in the onlookers' minds.

It was a deliciously ironic choice of music for the event. But, on this day, for this crowd, few songs could have been better than "America" from *West Side Story*. The story of misunderstood and shunned Hispanics trying to make their way in America was one they knew too well.

As the notes faded away and the band stomped to a halt, Joe Terronez stepped forward. He read out eight names. Then, a small huddle of dignitaries unveiled the new red, white, and blue street sign marking the corner of Second Street and First Avenue. It read, "Hero Street, U.S.A."

The spectators applauded wildly. Tears—sad, proud, and bittersweet—streaked the cheeks of men and women alike. It was a moment more than a decade in the making. All the fighting and all the frustration had finally paid off. They had won.

Terronez smiled.

The mass of people included friends and relatives of the eight men Terronez had named, journalists, and a U.S. congressman, Thomas Railsback of Illinois.

"I am proud to represent this neighborhood whose families generously gave the best they had to this country," Railsback told the crowd. "I question whether any group in this country has done more."

In fact, no other place had. It was barely a block-and-a-half long, a rocky earthen trail pockmarked with potholes, but that tiny street in that tiny railroad town had earned its new designation with the blood and tears of its residents. The Department of Defense examined the records and determined that the families of Second Street in Silvis, Illinois, had sent more of their children to serve in World War II and Korea than residents of any other similarly sized stretch in the country.

Despite that distinction and its lofty new name, the street remained an unpaved strip of dirt that turned to mud when it rained.

This was where the families had been forced to live—in abandoned railroad boxcars, away from the rest of the city's white residents—simply because their parents were Mexican. They had no electricity, no running water. They used outhouses even in the deep of winter. Snow blew through the cracks in the boxcar walls, and the kids had to punch through the ice in their washbowls to clean up in the morning. The children worked in the fields, topping onions, before they were even old enough for school, and they lied about their age to get jobs on the railroad when they got to junior high. The other schoolkids called them "dirty Mexicans."

Still, when war threatened the country they now called home, the men had stepped up to defend it.

One family sent seven; another, six. In all, the twenty-two families who lived on that one street sent fifty-seven of their children to fight. Eight died.

And not just anyplace.

Somehow, out of the thousands of battlefields where they could have fought, the eight had ended up at key turning points of both conflicts, engaging in crucial battles and participating in new, pivotal ways of waging war.

Death found them in many ways, and many places—in a distant jungle, a frozen forest, and trapped in the flaming wreckage of a bomber blown from the sky. One died going over a fence during the greatest paratrooper assault in history; another, in the biggest battle of World War II; yet another, riddled with bullets in an audacious act of heroism during a decisive onslaught a world, and a war, away.

Frank Sandoval toiled in the leech-infested jungles of what is now Myanmar, carving the Burma Road that served as a lifeline for America's Chinese allies and helping to push the Japanese back across the Pacific. The effort was part of what is now known as the forgotten front, the China-Burma-India Theater. It was a wild battle zone with its own rules—employing a mercenary air force and cutthroat natives—and gave rise to the stealthy commando tactics of Merrill's Marauders, the unit that gave birth to today's Rangers.

Tony Pompa wielded a double-barreled .50-caliber machine gun in the tail of a B-24, in the thin, dangerous corridor between flak and fighters in the sky over Italy. He was part of the newly evolving air war, where long-range bombers played a vital and devastating role in crippling Germany's war machine, against huge odds. Half the gunners died. In all, the Americans lost more than 18,000 combat planes and 79,000 men on missions aimed at destroying Nazi fuel depots and weapons factories. Willie Sandoval and Peter Masias were among the first U.S. paratroopers to jump into combat. Willie fought over the jagged, frozens mountains of Italy, got pinned down in the months-long horror of Anzio Beach, and jumped into Holland as part of the greatest airborne assault in history. Peter arrived on the most frigid Christmas Eve to hit Europe in more than one hundred years, brought in to rescue the decimated and panicked forces being crushed by a Panzer blitzkrieg, and died in the final airborne assault of the war.

Claro Soliz and Frank's big brother Joe joined the battle in Normandy, captured Saint-Lô, and fought through the fields of France and Belgium on the road to Berlin. Claro died fighting in the bitter cold of the Battle of the Bulge—Hitler's desperate last-ditch effort to halt the relentless Allied advance, the biggest engagement of the war. Joe made it to just a few miles from Hitler's bunker, and just a few days from Germany's surrender.

Peace returned to Hero Street, and so did the survivors. The men who continued to wear their uniforms found themselves in a peacetime military with duties far removed from the horrors of war, close to home or as occupation forces in Germany or Japan.

Then came another war, against a different enemy. Joe Gomez and Johnny Muños went to Korea to face freezing cold and hordes of Chinese, and to fight and die during the brutal, massive onslaught of the Spring Offensive, the largest single battle of the war. A half-million Chinese and North Korean forces sprang suddenly from hiding, screaming and blowing battle horns as they swarmed the

United Nations forces. Eighty thousand died or were wounded. The mortar-and-rocket exchange was so fierce it left the battlefield barren for months.

Joe earned a Silver Star for his actions, delivered posthumously to his widow and baby daughter.

They hadn't set out to be heroes. They hadn't even gone looking for a fight. Not that they wouldn't. There had been plenty of that growing up. They had balled their fists lots of times and gone wading into a melee with wide grins, ready to defend their friend, their girl, or their pride. Or just for fun. Almost all had taken a turn in the boxing ring at one time or another. Two had done well enough that there had been suggestions of professional possibilities. Willie's gloves had taken him to Chicago, for the regional Golden Gloves competition. Joe Gomez, known as "Cheppe" to his friends, came at his opponents hunched and hard to hit. He had more grit than style, but he seemed perpetually ready for a chance to duke it out, in or out of the ring.

This time, though, the fight came looking for them.

War came to Second Street the way it did to the rest of the nation—in a sudden, shocking jolt. The Japanese planes diving out of the bright, blue Sunday morning sky at Pearl Harbor struck into the hearts of Americans across the country. People stared at their radios, stunned into silence as the news poured simultaneously into living rooms in every corner of the land, and a collective shudder of shock swept the nation. It was as if a massive earthquake had hit the country all at once, and all Americans knew that the ground they walked on would never be the same again. A similar feeling was unknown until the terrorist attacks on 9/11.

Then, as outrage replaced horror, the men began lining up at recruiting centers. Claro Soliz grabbed his brother Maugie and headed for the station in Moline. Others may not have been in as big a rush, but as the call-up letters arrived in the mail, the men of Second Street stood up to do their duty.

When Korea came, they did it again. It was an unpopular conflict that few in the country backed, but they did what they had to do.

In these wars, everyone played a part—whether they felt wanted or not. To the Mexican-American families of Second Street, the fight wasn't about black or brown or white; it was about red, white, and blue. Men across the nation came together to stand against common enemies and to stand for common ideals.

Second Street, though, sent more. And suffered more—extraordinarily so, compared to the rest of the nation. Overall, just 2 percent of the American troops died fighting in World War II and Korea. Second Street lost 14 percent—seven times the national average.

Still, considering the places they fought, it seems astonishing that more didn't die.

Louis Ramirez fought the Japanese in the horrifyingly vicious battle for Guadalcanal. Lost in the jungle alone as thousands of Imperial Army defenders flooded onto the island, uncertain even of what day it was, he made a promise to God. If he could get home and get married, he would name his first child for the saint's day on which he was found. He came home permanently tortured by visions of what he had seen and forever reluctant to talk about what happened, but he kept his promise. He named his firstborn Martina, for St. Martin's Day.

Tony Pompa's cousin Luz Segura, known on the street as "Slugger," chased the Nazis across northern France and into the bitter cold of Belgium as part of an artillery crew—always within just a few miles of Joe Sandoval. They went through the hedgerow country and the death traps known as the "Valleys of Death"; across the land of the Walloons and into the Ruhr pocket, where resolute and unyielding SS troops resisted to the death; and they cowered in the snow-covered hills of the Ardennes as Nazi V-2s roared down on them. Luz saw men around him die and others try to kill him. But, amazingly, he came home unscathed, unbowed and ready to move on. He met the woman he would share his life with the week after he got home, and spent the next five decades adoring her.

Claro Soliz's nephew Frank faced suicidal kamikaze pilots hurling their aircraft at his ship off the shore of Okinawa, but lived to crack a warm beer the day the Japanese surrendered.

Phil Garza joined the Marines and followed his buddy Johnny Muños to Korea. He fought across the freezing mountains, wracked by fever and flu. He came home and married Willie Sandoval's little sister.

Manny Herrera. Tom Gomez. Bennie Montez. Tony Cedillo. Louis Belman.

The list goes on.

In all, the men of Second Street fought in jungles and in forests, on mountaintops and plains, in the air and on the sea. They carried their guns in blazing heat and blistering cold, in places where it never rained and places where it never seemed to stop.

Yet, despite all they had given and all they had done, when the surviving veterans of Second Street came home, they found that things hadn't changed that much. The street still wasn't paved. Most of the houses still lacked indoor plumbing. And the battle-weary veterans from Second Street weren't allowed to join the local VFW because of their Mexican heritage. They weren't "white enough."

That made Joe Terronez mad.

Terronez had grown up looking up to the Hero Street Eight.

They were the older boys whose sheer gumption earned them a place playing side by side with the white kids on the McKinley School basketball court, even if they were too poor to afford their own sneakers. They played in shoes discarded by their wealthier team-mates. Terronez trotted along beside them as they walked over the hill to school, and ducked as they pelted one another with green apples plucked from the orchard along the way. On Sunday morn-ings he bowed his head with them and watched as they traded fur-tive glances with the dark-eyed girls in the pews at the Our Lady of Guadalupe Catholic Church. And he knew that if a bigger kid from any of the other streets threatened a boy on their block, one of the older Second Streeters would come running to deliver justice.

So when Terronez saw the veterans turned away from the VFW, he decided it was his turn to stand up for them.

It would take a different kind of fight. One the Mexican-Americans were new to.

When Terronez began, it was the late 1950s. Times were tense. A divide remained between America's lighter and darker skinned citi-zens. They may have fought side by side in Korea—at least that much had changed since World War II—but back home integration was a long way off. The seeds of the Civil Rights Movement had begun to grow, but prejudice, discrimination, and, too often, vio-lence marked relations between the races. Restaurants posted signs that read, "No Mexicans, Niggers or Dogs Allowed." Lynchings were common—for Mexicans as well as blacks.

Segregation followed them even into death: Mexican-Americans were banned from many white cemeteries.

But change was in the air. Terronez knew that blacks were using peaceful protests and boycotting businesses to force change. But as a budding young activist in Silvis, he paid particular attention to the

NAACP's voter registration drives. Boycotts could accomplish some change, he realized, but ballots could do a lot more, and fast.

So Terronez and a friend went to work. They started paying the cost of citizen-application photographs for any Mexican-born Silvis resident. Then, with the photos in hand, they would shuttle the applicants over the bridge to the Rock Island courthouse where they could be sworn in. As soon as the ceremony ended, Terronez and his pal showed the newly minted United States citizens how to register to vote.

Then he ran for city council. It took a couple of tries, but in 1963 the Mexican-Americans in Silvis helped give Joe Terronez the votes he needed to win.

As the lone Latino voice on the council, he found it hard to get much done. But Terronez had a mission. Soon after he was elected, he made a motion to have Second Street renamed "Hero Street, U.S.A." and to turn Billy Goat Hill into a park honoring the eight who died.

The other aldermen on the council practically jeered as they rejected the plan. Boys from all over Silvis went to fight and die, they said angrily, not just Second Street. Joe agreed. But, he insisted, he doubted that any other street anywhere had sent as many. And he set out to prove it.

He wrote letters to Congress, the Senate, and the Pentagon. Finally, the Department of Defense's director of military equal opportunity determined that what Terronez suspected was indeed true. Second Street had sent more.

To Joe, the significance was obvious.

"When you are willing to fight—even die—for your country, who can say, 'It's my flag more than yours'?" he asked. "Those boys could have said, 'I'm going back to Mexico so I don't have to risk my life.' Instead, fifty-seven put their lives on the line for the United States, and eight of them died."

Their experience was like that of so many other immigrants who had come before, and who would come after. They fought in the wars, and they fought for acceptance. They represented what was happening across the country, where new arrivals from every race and ethnicity—Japanese, Italian, German, Jewish, Black, Hispanic, and more—came out to fight for the country they called their own. They were ready to defend it, and to make it a better place for all.

The story of Hero Street, Terronez knew, was a truly American tale of sacrifice, segregation, and the determination to succeed, set against the backdrop of a country struggling through some of its greatest trials—the throes of the Great Depression, the death of one of its greatest presidents, the dawn of the nuclear age, the fear and mistrust of the Cold War and the Red Scare, and the wrenching birth of the Civil Rights Movement—and, of course, two wars that defined the country in distinctive ways.

So, on that Memorial Day morning in 1968, Joe Terronez deserved to be proud. Renaming the street meant more than just changing its name. It was recognition of a truly American story—that began with the Mexican Revolution.

CHAPTER TWO

"*LA YARDA*"

The gunmen had waited three months for this moment. The nine of them had even pointed their guns down at the passing car ten days before, but held their fire as children from a nearby school spilled out into the street around the black soft-top vehicle and its illustrious passenger.

This morning, though, there were no children. It was shortly after 8 A.M. Pancho Villa said good-bye to one of his many mistresses and slipped behind the wheel of his 1919 Dodge Brothers roadster. In the passenger seat beside him sat his trusted and loyal comrade, Miguel Trillo. With them rode Villa's personal secretary and three bodyguards.

The scant entourage was an exception. Villa customarily traveled with fifty of his "*Dorados*," the "Golden Ones," the faithful remnants of his revolutionary army who lived under his patronage on his sprawling 25,000-acre ranch, with some of his many children and at least one of his multiple wives.

As Villa drove the clattering vehicle down the dusty street from Manuela Casas's house, to return to his hacienda, one of the assassins waited by the road. He took off his hat with his left hand. That meant the "Centaur of the North" sat behind the wheel. Using his right hand would have signaled that Villa rode in the passenger seat.

The other eight killers waited in ambush in rooms 7 and 9 of the hotel facing the intersection. As Villa's car rolled into view, someone shouted "Viva Villa!"

It was just the opposite: The gunmen opened fire, showering the car with bullets.

One of the first shattered the windshield and tore into Villa. The Centaur let go of the wheel and reached for his gun. The car veered and smashed into a tree. The shots kept coming—forty by some estimates, more than a hundred by others. Nine of them hit Villa.

Behind him, his secretary died almost instantly. So did at least one of his bodyguards. Another fell, mortally wounded, to die a day later. The third collapsed nearby, bleeding. As the assassins poured into the street to finish the job, that bodyguard raised his gun and fired, killing one of the attackers.

In a matter of minutes, the street fell quiet. Trillo's corpse dangled backward over the passenger side door, his lifeless eyes staring out toward the street. Villa, the legendary *bandido* and revolutionary war hero, slumped in the driver's seat, dead. He was forty-five years old.

It was July 20, 1923. The Mexican Revolution, by most official accounts, had ended three years before. But the people knew better.

The revolt began in 1910, during Mexico's Wild West period, when lawlessness ruled the backcountry, and hunger and poverty were the only things there were plenty of. The revolution's original goal of ousting the aging dictator Porfirio Díaz was achieved within just a few months, but the fighting continued for a decade more, as the victors and their armies turned on one another.

The death toll: as many as one of every eight Mexicans. And, even after the revolution was declared ended, the killing continued.

At its start, Francisco "Pancho" Villa was better known as a bandit chieftain, brutal but beloved for his benevolence—Mexico's "Robin Hood." Born Doroteo Arango, he killed a man who raped his younger sister and went into hiding when he was sixteen. He took as his alias the name of a bandit leader who had mentored him.

Between 1900 and 1909 Villa became a celebrated figure to the Mexican people as he raided ranches, robbed banks, and skillfully evaded the dictator Díaz's imperious and cruel *Rurales*. Then, in 1910, he heeded Francisco Madero's cry for revolution and quickly mustered an army of thousands to depose Díaz. During the back-and-forth division and betrayals between the four revolutionary commanders, Villa cemented his reputation as a folk hero, divvying up the land holdings and property of the rich to give to the poor and to the widows and children of his men killed in battle.

He also secured his standing as a charismatic and exceptional military commander, credited with opening the path to Mexico City and bringing Díaz's downfall. His skill on horseback earned him his nickname: "*El Centauro del Norte*." A renowned womanizer, he boasted a string of conquests off the battlefield, as well. He had twenty-three or more wives—each of whom he insisted on marrying to preserve their "honor"—and dozens of children.

The beginning of Villa's end came in 1915, in a series of four engagements—and four defeats for him—collectively known as the Battle of Celaya, in the Mexican state of Guanajuato. The worst for Villa came in the battle that took place at the city of Celaya. He pitted his army against the forces of his former revolutionary ally Álvaro Obregón, sending wave after wave of cavalry against Obregón's defenses. Villa's foe, however, had studied the trench fighting tactics of the world war then embroiling Europe, and he applied them with devastating effectiveness against Villa's heavy charges. Nearly 4,000 of Villa's men died, along with close to 1,000 horses. Another 6,000 men were captured, including 120 officers Obregón ordered summarily executed.

Villa never fully recovered. His power and influence fading, the Centaur surrendered in 1920. The government granted him 500,000 gold pesos and his sprawling Hacienda Canutillo, and he retired with a general's salary.

Obregón, however, never forgot. He bore a permanent reminder of his battle with Villa: A grenade had blown his right arm off at the elbow during the fighting at Trinidad and Santa Ana del Conde. The pain, he wrote in his memoirs, "was so prolonged and agonizing" that "I pulled a pistol from my belt and fired into my left temple hoping to consummate the job that the shrapnel had not finished."[1]

Lucky for him, an aide had cleaned his pistol the night before and failed to replace the bullets. A soldier wrestled the gun away, and Obregón lived on to become president in 1920, after leading an army against his predecessor.

Two years later, historians believe Villa sealed his fate when he gave an interview to *El Universal,* one of Mexico's largest newspapers. He said he supported an Obregón foe for president. Then he went further. "I am a real soldier," Villa said. "And I can mobilize 40,000 soldiers in 40 minutes."

In truth, his fate may have already been decided. No one knows for sure who ordered Villa's assassination, but suspicions surround Obregón. Once captured, none of the gunmen served more than a few months in prison for the killing, and several were commissioned into the army after their release.

The battles in which Villa and Obregón confronted each other may be the best known, but they were just a few of many confrontations that ravaged the central state of Guanajuato. The region had a bloody history nearly four centuries long by the time of the Battle of Celaya.

The first of the Spanish conquistadors arrived there in 1522, subjugating the indigenous people and killing any who objected. Seven years later, the explorer Nuño de Guzmán descended on Guanajuato in a murderous rampage, pillaging even communities already conquered.

Spanish settlements spread quickly after the discovery of silver mines in the area. They gave birth within a matter of decades to the cities of San Miguel, Guanajuato, León, and Celaya, where Villa and Obregón would have their fateful encounter.

It also was the birthplace of Mexico's independence movement, where the revolt against Spanish rule began in 1810 with Father Miguel Hidalgo's "Cry of Dolores." A hundred years later, the revolution against Porfirio Díaz enveloped Guanajuato and sparked an exodus of able-bodied men and, later, their families, drawn by the promise of peace and plenty of work to a place they called "*El Norte*."

So many died or left that Guanajuato's population dropped from 1,081,651 in the 1910 census to a twentieth-century low of 860,364 by 1921.

It wasn't all because of the revolution. Fortuitously, as men fled the revolution, American industry came calling. With World War I taking so many of America's able-bodied, the expanding railroads faced a manpower shortage. The answer, of course: Mexicans.

The railroad companies advertised in newspapers and on radio, offering jobs that paid anywhere from $1 to $2 a day plus transportation. Word spread. So did the Mexicans. For many, jobs in Texas, New Mexico, and California served as mere stopovers, as companies lured them into the Pacific Northwest and the Midwest. Worker camps became settlements, and grew into communities as the men summoned their girlfriends and wives.

During the first decade of the twentieth century, nearly fifty thousand immigrants crossed the border from Mexico. That was the official count, anyway. According to government calculations, Mexican immigration made up just .6 percent of the total immigration to the United States during those years. However, as one observer noted, Mexicans accounted for a full sixth of the section hands and extra gangs on the railroads in the Western division.

During the decade of the Mexican Revolution (1910 to 1920), the U.S. government reported, twice as many Mexicans entered the United States as in the decade before.

The totals were very likely far short of the reality.

Mexican emigration figures showed an astronomically higher flood of refugees fleeing the turmoil and scarcity of their homeland. In 1911 and 1912 alone Mexico tallied some 135,125 emigrants, most of them single males, crossing into the United States.

Plus, the U.S. government's reports seemed to contradict themselves. While the official account listed roughly one hundred thousand Mexican immigrants arriving between 1910 and 1920, border authorities reported as many as one thousand people a day streaming through the station at El Paso, Texas, alone. On a single day in 1914, the Labor Department advised that "approximately 8,000 panic-stricken aliens, mainly of the Mexican race, entered the United States in Eagle Pass, Texas, within a few hours" fleeing government troops "who were reported about to attack the town of Piedras Negras."[2]

The revolution provided the push. U.S. companies offered a powerful pull.

"Each week five or six trains are run from Laredo," according to a 1916 *Los Angeles Times* news story, "carrying Mexicans who have been employed by labor agents, and similar shipments are being made from other border points." The demand, concluded the *Times*, "is so great they are employed as fast as they cross the Rio Grande."[3]

A group from Guanajuato found work in a quintessentially American spot: in the Heartland, on the Mississippi, a few miles from where Ronald Reagan was born. The place was called Silvis, Illinois. It was home to a massive railroad and it was colder than anything they had ever known. Hours were long and wages were low, but there was peace, and possibilities.

The railroad itself had rolled into the area fifty years before the first known Mexican arrived. The first train, the "Rocket," chugged to a stop before an expectant crowd in the neighboring town of Rock Island on February 22, 1854. It was the very first to reach the Mississippi River. For more than two years, it would go no farther. Until the first rail bridge over the river opened, passengers wishing to continue west had to be offloaded and ferried across to the waiting tracks on the other side.

The trains opened a new chapter in American history and brought a burst of life for the cluster of settlements set on the Mississippi River now known as the Quad-Cities. Stations popped up on both sides of the Mississippi, and the network of tracks spread like tendrils, connecting the country with a vital means of—for the times, at least—"rapid" transit. People and supplies roared from place to place in a matter of hours or days, traversing distances that had taken weeks or even months of travel prior to the locomotives.

The Quad-Cities became an important hub in the nationwide transportation system, and in 1902, the Rock Island Railroad company built what was then the largest locomotive repair shop in the world. For its site, the company chose a nine-hundred-acre tract on the banks of the Mississippi just west of the railroad's original stopping place, in the small community called Silvis.

The railroad yards brought steady jobs and, soon enough, Mexican men to fill them. One of them was Joseph and Frank Sandoval's father, Eduviges. He crossed the border in 1917 and found work immediately.

"Those people were waiting at the border to offer jobs," another of Eduviges's sons, Tanilo, recalled, overlooking the railroad tracks that provided his father's livelihood.

Some came with their wives and young children, despite the difficulty of the journey. It was nearly a thousand miles just to reach the border. They had to skirt the snow-covered peaks of Mexico's Sierra Madre Oriental mountain range, thread through the hostile Chihuahua desert, and, finally, cross the Rio Grande. Some paid with their lives; others with the lives of their children. Eduviges and his young wife, Angelina, buried an infant son in the hard dirt somewhere near El Paso before continuing on to Silvis.

Another, unrelated family of Sandovals came shortly after. Carmen and Jose (or Joseph, as he came to be known in the United States) hailed from Guanajuato, as well, but the two sets of Sandovals of Silvis were like Smiths in a hundred other U.S. towns who share names, but no blood ties. Willie would be their second U.S.-born child, part of a clan that would eventually include eight boys and three girls.

Others came alone. Then, once settled, they sent for their girlfriends and wives in Mexico to begin families in this new place of opportunity and relative abundance.

But the newcomers found something else in the new land, as well: prejudice. They weren't allowed to live with the town's whites. They weren't allowed to sit in the pews at the "white" Catholic church; they had to stand in the back. And, truth be told, even the "opportunities" were limited because of where they hailed from and the darker tone of their skin.

"The only place a Mexican could get a job was at the foundry or the railroad," said Willie's younger brother Al . So they crowded together and slept in the tiny, two-room houses and empty boxcars the railroad gave them. It didn't matter how big the family was; homes were one-size-fits-all. They had no electricity or indoor plumbing. Water that sat in washbasins through the night would freeze, and the boys who would later be remembered as heroes had to break through the ice to clean their faces before school.

By 1915, some forty Mexican families made their homes in the railroad yards beside the tracks, a place they came to call *"La Yarda."*

A single potbellied stove provided the only heat for each of the immigrants' homes, and the children had a well-choreographed routine for scavenging fuel to feed it. They scrounged for discarded railroad ties to chop into firewood, or they waited for slow-moving trains to cross through the railroad yards, clambered aboard, and scurried to the coal wagon behind the steam engine. As the train continued to roll through, they stepped out onto the heap and kicked the lumps off to others trotting along beside the tracks. The tricky part was keeping their balance on the shifting pile as they toed the pieces over the side. The kids on the ground quickly gathered up the chunks and scampered home with their armfuls, knowing that what they carried meant the difference between a warm night's sleep and one spent shivering in the teeth-chattering cold.

The Mexican men were given some of the most backbreaking

and dangerous duties. They took jobs as linemen or "gandy dancers" on the railroad section gangs, using long metal bars to pry the tracks back into alignment or breaking out rotted crossties and hauling new 250-pound ones into their place, then sledgehammering in the spikes to hold the tracks steady. They made 35 cents an hour.

Sundays they rested. They went to church. And they played in *La Yarda*'s community brass band.

The birth of "*La Corporación Musical Mexicana de Hidalgo,*" as it was originally known, came thanks to two brothers from Zacatecas, Mexico. David and Manuel Macias both studied music as children, under the guidance of Catholic priests in their hometown. Manuel went on to play cornet in a military band unit, but fled to the United States in the midst of the Mexican Revolution. David was already there, working for a mining company in Bettendorf, Iowa, across the Mississippi from Silvis.

The Macias brothers made their way to the growing community of railroad workers in 1918. They found a welcoming, tight-knit, and increasingly restless group. The families there largely remained within the confines of their settlement beside the tracks and had little form of entertainment.

The two brothers offered to teach the men to play and read music, and the band soon swelled to more than fifty members—many, if not most, of whom had never held a musical instrument before. What they lacked in experience they made up for in enthusiasm, gathering regularly in the Silvis railroad yards to practice with their cornets and clarinets, tubas and trombones.

"My dad always played in the band. They all played in the band," Rufina Sandoval, Willie's kid sister, said. "Every Sunday, he'd be there with his clarinet. My uncle played trumpet."

They gave their first concert in 1921, followed by Sunday afternoon appearances in neighboring towns and, at least once, in Chicago.

Over time, the band changed its name, replacing "*Hidalgo*" with "*Banda de Silvis, Illinois*," and added a concert orchestra, a choral group, and a dance band. It also moved into its very own practice hall, made of two boxcars donated by the rail line, put together to form one large room. The building soon became more than a place for music. The Mexicans may have been banned from the "white" Catholic church in East Moline, but they hadn't abandoned their religion. Priests from nearby parishes visited the Mexicans to celebrate mass and hear confessions. The practice hall became the Mexicans' place of worship. To make it more churchlike, they added a peak. They dedicated it on Easter Sunday, 1927, and named it for Mexico's patron saint: Our Lady of Guadalupe. There they held their christenings and communions, weddings and wakes.

Life in the yards was hard, but good. The families shared friendships and, when needed, food. They worked together, sang together, played together, and prayed together.

But the peace they had found was short-lived. The war was still a long way off, but the Mexicans were under attack.

CHAPTER THREE

Clouds at Home, Storms on the Horizon

Barely a month after the families in the Silvis railyard dedicated their church, the Spirit of St. Louis lifted off from Roosevelt Field, Long Island. Its pilot, twenty-five-year-old Charles Lindbergh, landed in Paris thirty-three-and-a-half hours later, on May 21, 1927. It was the first solo nonstop transatlantic flight, and it earned Lindbergh the largest ticker tape parade in New York City's history.

The very same month, the 15 millionth Ford Model T rolled off the assembly line. It was the very last one Ford made. Ford waited until December to introduce its replacement. The new car was twice as powerful, 30 percent faster, and loaded with "modern" safety and comfort features. It even had windshield wipers. Standard. Ford dubbed it the Model A, signaling an all new automobile, and a new automotive era.

The flight and the Ford both fit the spirit of the times. The closing years of the Roaring Twenties seemed filled with possibility and promise. Men and machines stretched the limits of the attainable, setting new records and reshaping the world to fit their design.

In that same year, construction began on Mount Rushmore, the Holland Tunnel opened, and Babe Ruth hit sixty home runs, a record that stood for more than three decades. It was the year of the first "talkie," *The Jazz Singer*, and Al Jolson couldn't have been more prophetic when he said, "You ain't seen nothin' yet!"

The next year, Amelia Earhart became the first woman to fly across the Atlantic, Alexander Fleming discovered penicillin, and a cartoon character named Mickey Mouse was born.

Great things indeed were happening, and the spread of the railroads played a crucial part in helping to fuel the nation's prosperity. But the days of affluence and good times, of flappers and bootleggers, the Charleston and Al Capone, were coming to an end.

As the decade waned, the Mexicans in the Silvis yards could feel the increasing tension. A surge of bigotry had swept across the country. It gave birth to a renewed and emboldened Ku Klux Klan, with a membership that swelled from a few thousand in 1920 to an estimated 3 million just five years later. In a show of force in August 1925, forty thousand Klansmen paraded down Pennsylvania Avenue to the Washington Monument.

This new, postwar KKK proclaimed itself staunchly pro-American, protecting the white Protestant way of life from the threat of blacks, Catholics, Jews, and immigrants, including the Mexicans.

Signs reading "No Niggers, Mexicans or Dogs" dotted the windows and doors of businesses across a xenophobic swath of the South, Southwest, and Midwest. Mexicans and Mexican-Americans faced the same types of discrimination and segregation as blacks. They could be forced to use "colored" water fountains or restrooms and refused service in Anglo restaurants or hotels—and, as the Mexicans in Silvis knew, not be allowed to live among "whites."

The intolerance grew in intensity and fierceness, sparking various acts of brutality. As the Southern Poverty Law Center described it: "Violence first flared in a rampage of whippings, tar-and-feathers raids and the particularly gruesome use of acid to brand the letters 'KKK' on the foreheads of blacks, Jews and others they considered anti-American."[1]

Then it went further. Lynchings and shootings proliferated. As the SPLC reported, "many communities were firmly in the grasp of the Klan's terror. The victims were usually blacks, Jews, Catholics, Mexicans and various immigrants," but they could also include anyone Klansmen "considered 'immoral' or 'traitors' to the white race."[2]

A *New York Times* editorial in 1922 protested that "the killing of Mexicans without provocation is so common as to pass almost unnoticed."[3]

No one described that level of violence in Silvis, but the people of the neighboring towns often seemed almost eager to show their open contempt for the Mexicans. Even their children got in on the act, taunting and hurling slurs at the kids from the rail yards.

"They called us 'dirty Mexicans,'" Mary Garza, Willie Sandoval's little sister, remembered bitterly.

And there was no mistaking the meaning of the crosses set afire in the night at the top of Billy Goat Hill.

The discrimination grew worse as the days of abundance disappeared and the nation slid into the Great Depression.

The day it began went largely unnoticed in the rail yards. Black Tuesday, October 29, meant little more to the folks there than that four days remained before *El Día de los Muertos*, the Day of the Dead, known to most non-Mexican Christians as All Souls' Day. The stock market's collapse had as much significance to the families in *La Yarda* as did the stratospheric height the Dow Jones had reached just weeks before, on September 3. The Mexicans working for the railroad had no fortunes to lose on plummeting stocks. They had no fortunes at all.

But they had something that, as the depression deepened and more and more businesses closed and workers were turned out onto the streets, became even more valuable. They had jobs.

"By 1928, Mexicans represented 43 percent of track and maintenance workers on sixteen major railroads in the Chicago and Northwestern Indiana region and were working on the railroads in the string of cities from Toledo to Saginaw, with smaller numbers farther east."[4] And, as primitive as they may have been, they had homes, while others were losing theirs.

Silvis, with almost four hundred Mexican residents, had the largest *colonia* in the Quad-Cities area, "a veritable Mexican town of its own."[5]

Within six months, 4 million were out of work; by 1931, 13.5 million. And things grew increasingly desperate.

"On March 19, 1930, 1,100 men waiting in a bread line in New York mobbed two trucks headed for a nearby hotel and made off with their deliveries of breads and rolls."[6]

In 1930 more than one thousand banks closed. In 1931, twenty thousand people committed suicide. By the spring of 1932, in Chicago, "a group of fifty desperate men were seen in the back of a restaurant fighting over a barrel of garbage."[7]

As their frustrations grew, the people in the surrounding communities aimed at least some of their anger at the Mexicans. They complained that the residents of *La Yarda*, living as they were on railroad company property, paid no municipal property taxes. They demanded that the Rock Island Railroad evict them.

The railroad relented. The Mexicans were forced out of the yards, but they still weren't allowed to live among the town's whites. So they found a wooded spot between a creek and the foot of a sprawling hill away from the others, at the distant edge of town. They cleared the trees by hand and, with the railroad's blessing, hauled their boxcars to the new location, setting them along a dirt path that came to be known as Second Street.

There was no electricity or plumbing, and even after the city's other streets were paved, theirs remained a rutted patch that froze in the winter and turned to mud when it rained.

But it was home. And for the armies of kids looking for fun and adventure, it was practically paradise. They dug caves as hideouts in the hill and splashed in the cold spring runoff that coursed through the creek. Its official name was Honey Creek, but the kids called it simply "the ditch."

"Hell, we could go nude down there when we were kids and nobody would see us," Frank and Joe Sandoval's younger brother Tanilo said. "We used to damn it up and we'd go swimming. . . . It would probably be about chest high when we were kids. We thought it was deep."

In the winter, the trickle that ran through the creek would ice up. The kids strapped clamp-on skates on their shoes, and their swimming hole became their rink.

There were always more than enough playmates. There were ten children in Tanilo's family alone, six boys and four girls. The other Sandovals, Willie's family, counted eleven. Even the smallest of the Mexican families included two or three. And often enough, two or even three families crowded together in one of the narrow boxcars—aunts and uncles, in-laws, cousins and kids.

The stretch between the apple orchards at the top of the hill and the creek became their home, their stomping ground, their playground, and their window on the world of nature. "We learned about dragonflies. We learned about frogs. We learned about toads. We learned about minnows. We learned about tadpoles. In the spring, we'd go up sometimes and find baby owls," Tanilo said.

Tanilo's brother Frank gained a reputation as the best maker of slingshots, even if he wasn't any better than any of the other kids at using them.

"He'd go out in the woods and pick the perfect crotch, and then he'd go and stick it in my mom's oven to temper it. We used to use it for birds. But I never saw anybody kill a hell of a lot of birds with it," Tanilo said.

They had better luck chasing down wild rabbits with clubs, to bring home for some extra food to put on the table.

The kids played variations of games that all kids play, and made up some of their own. They played King of the Hill, marbles, and "Mexican Tag." They slid down the hill on makeshift sleds. And, when the fruits were in season, they plucked crabapples off the trees scattered on the hill and pelted one another in crabapple wars that no one really won, using garbage can lids for shields.

One of their inventions was a game they called "Hoy." They cut about three inches from an old broomstick and tapered the ends. That was the hoy. Another fifteen inches or so of a broom or mop handle became the bat. The object was to whack the hoy as far as they could. They got three tries. Distance was measured in bat lengths. They had to say, "Hoy!" as they batted, or they were out. If one of the kids in the field caught the hoy, they were out. If the fielders didn't catch it, they still had one final chance to win. If one of them could throw the hoy and hit the bat as it lay on the ground in front of "home plate," the batter was out.

When the winds picked up, one of the fathers, a handyman

named Luis Montes, made kites of bamboo for the kids. He painted them red, white, and green for the colors of the Mexican flag, and added a special touch that made them truly unique. "He'd stretch a strip of sheepskin over them," Tanilo said, with a wistful smile. "When they got up in the air, they would buzz."

The kids gave almost everyone a nickname; there was Cheppe, Charlie Chan, Rufus, Yatch, and Lunch. Pete Masias's brother Ray got dubbed BB because of his running skills. Somebody said, "You're faster than a bullet!" Ray grinned and shrugged it off. "No," he said, "not a bullet. A BB maybe."

It stuck.

Not everyone from the rail yards moved straight to Second Street. The other Sandoval clan, Willie's family, bought a house just a few blocks west of Honey Creek, in East Moline. They may have been allowed to buy close to the whites, but they were quickly reminded that they weren't welcome.

"There were two or three of us who went to St. Mary's [Catholic Church]," Willie's sister Rufina said. "And that priest told us not to come back. I'll never forget that."

By 1932, at the height of the depression, 25 percent of the workforce was unemployed. Add to it the effects of the great drought that was turning the nation's midsection into a barren dust bowl, and there seemed no place to escape the misery. Crops withered. "Black blizzards," giant, choking dust storms that buried fields and houses, blew across the Great Plains with increasing frequency and intensity. In 1932, there were fourteen. In 1933, thirty-eight. Farmers, like those made famous in John Steinbeck's *The Grapes of Wrath*, lashed the last of their belongings to their weather-beaten cars and trucks and joined the migrant hordes seeking work wherever it could be found.

Like the death of a thousand cuts, the railroads felt the effect of every faltering and failing farm and business. Slackening demand for goods brought weakening need for the brawny means of transporting supplies.

Soon enough, like desperate survivors on a leaky life raft, the railroad began pushing the weakest overboard. Willie's father, Joseph, lost his job on the Rock Island Line. Soon after, that branch of the family lost their house. They moved in with relatives, and Joseph worked some with the WPA. Things looked up when he landed a job at the Moline Ironworks. But when the plant closed down, their prospects turned bleak again. To feed his kids, Joseph did what he had to. He loaded the family into their black Buick and headed for the fields. Everyone, from oldest to youngest, worked.

Willie's brother Al was only five or six years old, but he went, too, catching up on his sleep on the floor in the backseat as the car bounced along, headed west.

"We went to the sugar beets in the spring," his brother Oscar said, "and we didn't come back until the fall."

Even little Al learned to use the specially shaped machete with the hook on the front for stabbing the beets and yanking them up from the soil. Then they'd lop off the leafy tops and toss the bulb on a nearby truck.

The farmers paid them $25 an acre. "The first year I think we did seventy acres," Ruben, the oldest of Willie's brothers, recalled.

When they finished harvesting the beets, they turned north to Minnesota, to top onions and pick potatoes.

"We worked from sunup to sundown. The farmer would give us gunnysacks, and we'd fill them up with hay, and that was our bed," his sister Rufina said. "We lived in the horse stalls."

Often enough, dinner depended on what the boys could catch—pheasants or pigeons their mother cooked.

Their lives as migrant laborers paid off, though. They sweated, scrimped, and saved day after day, across acre after acre. Within a couple of seasons, they had enough money to afford a place of their own on Second Street.

"My dad bought that house for nine hundred dollars," Rufina said. "The birds would fly in and out, but we didn't care."

Their new home had two bedrooms upstairs, plus a front room and a kitchen. The eight boys slept in the basement, on folding cots spread over the dirt floor. In the winter, snow drifted in through the cracks in the walls.

"We'd get newspapers and stuff it in the cracks to insulate the house a little bit," Al said. It didn't help much. "I'd wake up and there'd be a pile of snow on the bed."

With no electricity, they lit the house with kerosene lamps. They had a hand-crank pump in the yard for water and an outhouse in back. No one wanted to make that trek in the dark on a winter night, and not just because of the cold.

"That was worse than Missouri mud," Ruben remembered. "You'd walk, you'd pick up half an acre of mud."

At Halloween, the outhouses became a favorite target for pranksters. The boys snuck through the dark and tipped them over, into the creek.

"That wasn't very nice," said Joe Ramirez, one of Joe Sandoval's buddies. "It was a hell of a job to get those toilets back in place."

The potbelly stove in the kitchen had a dual purpose. In addition to cooking their meals on it, they used it to heat their home. As Rufina put it, "We were like Ma and Pa Kettle."

The chore of chopping the wood to keep the stove going fell to Al and his brother Charlie. One day they played instead of doing their duty. When their father got home from his night shift, there was no wood for the stove. He made the boys get up and get chopping. "We had to go out at midnight and chop wood," Al said.

Another time, Al tried to get creative with the fire.

"The potbelly stove went out, but the ashes were still there. So I threw in a lot of coal and it wouldn't light," he said. "So I got kerosene, a pretty good containerful, and threw the kerosene in there. And I was looking in there, and all of a sudden, boom! They were walking down the street, Slugger and Willie, and they saw all that smoke come out of the chimney like an atom bomb, and they ran to see what was going on."

They found Al in the kitchen, still blinking in shock.

"I looked like Al Jolson," he said.

Their little cousin, Bea, wasn't as lucky. When she was about five, she headed into the kitchen when no one was looking. She opened the potbelly stove and threw some things in to burn. The flames licked out and caught the front of her dress.

Terrified, she ran shrieking outside, not realizing that her panicked dash was fanning the flames and burning her stomach. Luckily, Willie was coming up the street and saw her.

"She ran out of the house and her clothes were on fire," Al recalled. "He grabbed her and threw her in the snow and put the fire out."

Willie would've been about fifteen at the time, but he already had a reputation as a quiet, religious, and hardworking boy with a strong sense of justice. And woe be to him who got him angry.

"Don't get him mad," Ruben said. "He didn't care about the world."

"That's why he was a good fighter," said Al. "He had those killer instincts."

Willie first stepped into the ring when he was about fourteen, the first in his family to discover the invigorating appeal of Bert Visconi's gym. Soon he had his brother Ruben, his best friend Slugger, and Pete Masias down at the gym with him. It wasn't long before it seemed that almost all the boys on Second Street eagerly awaited the school bell's ring so they could race to the gym at the police station and put on the gloves again.

"All the kids were fighting," Al said. "That's what kept us off the street, though. I'd go to school, but first I'd go running five miles in the morning before school. Harry would take us down a country road down there. Then we'd go to school, and after school we'd go down to the gym and work out till about nine o'clock at night. Time we got home, you're too tired to do anything else. Didn't have any trouble with us."

Some liked it more than others. Some got really good. Some found out the hard way that it wasn't really their thing. A few got good enough to be competitive. Among them, Ruben, Willie, and Al. All three, at one time or other, worked their way up through the eliminations to fight in the prestigious Chicago Golden Gloves Tournament.

None, though, wanted it as badly as Willie. He dreamt of someday going pro, and he dedicated himself to making it a reality. When he wasn't in school, doing chores or working, he trained. The folks on Second Street and far beyond got used to hearing the trudge of his shoes on the gravel at all hours of the day and night, and to seeing him in his familiar gray sweatpants running, always running, to build up his lungs and burn off the fat. His goal: to slip through the ropes ready and lean at 126 pounds.

Willie had a hard-chiseled chest and an easy, cockeyed grin. He had a steady gaze and quick hands. Most important he had those fundamental traits every true boxer needs—the courage and ability to take his hits, and the determination and sturdiness to dish them out, and make them count.

Still, he could win bout after bout, but winning the respect of the whites who watched him fight seemed forever beyond his reach. Even when he beat one of the area's best, the write-up in the local sports section focused more on the Anglo boy's prowess and surprising loss than on Willie and his win.

"Young Billy Russell," it read, "who scaled to the top of Quad cities flyweights with amazing speed, fell off his high perch when he dropped a close decision to Willie Sandoval."

The "close" decision, the article went on to note, was actually a unanimous one, with all three judges calling the win for Willie.

The crowd still booed.

It must have been music in his ears anyway. The chance to beat up one of the white kids like the ones who mocked all the Second Streeters was one of the reasons the Mexicans got in the ring. Boxing and basketball were ways they got even.

Willard Gauley, the basketball coach, believed in them. He had reason to. He taught them to play the game; they showed him they could win. In thirty-five years at the McKinley School in Silvis, he racked up thirty winning seasons. Even if some of his best players didn't have their own gym shoes.

"He was a great guy," Tanilo said. "If we didn't have shoes for gym class, well, one of these *gueros* or somebody discarded a pair, he'd salvage them and give it to the *Mexicanos*."

The Mexican kids played with a lot of heart. They also may have had a certain height, and age, advantage.

"Back then, if your grades weren't up, they'd hold you back," Tanilo added. "I think some of them were sixteen before they graduated from grade school."

Boxing, though, had a special appeal for Willie and his brothers. Especially in those desperate days of the Depression when it, too, became a way to make some money.

Technically, all the Second Street boxers were amateurs, but they'd pick up five bucks taking their lumps in an out-of-town fight, or pocket what they could putting on impromptu "exhibitions" at the American Legion or Eagle Club.

"We'd say to those guys, 'Do any of you want us to put on a fighting display?'" Al Sandoval explained. "They'd say, 'Sure, come on in.' My brother and I would put on the display. They'd throw money in there. We'd make five or ten dollars."

Money, and what it would buy, was almost always on their minds.

These were dark days for America, and life on Second Street was more similar than many might have realized to what the entire nation was going through.

The families grew vegetables and raised chickens and goats that they let wander to graze on the hill by their homes. That gave it its name: Billy Goat Hill. At least, that's what the Anglos called it. "We just called it, 'the Hill,'" said Tanilo.

Later, there would be stories of how the men from Hero Street learned to scale the hill like billy goats themselves. When they were growing up, though, the only goats were the ones they depended on for milk and meat and hide. If the boys forgot to bring them in, their fathers would send them out in the dark to get them, regardless of the time. On a moonless night the boys would go stumbling up the hill, doing their best to imitate the goats' bleats to try to get the animals to answer, and praying that the terrifying tales of "*La Llorona*" kidnapping children who hear her agonized wails in the night were only make-believe.

The families banded together to help one another with what little they could, and to care for one another when they got hurt or sick. When a mother gave birth, the other mothers served as midwives and took care of her other children. Sometimes it became permanent. When Luz Segura's mother died, his family moved in with his cousin

Tony Pompa's clan. Tony's mother became the woman Luz thought of as Mom, but Willie's mother, Carmen, was the one who fed him.

They bartered when they had, and shared when they didn't. Angelina Sandoval, Tanilo's mom, traded her goats' milk for the pale oleo and tins of corned beef Claro Soliz's mom got from the WPA after his dad got laid off.

There might not have been a lot to go around, but no one starved. Not even the hordes of train-hopping hobos who drifted through Silvis hunting for jobs that didn't exist.

"The number of unemployed transients caught illegally hopping rides on the Missouri Pacific Railroad jump from 13,745 in 1929 to 186,028 by 1931. In 1932, the Southern Pacific Railroad kicked 700,000 vagrants from its trains."[8]

Many got booted into the rail yards by Second Street, or jumped off as the train slowed, to avoid getting caught and possibly beaten by railroad "bulls." Almost all of them were hungry.

"During the Depression, the yard would be full of hobos," Tanilo said. "They came looking for something to eat. I don't think my mom ever turned one of them down. She gave them beans or tortillas and a couple of eggs."

The families were generous with strangers, and with one another. Claro Soliz gave his nephews their first bicycle, and Joe Sandoval bought the one Tanilo learned to ride on. That was in 1938.

"My brothers were my heroes," Tanilo said. "When they got their first jobs, they put in sewer and they put in electricity."

When the object was money, the kids got creative. The older ones would fudge their ages to take temporary work with the extra gangs on the railroad.

"You had to be eighteen to work on the railroad. So some of us lied about our age," Joe Ramirez said. "We were lucky to get on the railroad. There was nothing else. The WPA, working for the city, that was only when they called you in to work. You got grocery money."

The railroad, though, paid in cash, and the boys would skip school to work with the traveling gangs, fixing rails and replacing rotted ties. It took two men to lift one of the regular eight-foot ties, four for one of the ten-foot switch ties. They carried them with tongs like the ones the iceman used to deliver blocks of ice.

School took a backseat, too, at harvest time. The kids skipped school and headed for the onion fields across the river, in Bettendorf, Iowa. They'd make between 3 cents and 5 cents a bushel "topping" onions.

The younger kids also might make enough for ice cream or a movie ticket serving as runners for their dads or older brothers. The boys brought them the oversized beers known as "picnics" from one of the taverns at the "Happy Corners" in exchange for getting to take the empty back and keep the return money.

Others traded on their talents in different ways. Slugger's boxing buddy, Peter Masias, was known for his dark good looks and his silky baritone. "Oh, yeah, he was a crooner," said Ruben Sandoval. "Man, he could sing. He'd be walking down the street and he'd start singing. He was good."

Peter's brother Ray, BB to his friends, played guitar.

"He would play the guitar and we'd sing," Tanilo said. "We knew about three songs. And we'd go down to downtown Silvis. Because it was a big railroad town, we would go down there where all the trainmen would lodge while they were changing shifts or whatever. We'd sing those three songs, and people would give us a few coins, and that was enough to go the movies or buy popcorn or something."

Singing also worked as a way for the teens to get free drinks at the taverns, and to have a laugh at the non-Spanish-speaking audience's expense.

"We'd get up and we'd be playing and singing in Spanish," Al said. "And all the drinks would be coming over. They were all buying us drinks. They liked the music. I used to get a kick out of it because he'd be saying something bad about the people, but they wouldn't understand what he was saying. He'd be singing, '*Estos pendejos no saben lo que estamos diciendo.*'"

The drinks surely would have dried up if the listeners understood. Literally, *pendejos* means "pubic hairs," but Mexicans use it as a moderately vulgar way of saying "jerks." So, as pretty as the songs may have sounded to the English-speaking crowd, what the boys were saying was, roughly, "These buttheads have no idea what we're saying!"

While they had their fun, an evil wind was stirring in Europe. The Great Depression had a global impact. When their economies collapsed, the frustrated masses retaliated against the governments in power by putting new leaders in charge. In the United States, the people chose Franklin Delano Roosevelt. In Germany, Adolf Hitler.

By 1939, the cause that would pull the United States together, and back on its feet, was taking shape. On September 1, Germany invaded Poland. France and Great Britain had acquiesced when Germany rearmed after World War I and remilitarized the Rhineland. They signed over the Sudetenland, did nothing when Germany annexed Austria, and nothing again when Hitler's troops marched into Czechoslovakia. Both, however, had promised to defend Poland's border.

When Hitler invaded Poland, the die was cast. Two days later, on September 3, Britain and France declared war on Germany.

Those distant events meant little in Silvis. So Slugger didn't know what to think when he found Willie Sandoval sitting on the front step of his boxcar home, crying. He had never seen Willie cry before.

"What happened?" he asked.

Through his tears, Willie told him. Willie's mother, Carmen, was dead. She had given birth to twins three days earlier. It had been too much for her body to bear. The twins had been born dead. Now Carmen was, too.

She left her husband with nine boys and three girls. The oldest, Ruben, was seventeen. The youngest, Freddy, wasn't quite two.

They sent Freddy to live with his godparents, across the river. Raising the rest fell to the eldest daughter, Rufina. She was fourteen when her father pulled her out of school to care for the others.

Life went on.

The girls changed in pleasing ways; the boys became men. They held dances at the Eagle Club, attracting Mexicans from Galesburg, Davenport, and Moline. Daughters sat along the wall, under the watchful eyes of their mothers, and waited for boys to muster the courage to ask them out on the floor.

As prim as they may have appeared there, the mothers knew their daughters were fast becoming women. Most were married well before they left their teens. Many eloped. Several because they had to.

There may have been at least a shred of truth to Francisco Garcia's words, as he staggered drunk down the street singing:

Las muchachas de Rock Island
Ellas no quieren dar un beso.
Pero las de Silvis
Hasta estiran el pescuezo.

(The girls from Rock Island
They don't want to give one kiss.
But the ones from Silvis
Even stretch out their necks.)

Eventually, boys and girls from the different families intermarried, until they truly were "one big family." Joe Sandoval married Nelly; Joe Ramirez married her sister. Willie had a steady girlfriend. Peter Masias, the crooner, and Tony Pompa, with his movie star good looks, seemed in no hurry to settle down with any one girl.

Claro Soliz was the loner, a good-hearted artist who kept pretty much to himself. Or so it appeared to the others. One reason, though, may have been that he had taken on responsibility for his older sister and her kids after her husband was killed by a train.

Kay had married Joe Ramirez's older brother, Frank. On the day Claro's older brother got married, Frank's father had to work. He was down at the rail yard, loading coal onto trains. Someone said they should take him some food from the wedding. Frank volunteered. On his way back over the tracks, he stepped out of the way as one train thundered by. He didn't see or hear the one coming from the other direction.

As the thirties gave way to the forties and the boys graduated from school, they went looking for full-time jobs. Joe Sandoval got work at the John Deere lumberyard, cutting wood for making crates. Frank Sandoval worked on a section gang for a while, then got hired as a janitor at the Rock Island Arsenal.

In the summer of 1941, the war still seemed distant. Tony Pompa got fired from his job at the Arsenal when they discovered he wasn't an American citizen. So he lied about his age and joined the fledgling Army Air Corps, hoping to learn how to fly.

Folks who stayed on Second Street added on to their homes. Some put in basements. A few, like Joe and Frank Sandoval, had electricity and indoor plumbing installed. Little by little, the outcasts from the rail yards turned their modest boxcars into something closer to real houses, and their unpaved street into a place to call home.

Then, in December, their world changed again.

CHAPTER FOUR

A Star for Mom

At first, it seemed impossible.

Joe and Frank and the other Sandoval brothers huddled around the radio listening to the breathless reports, trying to grasp what they heard. Like most Americans, the news staggered them. The war had been stirring for years but had stayed like a storm on the distant horizon, thundering but never arriving.

Now it was inescapable. Yet, still, incredible.

The first report came as a bulletin interrupting the New York Giants–Brooklyn Dodgers football game at 2:26 P.M., Washington, D.C., time, 1:26 P.M. in Silvis. New York had just received a kick on the three-yard line. The receiver sprinted forward past the five, the ten, the fifteen. The swarm of Brooklyn players started to close in as he crossed the twenty and the twenty-five. Then, as a tackler brought the runner down at the twenty-seven-yard line, WOR's announcer broke in: "Flash, Washington. The White House announces Japanese attack on Pearl Harbor."

Within minutes, the other radio networks cut into their broadcasts with similar—and similarly sketchy—reports.

Tanilo Sandoval heard as he came up Second Street on his way home from the movies. It was Sunday, December 7, 1941. People on the rocky street were already talking about what had happened, as the details trickled in. By then the first report from on the ground in Honolulu had spilled across the airwaves, echoing the utter shock and disbelief that swept the nation.

"We have witnessed this morning the attack of Pearl Harbor and a severe bombing of Pearl Harbor by army planes, undoubtedly Japanese. The city of Honolulu has also been attacked and considerable damage done. This battle has been going on for nearly three hours," the newscaster intoned. "It's no joke. It's a real war."

Real, yes. But the report barely hinted at the level of destruction.

The Americans had been caught sleeping, many literally.

The first wave of Japanese planes came roaring out of the sky over Honolulu minutes before 8 A.M. on a cool Sunday morning, loosing their bombs first on the neat rows of Army Air Force planes tethered wingtip to wingtip at both Wheeler and Hickam fields. The Japanese aimed to destroy as many planes as possible on the ground so they could maintain dominance in the air.

They succeeded spectacularly.

By the time the dive-bombers and torpedo planes turned their sights on the rows of U.S. Pacific Fleet warships docked harmlessly in the harbor, 188 American planes were in pieces or in flames, another 159 damaged.

As the first bomb exploded on the helpless planes below at 7:55 A.M., the Navy Yard Signal Tower sounded the alarm with a terse message: "ENEMY AIR RAID—NOT DRILL."

Five minutes later, the first Japanese bomb hit the USS *Arizona*. It sat immobile, tied to the quay and surrounded by other moored ships along Battleship Row. The blast caused minor damage and started a small fire. The lethal blow, though, came just moments later, at 8:06, as sailors scrambled to battle stations. An armor-piercing bomb bored through the *Arizona*'s decking and detonated the battleship's forward ammunition magazine, setting off more than a million pounds of gunpowder. An eyewitness on a nearby ship said the force of the explosion made the massive ship "jump at least 15 or 20 feet upward in the water and sort of break in two."

It sank in less than nine minutes; taking 1,177 lives with it.

That was just the beginning.

The second wave of Japanese aircraft arrived almost exactly an hour after the first. Together, the successive flights involved 360 aircraft—104 bombers, 135 dive-bombers, 40 torpedo bombers, and 81 fighters. By the time they headed back to their waiting Navy ships north of the Hawaiian Islands, 18 U.S. ships were sunk, sinking, or damaged; 2,459 lay dead or dying, another 1,282 wounded.

Elizabeth P. McIntosh, a reporter with the *Honolulu Star-Bulletin*, went out into the morning of smoke and flames. She filled a notebook with what she saw.

"In the morgue, the bodies were laid on slabs in the grotesque positions in which they had died. Fear contorted their faces. Their clothes were blue-black from incendiary bombs. One little girl in a red sweater, barefoot, still clutched a piece of jump-rope in her hand."[1]

The number of injured quickly overwhelmed the hospitals. Lawns, mess halls, and school buildings became makeshift emergency rooms—

and morgues. At one point, the medical personnel could do nothing for the worst wounded but give them morphine, mark their foreheads with an "M," and move on.

The images that played out seared McIntosh's memory. On the way back to her office, she recorded more.

"Seven little stores, including my drugstore, had nearly completely burned down. Charred, ripply walls, as high as the first story, alone remained to give any hint of where the store had been. At the smashed soda fountain was a half-eaten chocolate sundae. Scorched bonbons were scattered on the sidewalk. There were odd pieces lying in the wreckage, half-burned Christmas cards, on one, the words 'Hark the Herald' still visible. There were twisted bedsprings, half-burned mattresses, cans of food, a child's blackened bicycle, a lunch box, a green raveled sweater, a Bang-Up comic book, ripped awnings."[2]

It was, until the 9/11 strike on the World Trade Center, the bloodiest foreign attack on American soil in history.

The next morning's newspapers still had scant details. What they did have painted a picture of mass destruction and inevitable war.

The *Pittsburgh Post-Gazette* summed it up neatly: "Tonight the war becomes a world war in grim earnest."[3]

In its first edition following the attack, *Time* magazine was downright belligerent: "It was premeditated murder masked by a toothy smile."[4]

Still, nearly twenty-four hours passed before the significance of the attack became a concrete reality. President Franklin Delano Roosevelt went before a joint session of Congress with an exceptionally brief and now famous statement, demanding a declaration of war.

"Yesterday, December 7, 1941—a date which will live in infamy," Roosevelt began, "the United States of America was suddenly and deliberately attacked by naval and air forces of the Empire of Japan."

It was 12:29 P.M., Washington time. Shortly thereafter, Roosevelt ticked off the list of attacks Japan had carried out in the elapsing hours since the surprise assault on Pearl Harbor. In the twenty-two hours since, the Japanese had unleashed war on key targets in the Pacific: Malaya. Hong Kong. Guam. The Philippines. Wake Island. Midway Island.

And then, the predictable words that nonetheless sent a shiver up the spines of mothers across the country: "I ask that the Congress declare that since the unprovoked and dastardly attack by Japan on Sunday, December 7, a state of war has existed between the United States and the Japanese Empire."

Congress granted Roosevelt's wish within thirty minutes.

The morning after, Florida's *St. Petersburg Times* captured the nation's reaction with its editorial prophecy: "We are in this thing, now, ALL THE WAY—and we are in to win. OUR VERY SUR-VIVAL DEPENDS UPON COMPLETE VICTORY. We have answered the defiance of a cowardly, back-stabbing foe who talked peace even while plotting undeclared war. THERE IS NO TURN-ING BACK NOW; THE DIE IS CAST."[5]

Within days, the boys from Second Street got used to seeing the lines of men outside the recruiting offices, signing up to go fight. A mixture of patriotic fervor, masculine passion, and wartime propa-ganda fueled their desire to wreak vengeance on the Japanese. But few of that fervent first wave of recruits would see duty in the Pacific. Four days after the attack on Pearl Harbor, Adolf Hitler played right into Roosevelt's hands.

The president viewed the Nazi conquests in Europe as a direct threat to the United States, but a strong isolationist movement in America had prevented him from joining the fight. In reality, hostili-ties already existed between the United States and Germany. Nazi

U-boats had torpedoed American vessels in the Atlantic, and the U.S. Navy had retaliated by hunting down German submarines. Despite this state of undeclared war and the urging of Roosevelt's friend and ally Winston Churchill, the United States remained on the sidelines. Roosevelt could do little more than lend material aid to the British.

The Japanese attack, however, vaporized the isolationist sentiment preventing the United States from going to war. Then, on December 11, Hitler did what Roosevelt hadn't been able to. Germany declared war on the United States, allowing Roosevelt to demand a declaration of war against the Nazis.

Germany's declaration had already been delivered to the U.S. ambassador in Berlin when Hitler went before the Reichstag to defend it and rail against Roosevelt.

Hitler called FDR "mad." He accused him of whipping up anti-German sentiment. He could not contain his loathing of Roosevelt, nor his delight over finally having this nemesis drawn into the war.

"I will pass over the insulting attacks made by this so-called President against me," Hitler sneered. "That he calls me a gangster is uninteresting. After all, this expression was not coined in Europe but in America, no doubt because such gangsters are lacking here."

The heads of Hitler's war machine—Joachim Ribbentrop, Joseph Goebbels, and Hermann Göring—flanked him as his invective surged with intensity and he accused Roosevelt of deceitfully forcing the Japanese attack.

"First he incites war, then falsifies the causes, then odiously wraps himself in a cloak of Christian hypocrisy and slowly but surely leads mankind to war," Hitler said.

When he finished, the members of the Reichstag jumped to their feet, applauding wildly. Hitler had his war.

So did Roosevelt.

"The long-known and the long-expected has thus taken place," he wrote in his message to Congress. "The forces endeavoring to enslave the entire world now are moving toward this hemisphere. Never before has there been a greater challenge to life, liberty and civilization. Delay invites great danger."

Since Italy's Mussolini had followed Hitler's lead and also declared war against the United States, Roosevelt asked for declarations against both.

He got them. Not a single member of the House or Senate voted in opposition. Roosevelt signed the resolutions less than three hours after his message was read, barely twelve hours after Hitler's tirade before the Reichstag.

In four days, America had stepped from being a tense bystander and into declared war against three enemies.

A small group of senators, congressmen, and the vice president watched as Roosevelt's pen moved across the papers. It was official. Japan. Germany. Italy.

Roosevelt looked up at the gathering around his small writing desk. "I've always heard things came in threes," he said. "Here they are."

Once the resolutions were signed, Senator Carter Glass of Virginia told the president, "Some men in the Senate Foreign Relations Committee wanted to soften the resolutions so as not to hurt the feelings of civilians in the Axis countries. I said, 'Hell, we not only want to hurt their feelings but we want to kill them.'"[6]

For the first time in its history, as the *New York Times* noted, the United States was at war in both the Atlantic and the Pacific.

Tours of service were set "for the duration" of the war plus six months, and the men soon learned that there were only three ways to come home: win, die, or be so badly wounded they could fight no more. The families of the dead got a gold star to hang in the window. Within months, a grim constellation dotted the country.

Claro Soliz, a gentle artist with a poet's way of describing the world, decided not to wait for a notice. The week after the Fourth of July—almost exactly a year after Tony Pompa enlisted—Claro grabbed his brother and headed for the recruiting office.

"Let's see who gets a gold star for Mom," he said.

He enlisted the same week a young girl named Anne Frank went into hiding in Amsterdam. The day Claro was sworn into the Army, she wrote in her now famous diary: "Until Wednesday, I didn't have a chance to think about the enormous change in my life. Then for the first time since our arrival in the Secret Annex, I found a moment to tell you all about it and to realize what had happened to me and what was yet to happen."[7]

Neither of them would see the end of the war.

Roosevelt and his commanders knew they could not muster the force they needed to fight on both fronts relying strictly on volunteers. The draft had been in place since 1940, but now the time arrived to ramp it up. Soon, draft notices started arriving in mailboxes across America, including ones on Second Street.

Joe Sandoval got his. But, newly married and with a baby on the way, he got a deferment letting him stay home. His single brother Frank, though, had no excuses when his letter came. In September, the older boys gathered on the hill to play guitars, sing, and say good-bye to the first of the Sandovals headed off to war.

The send-off had a Second Street flavor all its own. Benny Goodman and the jitterbug may have been the rage on radios and in dance halls across the land, but the good-byes on the hill hearkened back to the homeland of the boys' parents. They sang in Spanish— ballads and *rancheras*, the plaintive Mexican equivalent of country-western. And, as much as they knew the occasion that caused the farewell, they avoided talk of the dark possibilities that lay ahead.

On this night, as they joked and drank and sang and talked of a future Frank would never see, they knew the news of the war was bleak. Headlines screamed the dire facts day after day. The Nazis had advanced almost undeterred across Europe. France had fallen the summer before. It joined Norway, Denmark, Holland, Luxembourg, and most of the rest of Western Europe under the control of the Nazis or their allies. Along with the Italians, the Germans were handing British and Australian forces blistering defeats in North Africa.

In June, the Desert Fox, Erwin Rommel, finally crushed the heroic British resistance at Tobruk and seized the important Libyan port. British, Australian, and some Polish reinforcements had resisted repeated German and Italian assaults on the fortified harbor. They withstood a withering 242-day siege. Rommel's Panzers, though, eventually decimated the British Armoured Brigades in the desert around Gazala, destroying some 230 of the Eighth Army's 300 tanks and forcing the British to retreat to Egypt. On the morning of the 21st, the last troops still defending the Tobruk garrison surrendered. Rommel took more than 30,000 prisoners, 2,000 vehicles, vital fuel supplies, and 10 million pounds of rations.

The victory earned Rommel the rank of field marshal, the young-est ever. It also threw the British into a panic. At their embassy and military headquarters in Cairo, orders flew.

"Get that!"

"Burn it!"

Personnel dashed around in a frenzy, gathering up all the confidential documents by the armful and pitching them hastily into the flames. The Germans and Italians would soon be upon them, but they would have no secrets—only ash. Mussolini, too, expected Cairo to fall any day. He flew to Libya to be on hand for the victorious march into the city.

He was in for a surprise.

As the Germans swept across Europe and North Africa, the Japanese had continued to spread relentlessly across the Pacific. General Douglas MacArthur fled the Philippines in March. Bataan's fall and the infamous Death March followed in April. The number of American dead rose, and the country's spirits sagged. We had gone to war, and we were losing.

On April 18, the Americans struck back.

Sixteen B-25s did what no others ever had, or have since. They lifted off from an aircraft carrier bouncing on the steely gray Pacific, 650 nautical miles from Japan.

Never mind that none of the pilots had ever taken off from a carrier before.

The Mitchell bombers had been specially modified for the assignment. Work crews stripped out some of their machine guns and radio equipment to reduce weight. They added collapsible fuel tanks above the bomb bays to increase their flying range.

Even if they survived, none was expected to make it back to the carrier.

Landing a medium bomber on the deck of an aircraft carrier bobbing on the ocean was impossible. The plan called for the planes to hit their targets, then continue southwest and land in China.

They'd be cutting it close.

A Japanese patrol boat spotted the carrier a little before 8 A.M. They were still some ten hours and 170 nautical miles from their planned launch point. The lead pilot decided waiting was too risky, the mission too important.

His name was Jimmy Doolittle. The target: the Japanese homeland. It was the first air raid aimed at hitting the heart of the empire.

The mission was so dangerous, the odds so high, Doolittle only accepted volunteers.

And now, spotted by the picket boat almost two hundred miles farther from Tokyo than they had planned for, he called for an immediate takeoff. The last bomber left the deck of the USS *Hornet* less than an hour after that.

They flew single file at wave-top level to avoid detection. Six hours later, they reached Japan. They hit ten targets in Tokyo, another two in Yokohama, and more in Yokosuka, Nagoya, Kobe, and Osaka. None of the planes was shot down, but all of them were lost.

Running low on fuel, Doolittle and the majority of the other pilots either ditched their planes in the sea or crash-landed on the mainland. One, realizing he would never make it to China, landed in Vladivostok. The Russians seized the plane and held the crew captive for nearly a year.

Two crewmen drowned when their plane crashed into the sea off China. The Japanese captured the other eight on board. They executed three for alleged war crimes. Another, weakened by a near-starvation prison diet, died in captivity. By the time American troops found and freed the remaining four, they were emaciated. The copilot, Lieutenant Robert L. Hite, had dropped to just eighty pounds.

The raid inflicted little damage, but the feat itself exploded in the psyches of the people on both sides of the Pacific.

As Doolittle wrote later:

"The Japanese people had been told they were invulnerable. . . . An attack on the Japanese homeland would cause confusion in the minds of the Japanese people and sow doubt about the reliability of their leaders. There was a second, and equally important, psychological reason for this attack. . . . Americans badly needed a morale boost."[8]

The attack brought another, unexpected, result—that changed the course of the war. The strike on their homeland convinced Japanese military commanders that they needed to extend the islands' defensive perimeter and to eliminate the U.S. Navy as a threat in the Pacific. The answer: attack Midway.

Japanese Admiral Isoroku Yamamoto planned to draw the Americans into a trap and devastate the Pacific Fleet, yet again. Just the opposite occurred. Code-crackers intercepted the Japanese battle plan, giving the Americans the chance to prepare an ambush of their own.

The Japanese struck in June. The battle raged for three days. When it was over, four of the six aircraft carriers that had taken part in the strike against Pearl Harbor had been sunk, 3,057 Japanese were dead, and the Imperial Japanese Navy had been permanently crippled.

By the September morning when Frank Sandoval boarded the bus to take him to the induction center, the end of the war was already being written.

Like all but a tight and secretive cadre, the people of Second Street had no inkling, but the experiments leading to the creation of the atomic bomb had already begun in the New Mexico desert.

The month before Frank headed off, almost to the day, Major General Eugene Reybold, head of the Army Corps of Engineers, signed the Manhattan Engineering District into existence. The lengthy moniker soon shrank. It became known simply as the Manhattan Project.

The project brought together some of the best scientific minds of the time, focused on a formula, with no idea of what they were really creating. Many of them, when they recognized the true, horrible power they unleashed, would come to regret their role.

For the moment, the "atomic bomb" existed only as sets of mathematical equations scrawled on paper and chalkboards. What they proved remained the subject of debate. Even when they detonated the first one years later, the scientists who built it had no idea what would happen. Their predictions ranged from absolutely nothing to the vaporization of the entire Earth's atmosphere.

For now, the moment when they would know for sure remained years away and far beyond the imaginations of average Americans. What most knew of the war effort came from newspaper headlines, radio reports, rumors, and suppositions. The letters from the men who knew what was really happening arrived home looking like Swiss cheese thanks to the censors' razor-bladed excisions, or filled with empty allusions to nameless faraway places.

The families on Second Street learned more from their shifts at the Rock Island Arsenal. Several of the women did duty as Silvis's version of Rosie the Riveters. Instead of building planes, though, they worked on the lines assembling .30-caliber machine guns and the disintegrating belt links for the chains of ammunition that fed them and their .50-caliber cousins.

The war provided, and the war took away. Frank left, but his brother Joe remained, clinging to the safety of his deferment and making a decent salary cutting wood for crates in the John Deere lumberyard.

The families on the home front got used to the ration books and the balding tires on their cars. Tires became one of the first things rationed after the Japanese seized the Dutch East Indies and its trove of rubber plantations. A month later, in February 1942, cars, too, joined the list of limited items. Sugar made the list in May, for the same reason: to make bombs and bullets and the machines of war.

An emergency statement from the U.S. War Production Board explaining the need appeared in newspapers in April.

"Unless we dig out an additional 6,000,000 tons of steel and great quantities of rubber, copper, brass, zinc and tin, our boys may not get all the fighting weapons they need in time. . . . Even one old shovel will help make 4 hand grenades."[9]

Frank's sister Georgia carefully managed the ration book she got from the government, pulling out the stamps that entitled her to her meager allotment of sugar or meat. One coupon permitted the bearer to buy two pounds of sugar a fortnight. Families could earn extra ration coupons for every pound of kitchen grease, bacon fat, meat drippings, and cooking fat they brought to the butcher. Grocers and butcher shops posted bulletins from Washington explaining why: "Fat makes glycerine. And glycerine makes explosives for us and our Allies—explosives to down Axis planes, stop their tanks and sink their ships. We need millions of pounds of glycerine and you housewives can help supply it."[10]

The actress Helen Hayes appeared in a magazine ad in December, photographed in her kitchen with two sailors, demonstrating how she supposedly strained fat into a can. "I'm told that a single pound of kitchen grease will make two anti-aircraft shells," she said. "So you can bet that not one drop of waste fat in my house ever goes down the drain."[11]

To supplement their food supplies Americans planted "Victory Gardens," which on Second Street looked a lot like the plots of tomatoes and peppers and pumpkins they had grown all along. Others might feel constrained by the sacrifices they were required to make. On Second Street, though, they already knew how to squeeze every last penny until it bled.

The summer before he went into the Army, Frank bought a suit to wear to his high school graduation. A year later, his brother Emidio wore it to his. In 1944, it was Tanilo's turn.

"It was kind of an odd color, a little bit of gray in it, or tin in it," Tanilo said. But there was no denying it was made to last. "It was a good suit."

The war didn't open many new doors for the Mexican-Americans on Second Street. They continued to suffer the usual indignities, but not the new ones meted out in a legalized mixture of hysteria and hatred. Those fell to the Japanese-Americans. Just two months after Pearl Harbor, Roosevelt signed Executive Order 9066. It allowed the "exclusion" of anyone from anywhere without trial or hearings.

Six days later, Japanese-Americans living on Terminal Island by the Los Angeles harbor were told they had to move within forty-eight hours.

The internment camps came later. They fell under the authority of the War Relocation Authority. There were ten in all, scattered across remote areas of the country—in New Mexico, Arkansas, and, the best known of all, at Manzanar, California. Within months, 110,000 Japanese-Americans—men, women, and children—had been forcibly removed from their homes and locked behind fences and barbed wire, watched over by armed guards.

One of them was George Takei, best known as *Star Trek*'s Mr. Sulu.

"I was 5 years old when my parents got us up early one morning and hurriedly dressed us," he said. "My brother and I were in the living room, looking out the front window. I saw two soldiers with bayonets on their rifles come marching up the driveway. They stomped up the front porch and they banged on the door. . . . We were ordered out of our home."[12]

The family spent the next four years in an internment camp in Arkansas.

Takei turned the experience into a musical, *Allegiance*, which debuted in San Diego in late 2012, and a TED Talk.

"Our only crime was looking like the people who bombed Pearl Harbor," he said. "I remember the sentry tower with machine guns pointed down at us. I remember the searchlight that followed me when I made night runs to the latrine. As a 5-year-old kid, I thought it was kind of nice that they lit the way for me to pee."[13]

The government's justification was perhaps summed up best later by the head of the Western Defense Council, before the House Naval Affairs Subcommittee.

"A Jap's a Jap. There is no way to determine their loyalty. . . . This coast is too vulnerable. No Jap should come back to this coast except on a permit from my office," General John L. DeWitt said.[14]

DeWitt swore the West Coast faced the threat of imminent attack by the Japanese, even though he presented no evidence to support his assertion. Still, the concern might have seemed reasonable given the advances of the Imperial forces.

Despite the crushing defeat of its navy at Midway, Japan continued its island-hopping conquests across the Far East. In July, the Japanese added Guadalcanal to a string of possessions that stretched from China down through the Solomon Islands, and tightened their hold on a distant and foreign place called Burma.

It was a place that everyone on Second Street would know soon enough.

Frank went off to training at Camp Wolters, outside Mineral Wells, Texas. The town, as its name implies, was once famous for its "medicinal" mineral waters, discovered by one of its earliest settlers. Mrs. James Alvah Lynch's rheumatism went away after she drank the water from a well sunk on her family's land. Within a decade, Mineral Wells had grown into a world-famous health resort, attracting as many as thirty-three thousand visitors a year on the railroad that ran into town.

As the water-fueled boom died off and the winds of war swirled, the folks of Mineral Wells actively sought an Army base. They offered a 2,300-acre ranch where Texas Longhorns with "thorn-raked flanks" had once roamed.

It was a place of coots and cuckoos and black-tailed jackrabbits, rolling hills and sizzling summers. And by the time Frank got there in the fall of 1942, it had cemented its reputation as the largest infantry replacement training center in the country. Nearly five hundred thousand troops came through during the war. They learned to fire and care for their M1 Garand rifles, to lob grenades, to fire mortars, and to hone their bodies into what was for most the best physical shape of their lives.

The demand for men on the multiple fronts made basic training exactly that—a speedy introduction to fundamentals before they moved on to advanced training.

Frank's stay lasted barely six weeks before he shipped out to Northern California, and a base that encompassed what in the days of the Gold Rush had been known, appropriately, as Camp Far West. Far West was the earliest U.S. Army outpost in Superior California, set at the sloping foot of the Alta Sierra Mountains, almost directly due west of Lake Tahoe. It was named after the man who convinced the United States in 1855 to form the American Camel Corps. The aim: to test the animals for transporting men and supplies across the deserts to the westernmost postings. It was a failed experiment.

Nonetheless, Edward Fitzgerald Beale gave his name to what was, by the time Frank and his friend Charles Monroe arrived, the principal training center for combat engineers. Camp Far West became known as Camp Beale, a place where recruits learned basic tools and vital skills—how to fell a tree, strip a log, read a compass and a map. By the time the rain and fog of winter blanketed the valley, they knew rope rigging and had spent a full week roughing it in pup tents as they helped build their first pontoon bridge.

"Training continued rain or shine, building bridges, built a dam, going to the rifle range, doing all kinds of field training," Monroe said years later in a letter to Frank's mother. They marched "10, 15 and 20 miles with full field pack which included are [sic] rifle," he continued. "Every day except Sunday we went through exercise, which kept our bodies in top shape."

Training lasted nearly a year, with long stints at Camp Young at the other end of California. It couldn't have been more different from where Frank was headed.

Camp Young sat on a stark patch of the Mojave Desert dotted with saguaro cactus and Joshua trees. It was a moonscape of broken rock, lava cones, and seven-hundred-foot-tall sand dunes that thundered as they shifted in the night. General George S. Patton picked it to train tank crews to meet Rommel in North Africa.

It was deliberately harsh—scorching hot in the summer, cutting cold in the winter, bleakly barren, and dry as bleached bone. East of Coachella and Indio, just north of the Salton Sea, it served as a stand-in for the deserts of North Africa. And, as the Bureau of Land Management proclaims proudly to this day, "this simulated theater of operation was the largest military training ground in the history of military maneuvers."

The Desert Training Center sprawled over eighteen thousand square miles—as big as Massachusetts and New Jersey together, with a few hundred square miles to spare. It stretched from Pomona, California, to within an hour's drive of Phoenix. North to south it ran from the Nevada state line until it butted up against the out-skirts of Yuma. And not a bit of it offered someone from the banks of the Mississippi like Frank enough water to work up a spit.

Frank hated it—although he worded it more delicately in his let-ters home.

"Truth is I don't like it," he wrote in June 1943, "but what can you do? This is the Army. This camp is up in the mountains, but is des-ert. We live in tents."

He found at least some of his superiors as inhospitable as the des-ert. He "caught hell," he said, when he got caught slipping into Spanish. Unlike blacks or Japanese-Americans, the Mexicans served in white units, but that didn't give them the liberty to converse in a language other than English.

About the only thing similar to Burma was the snakes. Even then, though, the rattlesnakes of the Mojave Desert by comparison seemed kindly, polite enough to sound a warning bell before they sank their fangs into whatever ignored it. Plus, rattlesnakes stayed pretty much to the ground, not dangling up in some tree ready to drop down the shirt of some hapless passerby.

"This was a very hot and dry location," Monroe told Frank's mother. "The temperature would reach as high as 120° in the shade. . . . During our stay at this camp, we were moved for a few weeks to Arizona on the Colorado River where we built roads for the eighth [sic]Army that was located there. We returned to camp young [sic] and one weekend later we went to the Salt [Salton] Sea, which we enjoyed very much. The water was so salty we could just lay on the water and float like a cork."

In September, the newly minted combat engineers were taken to Indio and put on a train. Their destination remained a secret. All the men knew was that they were finally going to war. And that, for now, the train was headed east.

Along the way came a sad irony: The troop train stopped briefly in the railroad yards in Silvis. Frank leaned out a window and spotted a worker he knew.

He called out to him.

"Go see if you can find my dad."

The man went looking. The train pulled away.

By the time Frank's dad got to the tracks, his son was gone.

No one from Silvis would ever see Frank again.

CHAPTER FIVE

ALL-AMERICAN, ALL THE WAY

By 1943, the call-ups were coming fast and furious. America's losses were mounting, the need for fresh—and more—troops growing.

In February, the other Sandoval family on Second Street got its first notice. Willie, the hard-hitting boxer who dreamed of going pro, got the Selective Service letter with the ironically cheery greeting. "Welcome," it began, when everyone knew it was anything but. He reported for duty two days after Valentine's Day.

A month later, nearly to the day, Peter Masias, the ladies' man with the rich baritone, got his note in the mail. Barely a week later, Slugger got his.

And off they went.

Second Street was mostly mud by then, Honey Creek starting to flow. March was the time of year when the days were warm enough to thaw the ice, nights just cold enough to refreeze the tops of shallow puddles. A sharp wind sliced up the street, stinging faces and fingers. But it was nothing like the cold Peter and Slugger would know in the winter of '44.

It was merely coincidence, of course, that Slugger and Peter got summoned so close together. They lived next door to each other. They played together. Neither volunteered. "We used to box together," Slugger said. Once we fought against each other. They ran out of fights or somebody didn't come. So we had to substitute for them in Davenport. He was a good friend."

Before that, they boxed in the basement of the Silvis library. "We'd sweat like crazy in there," he said.

That night in Davenport, though, Slugger discovered he was a bit too kindhearted to be much of a fighter.

When they were pushed by the coach to box each other, Slugger came out with a hard swing that caught Pete square in the face. The minute it landed, Slugger knew his friend was hurt. Bad. As Pete tried to blink away the pain, Slugger dropped his gloves and begged forgiveness.

"Oh, gee, Pete," he said. "Are you OK? I'm really sorry."

Coach Visconi went nuts.

"That's not what you do!" the coach shouted. "You're *supposed* to hit him!"

Still, boxing was how Slugger earned his nickname. Not because he was good. Just the opposite. They called him Slugger because he was anything but.

"I didn't do it too long," he said.

When the carnival rolled into town, Slugger and Peter met in the vacant lot between their houses and raced to the site where the trucks pulled in to unload.

"They used to hire guys," Slugger said. "They'd give you one dollar. We used to help them put the tent up. I never forgot that. We worked on the tent with the wrestlers."

The war changed everything. As soon as they put on uniforms, the Silvis boys all went their separate ways.

Slugger went into antiaircraft artillery—a unit that would have him within miles of Joe Sandoval from England to Berlin. His title: cannoneer, 601. His job: bring down German aircraft.

He trained on the North Carolina coast, in an upland swamp filled with mosquitoes men swore were as big as the gliders they used for target practice. Locals called it, appropriately, "dismal." On maps it showed up as the Holly Shelter pocosin, a place of pine flatwoods, alligators, and rattlesnakes. The military viewed it as a suitably isolated location for one of seven AAA training centers. Camp Davis had the distinction of offering five practice areas that included tens of thousands of acres of remote wooded terrain and a flat sand oceanfront range, places where the thunder of cannon fire could echo across the sea and shake the trees and disappear on the wind.

"Nor is this the first time that the noise of war has broken the peace of these lowlands, still haunted by the memories of Indians and pirates, slavers and Spanish marauders, Regulators and Taxmasters, Green and Cornwallis," the camp's commander, Colonel Adam E. Potts, pointed out, "and climaxed by the greatest naval bombardment in the world's history at Fort Fisher."[1]

By the time Slugger arrived in the late spring of 1943, the steady thud of ack-ack fire pounded through the pocosin, and the heavy booming of large guns roared along the shore.

He got there just before the WASPs. It was a first for the Women Airforce Service Pilots. Until then, they'd been relegated to transporting planes from far-flung factories to military bases around the country. Camp Davis gave them a fresh opportunity. They became the tow-plane pilots, flying A-24s and A-25s with targets trailing behind them for the trainees to riddle with fire.

"When they landed, we'd look and see if we hit them," Slugger said.

His time there also gave him his first view of the Atlantic Ocean. One of the most active parts of the base sat fifty miles from Camp Davis, on a spit of sand between the ocean and the Cape Fear River. That was Fort Fisher, where Slugger and the others learned to fire the 40mm cannons at targets in the air and at sea. They trained six days a week, working in six-man crews.

Once they got into the war, the number would double so that one crew would always be in reserve. It only took three men to aim, load, and fire a gun once it was in place. The driver, assistant driver, and backup gunner served as ammunition handlers, unpacking the shells and passing powder charges to the loader.

"While we were there was the first time I ever heard of the German submarines being on the coast—our coast," Slugger said. "We went out there patrolling. We went one mile one way and a mile back the other way."

He never saw any, but rumors persisted long after the war that one of the U-boats actually shelled the area.

It happened, supposedly, while Slugger was there, just a couple of miles up the beach from Fort Fisher. During the night of July 15, 1943, one of the Nazi submarines surfaced and fired five rounds at the Ethyl-Dow chemical plant. The shells missed. They overshot the target and fell harmlessly into the Cape Fear River.[2]

The incident, if it occurred, remains shrouded in secrecy. No news of it ever made it into the local paper or onto the radio.

It was, or wasn't, the closest the trainees came to a real fight at the base. Their months of loading, sighting, and firing all aimed at targets that didn't fire back. That ended as the cool nights of fall slid across the Carolina coast.

Slugger's unit shipped out ten days before Halloween. He loaded onto a troopship in Boston with the 430th Antiaircraft Artillery Automatic Weapons Battalion (Mobile). They set sail the following day, in a convoy of nearly three dozen ships. Some one thousand men crowded onto the freighter for the crossing. For many, like Slugger, it was their first time at sea. By the time they docked in Liverpool, many were noticeably thinner than when they'd left.

"I had never been sick in my life," Slugger said. "And I was there. Seasick. We were all throwing up all over the place. Man, I was glad when we got to Liverpool."

They weren't there long. The Americans were massing at clusters of camps throughout England, readying for an invasion only a tiny group of planners even knew was in the works.

As the dreary fall gave way to winter, the 430th settled in at a thirteen-hundred-year-old town a short distance from Liverpool called Huyton. German bombers had hit the town a couple of times early in the war, but not after the American artillery units set up their guns and resumed practice. The booming of the 40mm cannons may have been a nuisance to the nearby townspeople, but it also provided the comforting assurance that the Germans faced a gauntlet of antiaircraft fire if they chose to attack again.

Slugger had been assigned to the job of cannoneer, and gave thanks he wasn't in the infantry. Willie and Peter took a different route. They both volunteered for a new and untested form of American fighting that would prove crucial in shaping the outcome of the war. It relied on rugged individuals highly trained in the arts of killing, who could parachute directly into combat or behind enemy lines and operate alone, if necessary, to cause maximum damage to the enemy.

They were called paratroopers, and the combination of deadly skills and their distinctive uniform with loose-fitting pants tucked in their boots would later earn Willie's unit a battlefield nickname, discovered in the diary of a German officer: "Devils in Baggy Pants."

Willie's unit was among the original members of the fledgling 82nd Airborne. It was the first unit of its kind, despite the number in its name. Just a few months later, it became the first American force in history to jump into combat—with disastrous consequences. It was made up of rough-and-tumble men from all different backgrounds—Irish, Italian, German, English, and, thanks to Willie, at least one Mexican-American kid from Silvis. Appropriately, the 82nd was known as the "All-American" division.

Their initial training began at Fort Benning, in a program designed to test the best and wash out the weak. The base presses against the winding bank of the Chattahoochee River that forms the border between Georgia and Alabama. The area is on the Fall Line, where the rolling hills of the Piedmont Plateau bump into the flat-lands of the coastal plain. The fort sits just south of Columbus, Georgia, and across the river from Phenix City, Alabama, which, when Willie arrived, was cementing a reputation as a hotbed for organized crime, prostitution, and gambling. Not surprisingly, the soldiers from the training center fueled much of the booming criminal enterprise—and wound up drugged and rolled by the "hostesses," beaten and robbed by bouncers, and, on more than one occasion, found floating facedown in the river.

The bars had names like the Bucket of Blood, the Silver Dollar, and the River Front, where the owner gave a free beer to anybody who could throw their empty and hit one of the rats crawling through the place.

"On payday at the fort," the documentary filmmaker Robert Clem recounted, ". . . the mob that ran Phenix City would dispatch 'mobile units' to meet the extra demand, with girls handing out their favors under a tarp in the back of a truck."[3]

No surprise then than U.S. Secretary of War Henry Stimson damned Phenix City as the "wickedest city in the United States."[4]

In the spring of 1943, when Willie got there, the volunteers hoping to be part of the airborne faced a grueling four-part training schedule. More than half wouldn't make it to the end.

The "A" stage pushed, tried, hardened, and eliminated. It was about endurance, strength, and discipline. The candidates ran nine miles before breakfast, climbed ropes, did calisthenics and too many push-ups to count.

"You had to be able to by the end of the week climb a rope thirty-five feet high; climb up and then hold it until they told you, and then come down," Private W. A. Jones recalled. "You had to be able to do a minimum of thirty push-ups and a 5 mile run. . . . If you didn't you were out."[5]

The instructors, Jones said, "were the meanest son of a guns in the world. I still think so. I was afraid of them. . . . We had sawdust in the building where you climbed the ropes. This one guy spit in the sawdust. The instructors made him get down with his mouth and pick it up, and go outside and spit it out."

The challenge began almost immediately. When PFC John B. Isom stepped off the transport plane that brought his group to Benning, the NCOs ordered them to run around the airfield for seven miles. Several men dropped out. Isom thought he might, too, "until

I got what they call a second wind and I thought I could run around the whole world. When we came back to the camp I guess I drank half a gallon of water. I was so thirsty. They warned us not to do so, but I managed all right."[6]

For someone in peak physical condition like Willie, the demand that they double-time everywhere on the "Frying Pan" came easy. And he had done enough push-ups in his time to easily rank among the best. But other challenges lay ahead.

In "B" stage, the men learned about the parachutes. How they worked. How to control them in the air. How to land. They learned to count off three seconds when they jumped from the plane. If their main shoot hadn't opened by then, it was time to pull their reserve. They learned to hook their tethers to the static line running down the middle of the plane, how to check their equipment, and how to sound off before the green light signaling they were at the drop zone came on. They learned that the faster they followed one another out the door, the closer together they landed and the faster they could regroup.

In the "C" stage they also learned to pack their parachutes. Everybody packed his own. That way, if it didn't open, they could only blame themselves.

During this next-to-last stage, they also got to put some of the theory into practice, on the towers. The 34-foot ones claimed several of the volunteers. They were strapped to a cable at the top and were expected to jump, to land in a pile of sawdust. More men washed out there than on the taller, 250-foot towers. The bigger ones, though, came as close as they could get to the experience of a real jump—without a plane. A parachute was connected to the tower. Willie, like all the others, strapped on the harness and was lifted to the top of the tower, then released. Now came time to remember everything he'd been taught about landing. Failure had a heavy price. It could leave a man with broken legs and, once they healed, a ticket back to the infantry.

When the chute was released, Willie had to look out at the horizon, not at the ground. He had to keep his legs slightly bent and, as he felt his boots touch the ground, roll. This was the time to perfect his technique, not just to test his mettle. It would only get harder once he loaded up with ninety to a hundred pounds of battle gear.

"D" stage was decisive. Every one of the paratrooper candidates had to make five jumps out of a C-47 "Dakota" transport plane, including one at night.

The men loaded on in "sticks," groups of twelve men, holding the hooks on their tethers tightly. They sat stiffly, clutching the hooks, along the sides of the rumbling planes. The planes flew at about twelve hundred feet, at about 130 mph. The roar of the engines and the howl of the wind in the open cargo door washed over them as they ticked off the steps ahead in their minds—again and again.

As they neared the DZ, the jumpmaster ordered: "Stand up and hook up!"

Willie stood and snapped his tether to the static line.

"Check your equipment!" the jumpmaster commanded.

After a few seconds, he called out, "Sound off for equipment check!"

They started with the last man. "Number twelve OK!" he shouted, and slapped the back of the soldier in front of him. So it went, down the line. Willie called out his "OK!" and slapped the next jumper.

"Stand in the door!" the jumpmaster shouted.

The first in line stepped into the open doorway. The others slid their tether hooks along the static line as they shuffled forward. Then the green light came on and they poured through the door, one after the next, as quickly as they could.

Despite the training, their hearts raced as they spilled out into the sky and saw the ground so very, very far below. Before most could remember to count, their chutes billowed with a pop that yanked them skyward with a hard snap.

The rest came all too fast. They barely had time to grasp the awe of floating, the flutter of the lines in their hands. Some remembered to look at the horizon. Many didn't. They looked down. Lost their bearings. Hit hard.

They got better. Or they left.

On Friday morning of "D" week, June 25, 1943, the candidates lined up on the parade ground. The sun had come up some two hours before, and the temperature under a nearly cloudless sky was climbing fast. The mercury would reach eighty-seven degrees at its peak that day, but it still had a ways to go before it helped the "Frying Pan" live up to its nickname. A puff of breeze from the east offered little relief, and soon the rows of ramrod-straight recruits would have trails of sweat stinging their eyes.

They didn't care. The day was special. On that sunny morning in Georgia, they stopped being candidates. They became graduates. They became Airborne. Exactly how elite that cadre was showed in how thin their ranks had become since the day they arrived. Fewer than half of those who'd started now stood on that parade field.

One by one, the men stood firmly at attention as the silver wings, the Basic Parachutist Badge, was pinned over their left pockets. They had made it. They could call themselves paratroopers and blouse their uniform pants in the tops of their boots—the famed "baggy pants"—wherever they went.

Willie sent home a card celebrating the event. It had a photograph of a paratrooper drifting beneath a fully opened chute, with a transport plane high above.

"Today is the day," it proclaimed, followed by a poem:

For weeks and weeks,
I've worked darn hard,
Doing tumbles, pickups and such;
But today's the day,
I'm on my way,
I'm a qualified jumper.
There's thrills and chills,
Scares and cares,
When going out of that plane;
But today is the day,
I can proudly say,
Geronimo, I made it.

Willie let the poem speak for him. He wrote the date under it and signed it, simply, "William."

Graduation, however, was just the first step. The new paratroopers could be assigned, as needed, to any airborne division. Willie's orders sent him to the 82nd. Within days of earning his wings, he boarded a train that took him north to another base along the Fall Line. The train stopped at Fort Bragg, next to Fayetteville, North Carolina.

It was a lowland place settled by Highland Scots before the Revolutionary War. And, although neither of them knew it, the fort stood just over two hours up the Cape Fear River from where Slugger was blasting at targets by the sea.

Benning had made Willie an Airborne paratrooper. Bragg would make him an "All American."

The volunteers were, invariably, rugged individualists. At Fort Bragg, they became a team. A highly honed one. The intensive training phase called upon them to make several more jumps, by day and night. They ran obstacle courses, learned jujitsu, marched for miles in full combat gear, and learned to quickly assemble into a deadly attack force once their feet hit the ground.

Best of all for Willie, the commanders encouraged competition between the regiments, especially boxing. Once again, the fighter from Second Street put on the gloves, stepped into the ring, and proved he was fearless.

For all the work, for all the challenges, he was having the time of his life. It showed in his cockeyed grin in the photo with his unit boxing team: Sixteen shirtless fighters bunch in a group for the camera like a high school wrestling team. They wear their trunks and boxing shoes. Several have their hands taped like they had just pulled off their gloves. A smiling boxer at the center holds a trophy. Willie crouches in the second row, the curl of his smile tugging at his lip.

That summer in North Carolina—of chow lines, competition, and camaraderie—turned the band of mavericks into a band of brothers and readied them for war.

Peter wasn't far behind. By the time Willie got to Fort Bragg, Peter was in jump school, going through all the drills and tests Willie had faced just weeks before.

Their paths diverged from there.

Peter was destined for the newly formed 17th Airborne Division, not the 82nd. He became a member of the 139th Airborne Engineer Battalion, expert in the dangerous tasks of both construction and destruction under fire. In addition to building battlefield routes and runways, engineers served as demolition experts, cleared minefields, and disabled charges set to destroy vital bridges.

Again, though, their coincidences converged. Peter went through his advance training barely an hour south of Willie, and almost as close to Slugger, at Camp Mackall, North Carolina. He learned to rig explosives and to disarm mines; and he continued to jump from planes and run and do push-ups just as he had done at Fort Benning. He spent the summer, fall, and most of the winter there and continued training long after Willie and Slugger packed onto ships and sailed off to war.

The engineer soldier's handbook issued on June 2, 1943, while Peter was going through jump school, described the duties, and the stakes:

WHAT IT MEANS TO BE AN ENGINEER—You are an engineer. You are going to build bridges and blow them up. You are going to stop tanks and destroy them. You are going to build roads, airfields, and buildings. You are going to construct fortifications. You are going to fight with many kinds of weapons. *You are going to make sure that our own troops move ahead against all opposition, and you are going to see to it that enemy obstacles do not interfere with our advance. You are an engineer.*[7]

It was a tradition stretching back to the Revolutionary War. The first ones primarily built field fortifications. The Corps of Engineers came into its own during the First World War and grew from 2,500 men to almost 300,000. By the Second World War they had become a vital part of military operations.

The first part of the mission, construction, required Peter to gain skill at clearing trees, building roads, and laying bridges. By the time he finished, he had to understand I-beams, floor beams, girders, and trusses. He had to be able to tie up a bowline, a timber hitch, a sheep shank, a fisherman's band, and a half dozen other knots, and know how to build a raft using fifty-five-gallon gasoline drums, three-inch planks, and three-quarter-inch rope.

The second part of an engineer's job involved destruction, and death—both causing it and preventing it. As the manual put it:

> One of your most important jobs is the handling of explosives and demolition tools. . . . You must learn this job thoroughly. It is a great responsibility. When you are given the job of blowing up a bridge, a road, or a building, that bridge, or road, or building *must be destroyed at the specified time.* There can be no mistakes. Demolitions are usually ordered at critical times; and the failure of a single demolition may cost the lives of hundreds of men. You must not fail.

The half-pound blocks of TNT, they learned, were the safest of the explosives they handled. They needed a special cap or detonating cord. The TNT wouldn't just go off if it was hit, no matter how hard. And it could be used for underwater demolition.

Dynamite, on the other hand, was much trickier. The half-pound sticks were just as powerful as TNT but could be set off by an errant blow or flying sparks. And, as would be of particular concern to Peter later on, "when frozen it is especially dangerous and must be handled with extreme care."

The fledgling engineers became adept with bangalore torpedoes, at charging forward with the five-foot tubes packed with ten pounds of high explosive, throwing themselves at the ground, thrusting the weapon's nose through the bands of barbed wire they planned to clear, and setting them off with Primacord.

They learned to lay minefields in the patterns most effective for stopping tanks, and men. And as they worked their way through the humid summer and the crisp fall, they learned the dangerous opposite: how to sweep a field while cautiously listening for the telltale hum of the metal detector, and how to use their bayonets to gingerly dig up and disarm a mine that could easily blow them in half.

It was a delicate, painstaking, and nerve-racking task that took its toll on men like no other. The men had no extra protective gear. They relied solely on their skill to succeed without losing their hands, their eyes, or their lives. Understanding the power and sensitivity of what they were handling only made it worse. It frayed their nerves and tortured their sleep, and more than one man cracked and had to be transferred.

Peter persisted. As the temperatures rose through the long summer, he polished his abilities at making his team safe and at laying waste.

The first to arrive amid the fields and woods of North Carolina also was the first to leave. As Peter and Slugger continued their training, Willie got to go home and show off his uniform. It was the last time he would see Second Street before the United States plunged him head-on into the war against the Nazis. And the last time anyone from Second Street would see him.

The stage had been set the November before, in North Africa. Over the months that followed, it pitted the Americans against Germany's brilliant "Desert Fox," Field Marshal Erwin Rommel, and opened the way into Europe through the soft toe of Italy's boot.

The first combat experiences proved to be costly lessons for the raw American troops facing the battle-hardened Germans. The green and untested U.S. fighters suffered humiliating losses. They were ill-prepared, ill-equipped, and ill-informed.

It showed the very first day of combat, even against an outnumbered French force using outdated equipment. British and American commanders, all the way up to Roosevelt and Churchill, had debated for months about the best strategy for bringing the United States into the European war.

Initially, the Americans pressed for a direct assault against the Germans at Normandy. The British, fearing that too early an attack against the heavily fortified French shore could end in insurmountable failure, persuaded their allies to come in on the Germans' Southern Front in North Africa.

The stakes were high. In the first full-fledged involvement of the Americans in the European Theater, failure would have been critically, and perhaps permanently, demoralizing. The U.S. commanders knew it. During a planning meeting at the White House, Major General George S. Patton Jr., dressed, as always, in a crisply creased uniform, told the president, "Sir, all I want to tell you is this—I will leave the beaches either a conqueror or a corpse."

The way things turned out, it could easily have been the latter.

The mission called for the simultaneous landing of nearly one hundred thousand men at three key cities in Morocco and Algeria: Casablanca, Oran, and Algiers. With the Nazis bogged down in Tunisia battling the British at El Alamein, all three cities were under the control of Germany's nominal ally Vichy France.

The combined British and American task forces were superior in numbers and strength. The French had only slightly more than half as many troops as the invaders. They had outdated tanks.

Whether the American equipment was much better was debatable. Most of the GIs carried the same kind of bolt-action Model 1903 Springfield rifles U.S. soldiers had fought with in the First World War. The U.S. Sherman tanks carried powerful 75mm guns that would prove effective against the German Mark IV tanks, but the American tanks had a tendency to burst into flames when hit. It was so bad, in fact, that tank crews nicknamed the tanks Ronsons, after the cigarette lighter maker.

Nonetheless, the Americans expected the Vichy French to break off their loose loyalty to the Nazis once they saw that the United States and Britain were finally throwing their full might against the Germans. At most, the Americans expected minor resistance.

They were wrong.

In Morocco, the problems began even before H-hour. They intended a predawn attack, at 4 A.M. on November 8, 1942. They had to wait. An unexpected current scattered the formation of transport ships. Some wound up as much as seven miles off course. Rough seas and crashing waves smashed landing craft against the rocky shoreline or sent them miles from their assigned beaches. Hundreds of troops drowned. Tons of equipment sank.

The attack force at Fedala fared the worst. Nearly half of the landing craft were lost. Sixteen of the transport *Thomas Jefferson*'s thirty-one landing craft went down in the first wave. The transport *Leonard Wood* lost twenty-one. The *Carroll* lost eighteen in the first wave and five in the second, leaving it with just two boats for taking men and equipment ashore.

Aboard the USS *Tasker H. Bliss* the morning of the assault, Charles "Chick" Bruns of the 10th Combat Engineers noted in his diary:

Wow! all hell has just broke out. I'll finish this latter. [*sic*] It is now 10:00am and the navy's big guns are still blazing. Boy oh boy, what a battle. I have been out on deck all during and you can see the big shells falling all around the ships. The coast is just literally being blown to bits. Wave after wave of men are going in. One destroyer just came by and it had the back end of it shot off. About 20 big, four motored German bombers came over escorted by fighter planes. Man did they ever start bombing us. Bombs just fell like rain.[8]

On shore, the displaced and disoriented landing parties attempted to regroup and complete their missions. One team, realizing it had landed five miles from where it was supposed to, had to march across the desert. It finally arrived at noon, abandoning its artillery along the way. Another group, tasked to seize the airfield, burst into a building they thought held Vichy troops, only to find they had captured a French café and about seventy-five of its customers.

Oran was no better.

Two former U.S. Coast Guard cutters given over to the British as part of the lend-lease program had a singularly important job. The HMS *Walney* and the HMS *Hartland* were to race into the Oran harbor, seize the docks, and keep the Vichy French from destroying them. They wound up sailing into a massacre.

Both ships were caught in a deadly cross fire from four shore batteries, raked by fire from the thirty-one French ships in the port, and, with their engines knocked out and listing badly, pounded by close-range broadsides from two French frigates. Casualties reached 86 percent—183 dead and 157 wounded, out of 393. The survivors were captured.

A similarly disastrous scenario was playing out some 275 miles away, in Algiers. There, a dozen shore batteries protected the harbor. This time, the landing force was made up of six hundred American fighters aboard two British destroyers. The French opened fire within minutes of the ships approaching the harbor entrance and disabled the HMS *Malcolm* almost immediately. Severely damaged, with ten dead and twenty-five wounded aboard, the *Malcolm* limped back out to sea.

That left the HMS *Broke* to continue alone. It was able to break through the harbor boom and get its troops to shore, but it came under heavy fire as it withdrew. Crippled by repeated hits, the *Broke* sank two days later.

The American troops who made it to shore fought for seven hours. Then it was over. French forces surrounded them and forced them to surrender.

As the military historian George Howe put it: "The situation of [the landing] force at nightfall, 8 November, was insecure and even precarious."[9]

Still, the grossly outnumbered and outgunned French quickly capitulated. They signed an armistice with the Allies on November 10. The Americans and the British could now turn their attention to driving the Germans out of Africa. In preparation for that fight, and their still distant assault on Italy, the Allies continued to stream troops and equipment into North Africa. By the end of November they would have a force 253,213 strong in place. But the Americans still had a lot to learn.

The lessons came quickly, and harshly. The Americans raced to confront the Germans in the Nazi stronghold of Tunisia. They made it to within sixteen miles of Tunis two days after Thanksgiving. Then began the string of humiliating losses that would push them back more than eighty-five miles, decimate American forces, and send GIs fleeing in panic.

Even their retreat was embarrassing, and costly.

"This constituted the foremost advance towards the TUNISIAN capital that we were ever able to attain before the conclusion of the campaign, six months later. Here we were stopped, and elsewhere our progress had already slowed," the commander in chief of Allied forces, General Dwight D. Eisenhower, wrote in his after action report.

Heavy rains hampered them even more. It got so bad, the troops took to saying "Captain Mud" was with the Germans.

Eisenhower went on: "More and more in time the weather appeared to be our worst enemy, crippling both our offense and defense, and making it increasingly difficult either to advance or to withdraw. Rains saturated the valleys of Northern TUNISIA, and made a quagmire of the airfields."[10]

"Incidentally," he continued, "the weather hampered the movement of our forces under General Anderson in withdrawal, although fortunately that withdrawal was accomplished with a minimum of enemy interference. However, United States Combat Command 'B' became badly mired and finally had to abandon the larger part of its equipment, retrieving only three of its eighteen 105 MM Howitzers; twelve of its 62 medium tanks; and 38 of its 122 light tanks.

"It was a crippling loss, well-nigh irreplaceable because our supply system was already overtaxed, and because our losses now hindered still further our efforts to compete with the rate of Axis build-up."

The Germans counterattacked on December 2. By Christmas they had pushed the Allies off the high ground of Longstop Hill outside Tunis and were driving forward. The Nazis continued their advances through January and, on the 30th, began what would be the first major encounter between German and U.S. forces. For the Americans, it would be a devastating and humiliating defeat and proof of how unprepared they were for battle against the Nazis.

"The German Army makes war better than we are now making it," a French Army observer sent in to analyze that first searing loss reported. "Unless this is realized and unless steps are taken to improve the quality of our fighting forces, we are bound to suffer defeat when meeting it on anything like equal terms."[11]

The rout began at Faid, where the German infantry and Panzer tanks poured through the dusty narrow pass between two rises to attack poorly equipped French forces. Armed with World War I–era artillery, the French nonetheless put up a valiant fight and caused heavy losses among the Nazis before they were forced back. As they fell back, the American 1st Armored Division charged in with fifty-one Sherman M3 tanks. They quickly destroyed a few of the German Panzers, and the Nazis turned and ran.

The Americans chased after them. Then the trap sprang. The Germans caught the Shermans in a lethal barrage of antitank fire. The gas-fueled "Ronsons" burst into flames when they were hit. Forty-four of the U.S. tanks were lost.

"It was murder" is how Edwin Westrate, an army forward observer, described it. "They rolled right in the muzzles of the concealed eighty-eights and all I could do was stand by and watch tank after tank blown to bits or burst into flames or just stop, wrecked. Those in the rear tried to turn back but the eighty-eights seemed to be everywhere. I don't know how many tanks we lost altogether that day but it was a sickening few which escaped in our zone."[12]

Now unopposed, the Panzers advanced easily. On Valentine's Day, they handed the inexperienced American forces one of their most shameful losses. The Germans attacked with 140 tanks at 4 A.M., concealed by the howling winds of a Saharan sandstorm. The cover was good, but the American mistakes proved critical. Their tanks were spread too thin. Their infantry took positions atop hills, where they stood silhouetted against the sky and too far apart to support one another or their tanks on the valley floor. And their lack of real battleground familiarity sapped the nerve of the troops and fed the overconfidence of their commanders.

Colonel Thomas D. Drake "issued instructions to all officers that no one would leave the line under fire," Major Robert R. Moore, commander of the 168th Infantry, 2nd Battalion, stated in his after action report. "They would be ordered back to the line by an officer and if they disobeyed they were to be killed at once. 'Teach all personnel to beat the Germans and to kill them at every opportunity. I will notify you when I want prisoners taken.'"[13]

Captain Ernest Hatfield, an aide to the 1st Armored Division's commander, described the confusion and overwhelming force of the assault in his diary:

Awakened at 0700 hrs by telephone call from CCA. Germans are attacking Lessouda in force with tanks and artillery. Stukas bombing their CP. Tanks (30 German) surrounded Lessouda hill and overran B Battery of 91st Field Artillery. Thirty tanks striking south from Lessouda toward Sidi Bou Zid—unknown number of tanks striking toward us at Sbeitla. . . . Fighting is very hard and bombing is ongoing. Our air support isn't too good. Hightower reported only five medium tanks left in one company, one company is unheard from and another is unheard from and there is no information about it. General [Ward] asked Corps for reinforcements . . . they got here about 1230 hours. . . . I got a report from Dixon, II Corps G-2, that reconnaissance elements of the 21st Panzer were on the Sidi Bou Zid-Gafsa road . . . and that 34 enemy tanks were seen at 1300 hrs coming toward Sbeitla."[14]

Colonel Drake watched the unfolding disaster perched atop Djebel Ksaira, a rocky 1,840-foot mountain north of the pass. With him, he had about 1,000 men from the 165th Infantry and 650 sundry troops.

They, too, served as an example of how poorly prepared the Americans were for battle. About 200 of the men at Ksaira had arrived as replacements two days earlier. Some came without weapons. Some had never fired a rifle.

Drake received several truckloads of new bazookas the day before the Germans attacked, but none of his men knew how to work them.

Unable to do much else, Drake phoned the command post at Sidi Bou Zid to tell them he saw signs of panic in the artillery below. He was told the men were merely "shifting positions."

"Shifting positions, hell," Drake said, "I know panic when I see it."[15]

It was too late. The Germans crushed the American tank defenses and surrounded the isolated infantry units on the Ksaira and Lessouda hills.

An American counterattack on the 15th, aimed at rescuing the trapped infantrymen, met similarly disastrous results. The Shermans rolled forward at 12:40 P.M., kicking up such large dust plumes that they might as well have sent up flairs to mark their progress. The dust blinded crews in the old-style cavalry V formation and made them easy for planes and spotters to track.

The Germans used the terrain to their advantage. As the advancing Shermans clustered at a suitable point to cross a deep, dry riverbed known as a wadi, four Nazi 88mm and two Nazi 47mm antitank guns hidden in nearby olive groves opened fire. Breaking through to reach the village of Sidi Salem, German Panzers and Tigers swept in on the flanks for a point-blank tank battle.

It was hardly a match. The battle-seasoned German crews annihilated the U.S. force, captured its commander, and left fifty American tanks smoldering.

The entire 2nd Battalion was lost. But, from their vantage point at the 1st Armored Division's command post, the Americans didn't know. Watching the bright flames from the village licking at the night, the division's commander reported, "We might have walloped them or they might have walloped us."[16]

While the tanks were engaged in the village, the Germans overran the infantry hill positions. They captured Drake and all but about three hundred of what remained of his force.

Luckily for the United States, the German field commanders, Irwin Rommel and Hans-Jurgen Von Armin, argued over how to proceed. While the debate raged, the Americans were able to regroup for a last, determined stand at the Kasserine Pass. Or, as Major General Lloyd Fredendall, commander of the American II Corps, demanded: "I want you to go to Kasserine and pull a Stonewall Jackson."

Fredendall meant, of course, that his forces should make an impenetrable stand like the one that won the Confederate General Thomas Jackson his better-known nickname.

February 19 dawned cold and wet. An icy wind rushed over the mountains and through the pass. Heavy rains soaked the waiting U.S. soldiers. The green U.S. troops beat back the Germans' first attack. But once night fell, Nazi infiltration teams slipped through the crevasses and cracks of the rocky ridges and wreaked havoc on the rattled GIs.

The Americans panicked. They fled in droves, abandoning vehicles and equipment as they raced headlong over the rocks and sand.

In four days of fighting, the Americans were pushed back eighty-five miles. The losses: 2,546 missing, 103 tanks, 280 vehicles, 18 field guns, 3 antitank guns, and 1 antiaircraft battery.

The Germans, however, were victims of their own success. Their blitzkrieg assault left them overextended and short on supplies. The thirsty tanks desperately needed fuel and ammunition to press the attack. And the farther they advanced, the more Allied troops joined the fight. The Germans' heady progress stalled.

On February 22, Rommel called off the assault. The Germans withdrew. The Americans had suffered an embarrassing and costly defeat at the hands of the battle-tested Nazis, but they learned valuable lessons.

As Major Allerton Cushman's observer's report noted: "Both officers and men are psychologically unprepared for war. All ranks are not yet imbued with the spirit that makes them willing to die rather than fail in any assigned mission. We cannot consider ourselves a first-class army until all echelons make a conscientious and determined effort to instill just such a spirit in every officer and man."[17]

Eisenhower learned quickly that the problem began at the top in North Africa. He sent 2nd Armored Division commander Major General Ernest Harmon to investigate. Fredendall, Ike learned, had hidden in a solid rock bunker seventy miles behind the front line during the Kasserine Pass humiliation. Harmon described the II Corps commander as a "moral and physical coward."

British General Harold Alexander put it more politely, but no less bluntly. "I'm sure you must have better men than that," he said.[18]

A furious Eisenhower ordered the purge of lackluster and incompetent officers, relieved Fredendall of duty, and replaced him with the man who would take American tanks all the way to Berlin: George S. Patton.

Within days, Patton let the difference be known. His message was clear: They would be the best soldiers in the world and look the part. That included wearing neckties, despite the desert heat.

By mid-March, the Allies were on the attack. The British struck at the Germans and the Italians along the southern flank and, in the course of a month, drove them back more than 150 miles, to within 50 miles of the Tunisian capital. As the British hammered away, Patton struck in the north.

"This north country is entirely different from the semi-desert where we Americans spent the winter. Up here the land is fertile and everything is violently green," the famed war correspondent Ernie Pyle wrote in March. "Northern Tunisia is all hills and valleys. There are no trees at all, but now in spring the earth is solidly covered with deep green—pastures and freshly growing fields of grain. Small wildflowers spatter the countryside. . . . Villages are perched on the hillsides, and some of them look like picture postcards."[19]

Ironically, the battering at Kasserine Pass gave the Americans an unexpected benefit. The Germans, unimpressed by the lack of skill and will on the part of the U.S. troops, assumed an overconfidence that caused them to underestimate their enemy in future encounters.

Patton made them regret it. He brought 88,287 men against the Germans. And in the few weeks since he had taken command, even Pyle noticed the difference.

"The most vivid change is the casual and workshop manner in which they now talk about killing," Pyle said in an April 22 dispatch. "They have made the psychological transition from the normal belief that taking human life is sinful, over to a new professional outlook where killing is a craft. To them, now there is nothing morally wrong about killing. In fact, it is an admirable thing."[20]

By the beginning of May, the Germans lay confined to a single sector in Tunisia. The Allies clearly held the momentum. But the cost of the advances was brutal and bloody, and gouged at the men's psyches.

"The Germans lie on the back slope of every ridge, deeply dug into foxholes," Pyle explained. "In front of them the fields and pastures are hideous with thousands of hidden mines. The forward slopes are left open, untenanted, and if the Americans tried to scale these slopes they would be murdered wholesale in an inferno of machine-gun crossfire plus mortars and grenades."[21]

So the Americans pounded the Germans with artillery by day and moved on them by night, around the sides and from the rear. That, too, though, took its toll.

"Sgt. William L. Nelson gave his 9th Division comrades one such example. From an exposed position Nelson directed mortar fire effective enough to stop a German counterattack, an act which brought down on him a rain of enemy grenades. Though mortally wounded, Nelson crawled to another position and directed more devastating fire on the enemy. For his heroism, Sergeant Nelson was posthumously awarded the Medal of Honor."[22]

The Nazis laid mines by the thousands to stop the Americans. Pyle counted more than four hundred dug out in one field. Sweeping with mine detectors was too slow to keep the pressure on the Germans. Instead, the men stumbled over the uneven ground, slipped on the loose rocks, lost their footing in holes and gullies and wadis, fell hard in the darkness, and, in a primitive and violent way, found the minefields.

"Naturally there are casualties," Pyle wrote, "but they're smaller than you might think—just a few men each day."[23]

Churchill had said it months before, after the Americans and British poured ashore in North Africa. Now his words seemed even more prescient: "Now this is not the end. It is not even the beginning of the end. But it is, perhaps, the end of the beginning."[24]

History would prove him right. The end remained a long way off, and there would be more sickening failures on the way. But the final phase of the North African fighting—exposing the "soft underbelly of Europe" Churchill spoke of just months before—came in May.

The Americans attacked Bizerte. The British attacked Tunis. The Nazis fell back from the rocky mountain passes, across the green plains, through the ancient Kasbah of Bizerte, and into a corner by the sea in Tunis.

The Germans crumbled.

"Enemy troops were surrendering in such large numbers that they clogged roads, impeding further advance. In the second week of May enemy prisoners totaled over 275,000. When Axis generals began surrendering on 9 May the six-month Tunisia Campaign entered its final days. As General Bradley turned his attention from fighting a determined enemy to governing large numbers of civilians and prisoners, his troops composed doggerel about a memorable lady they had discovered: 'Dirty Gerty from Bizerte.'"[25]

Barely a month later, the Allies were ready to leap the Mediterranean into Italy. The first step: Sicily, and one of the worst "friendly fire" tragedies of the war.

Sicily had a long, belligerent history. Greeks, Romans, Arabs, Normans, vandals, Ostrogoths, and Byzantines had all fought and died for the largest island in the Mediterranean Sea. Now, as summer loomed, the Allies targeted the rugged, hilly island as the stepping stone to the Italian mainland.

Willie's unit played a key role in the invasion. But inexperience and fouled communications turned it into a deadly debacle of Americans killing Americans. Hundreds died, slaughtered as they drifted down helplessly, riddled by friendly fire from GIs on the ground who mistook them for attackers.

The first wave of 82nd Airborne paratroopers took off from airfields in Tunisia as the sun set on July 9. They planned on a four-hour flight, east over Malta, then northwest along the southern coast of Sicily. They didn't count on a strong headwind that slowed them down, scattered the formation, and threw their navigation efforts into chaos. They wound up strewing paratroopers across the countryside miles from their designated drop zone. A chorus of hushed countersigns—"George," "Marshall"—sounded through the dark as individual troopers wandered through the fields, farms, and olive groves, trying to link up with other members of their units. Days later, barely two-thirds of the 3,400 paratroopers who jumped had regrouped.

The night of the 11th, though, would be much worse. That's when the bulk of the 504th Parachute Infantry Regiment flew in to join the rest of the 82nd Airborne on the ground. The 144 planes in the flight group stayed together, unhindered by headwinds. They reached the coast of Sicily about 10:30 P.M. and turned toward their target, Gela.

"As the lead plane reached Lake Rivierre a burst of machine-gun fire came from the beach below," Captain Harry F. Jost recounted.

"It was as though the burst was a signal for everything below to open fire on the elements of the flight all along the coast. Antiaircraft fire from the Allied ships and from batteries on the beaches tore into the slow moving transports full of human cargo. Many of the planes crashed downward in a vivid arc of flame, while others tried, hopelessly, to swing clear of the hail of fire. Planes forced down along the coast were fired on by the shore guns as the troopers tried to launch the rubber life rafts from the riddled hulls of the fallen aircraft. Of 23 planes shot down, only 6 crashed carrying their cargo of troopers with them. However, jumping from a burning, crashing craft was, in many instances, like jumping from the frying pan into the fire. In these instances numerous troopers were, during their parachute descent, fired on and killed by American troops on the beaches."[26]

The ground fire caught the raw pilots completely off guard.

"A few minutes before reaching the drop point with the paratroopers," one of the C-47 flyers recalled, "a shell smashed into the starboard side of the fuselage and knocked out a hole, four by six feet, while a fragment from the shell slit the aluminum and every rib from hole [*sic*] to rudder. Passing through the plane the fragment ripped off a door as a second ack ack blast carried away a portion of the left stabilizer. The explosions also blew away a large piece of equipment, and the impact was so great that it felt like a motor crash in the pilot's cabin.

"The airplane spun at a right angle and nearly pulled the controls from my grasp. For a second I didn't realize what happened, then finding myself out of formation I began a violent evasive action. I saw three planes burning on the ground and red tracers everywhere as machine gunners sprayed us as if potting a flight of ducks."[27]

The paratroopers could do nothing.

"We felt like trapped rats," said Captain Adam Komosa.[28]

Jumping didn't improve their odds.

"We jumped into a steady stream of AA fire, and not knowing that they were friendly troops," related First Lieutenant C. A. Drew, Company F, 504th Parachute Infantry Regiment. "There were 4 men killed and 4 wounded from my platoon. Three of these men were hit coming down and one was killed on the ground because he had the wrong password."[29]

Eight planes limped back to Tunisia. They brought with them four dead and six wounded. The plane carrying Brigadier General Charles L. "Bull" Keeran, the assistant division commander, went down into the sea. His body was never found.

After the plane carrying the 504th's commander, Colonel Reuben Tucker, landed, ground crews counted more than two thousand holes in the fuselage.

In all, friendly fire downed twenty-three planes and damaged thirty-seven. Some two hundred troops died, including sixty pilots and crewmen, at least fifty-one men from the 504th, and thirty-five from the 376th Parachute Field Artillery Battalion.

The mission, however, succeeded. By mid-August, the last of the surviving Axis troops fled across the narrow Strait of Messina for the Italian mainland. The dearly won toehold had been gained, and the Allies' long, brutal march up through Europe began.

CHAPTER SIX

BETWEEN FLAK AND FIGHTERS

The victory in Sicily gave the Allies a small but valuable purchase on the continent, a springboard from which to attack Italy and Churchill's "soft belly" of Europe.

They began with bombing runs along the heel and sole of the boot, pounding the air bases and fortifications the Germans and Italians had relied on to attack the British and American forces in North Africa. The targets included a little-known airfield on the Salento Peninsula, in a place called Grottaglie.

The peninsula jabs south from the Italian mainland like a limestone spike, dividing the Ionian and Adriatic seas. It has been fought for, and over, since ancient times. By the Messapii and the Mycenaean Greeks, the Byzantines, and the Normans.

Grottaglie sits on a rocky plane just inland of Taranto and has distinguished itself from the days of Greater Greece as a center for the making of distinctive ceramics. It is, as the Latin root of its name suggests, cut by deep and plentiful ravines. It is also dotted with olive trees and pockmarked with caves carved into the limestone ridges, where medieval peoples hid from the invading Saracens as the Muslims pressed their expansion north of the Mediterranean.

Most important now, though, was its location. Grottaglie was ideally situated to put the long-range American B-24 bombers within striking distance of strategic Axis targets and allow the Allies to begin their relentless assault on the Germans, chipping away at Nazi defenses, vital oil production facilities, and factories supplying Hitler's war machine.

When the Americans arrived in the final days of December 1943, Grottaglie was home to a runway cratered by Allied attacks and bombed-out buildings with broken floors and wind howling through holes in the walls and roofs. The bare, charred skeletons of two dirigible hangars cast eerie shadows on the airfield.

The 12th Air Force, out of Tunisia and, later, Sicily, had done an exceptional job of destruction. As the 449th's group historian, Second Lieutenant Damon Turner, described it: "Debris lay everywhere about the field. Some booby traps could still be found, although the area in which the group was living had been cleared of these menaces. Gaping holes marked most of the buildings, while every structure had been scarred above the ground level by bullet holes and bomb fragments. Bomb craters had been filled in, but the recency of destruction filled the air."[1]

The sun, rain, and cold poured in through the punctures cleaved in the roofs of the buildings left behind by the Italians. There was no running water, no light, and no heat, but that didn't stop the Americans from turning them into officers' barracks for the 449th Bomber Group, Fifteenth Air Force, where weary pilots, navigators, and bombardiers curled up on the cold marble floor between missions.

"Two squadrons and headquarters personnel are living in the

headquarters building," Turner noted. "Shaving is done in water heated in helmets—it's not done often. . . . A four-hole latrine had been dug, and men stood in line."[2]

Second Lieutenant Elliott "Tommy" Thompson was twenty-three when he landed in Grottaglie. He knew cold from growing up in New Jersey, and hard times from losing his father when he was seven, during the Depression, and having to go to work to help his family as soon as he got out of high school.

None of it compared to Grottaglie.

"It was horrible. We had nothing there. We had no beds. We had no mess hall. We had no barracks," he said. "Grottaglie used to be Mussolini's pride airfield. It was bombed to hell. The buildings were all collapsing apart. I slept in a bombed-out building where it had a partial roof over one corner of the building, so at least we had some protection when it rained.

"You had to find your own little spot. . . . It was wherever you could find a spot," he continued. "I slept on a marble floor. The only thing I had underneath me was a couple of blankets. You can imagine how tough that was."[3]

Some of the men found oil lamps to use for light. And some fought back against the cold with improvised heaters fueled with gasoline. But there was a downside.

"Gasoline stoves made of empty cans give heat but are dangerous," Turner noted. And, later, "There have been several bad gasoline fires. This evening one severely injured several men."[4]

With no mess hall, officers and enlisted men shared the same chow, and the same chow line.

"We'd stand in line in with our mess kits in the pouring rain waiting for chow," Thompson said. "And you couldn't eat the crap they were giving us. But at the end there were always these little kids

4, 5, 6 years old, with tin cans in their hands. Anyway all these Italian kids would stand there where the garbage can was and beg us for the rest of our food. 'Not in the garbage, please!' Put it in their little tin cans so they'd have something to eat."[5]

The gunners and ground crews slept in tents outside. Tony Pompa, a tail gunner on a B-24 named the "Lurchin' Urchin," was among them. But no one there knew the dark-haired kid by that name.

When Tony had left Silvis in 1941, the war was a distant prospect. Let go from his job at the Arsenal after they discovered he wasn't an American citizen, he headed to Chicago. Then he took a detour.

Weeks went by before he explained what had happened in a letter to his sister on July 22, 1941:

> Hi Clara P
> This letter is addressed to my mother only I kind of changed her name to Lopez, but don't worry, changing my name won't do any of us any harm.
>
> I guess I might as well tell you where I'm [sic] or maybe you already know, before I left I told you's [sic] that I was going to work in Chicago, well after-wards I thought it over and figured I wouldn't be gaining anything, just working for my board + room, so I stopped in Peoria and signed for the Army Air Corps. And here I am at Scott Field a little past East St. Louis. . . .
>
> I'll be up here maybe three years, I would probably feel better up here if I could have taken lessons to be a pilot in the Air Corps, but they told me I had to have two years of college, and if I still want to take that trade, I have to go about two years of school here. I don't want to do that so I'm going to try and study mechanic.[6]

That didn't happen either.

They made him a gunner and sent him up in mammoth B-24s to pepper targets with rounds from a .50-caliber machine gun. He was seventeen.

The Army didn't know. And they didn't know his real name.

In his letter to Clara he closed, "Remember, my name is Tony P. Lopez."

Training for the gunners was long and intense.

They learned how to sight. They learned how to shoot. They learned to assemble their M2 .50-caliber machine guns blindfolded.

They fired at targets on the range and at targets in the sky. They rode in the back of a pickup truck aiming a mounted shotgun to learn how to track and lead their aim to hit a moving target. They learned what to expect from the enemy fighters that would be swooping in to attack—how they would close in like sharks cutting through the water, then roll and charge them at an angle with their machine guns blazing.

When they were good enough, the would-be tail gunners like Tony stepped into turret trainers mounted on trucks to learn to level their guns as they twisted and turned.

The goal was to make the guns feel as natural in their hands as their own fingers and to make controlling the carnival ride whirling of the turret feel like an extension of their minds. As one turret training manual put it: "Once you have developed the touch, the turret practically runs itself."

Almost a year after he enlisted, they sent him to radio operator school in Sioux Falls, South Dakota. His time in the military away from home, and the cold of a South Dakota winter, wore on him.

He met a girl, though, a pretty, tall German-American teenager with light brown hair. She ran a café with her mother. Her name was

Dolores. He called her Dee. She fell for his dark good looks. He fell for her pale complexion and welcoming blue eyes.

She got pregnant. It was a not-so-welcome surprise he hinted at in a letter to his sister on February 21, 1943.

Dear Clara:

Guess I should of [sic] *written you a card as soon as I arrived but I've been feeling so low + disgusted since I left the quad cities that all I feel like doing is laying down + die, not a bad idea huh? maybe* [sic] *if I still feel this way a few weeks from today I'll tell you one reason why I feel this way. The other reason is because I like the idea of coming home but I don't like the idea of leaving. I guess I wouldn't mind it much if we were doing something important, maybe it's because I'm getting tired of the way I live. I would like to look into the future + and find out whether I'm going across or not, when the war will end so all of us prisoners will be pardoned from prison. I got myself in so I guess that's about all the squawling I can do, anyway I'm still dreaming of the day when I will be able to go back and live the life that I didn't appreciate to live, what do you think?*[7]

Tony may not have been thrilled to have a child coming so soon, but there was no mistaking his feelings for Dee.

Her parents were divorced, but her father lived in Sioux Falls, too. When she and Tony were getting married, they went to see her dad. He didn't take the news well. When he got belligerent with Dee, Tony stood up to him. No man was going to mistreat the mother of his child, not even her father.

The young lovers had a civil wedding before Tony Jr. was born in July. Dee had just turned seventeen. Tony Sr. was nineteen.

The baby was barely two months old when his father got transferred to the final phase of his training.

It was time for Tony to take to the air, to hone his skills firing the twin machine guns at targets trailing behind tow-planes, and to join a crew—the one he would be with from there until they came home, or didn't. His crew: 7-16. His pilot: Tommy Thompson. Together, they would learn the reality of flight aboard the combat plane Ford was making at the rate of 650 a month.

For all its massive size and staggering might, the B-24 had an aluminum skin so thin it could be cut with a knife. It might as well have been made of canvas for all the protection it gave against flak and enemy bullets. In the tail turret, however, Tony was surrounded by one-and-a-half-inch bulletproof Plexiglas and a half-inch armor plate.

The gunners wore a heated flight suit—which frequently failed—and an oxygen mask. Powerful as the Liberator was, it had no luxuries. At twenty-six thousand feet, the usual cruising altitude for the bombers, temperatures inside dropped to thirty, forty, or even fifty degrees below zero. The air grew so thin a man would pass out in just a few seconds if his oxygen was cut off.

That happened with alarming frequency, especially as men heaved and twisted, huffing from nerves and effort as they shuddered and shook through fields of flak or fought off swarms of fighters. A seal formed between their faces and the rubber on their masks. The condensation in their breath froze and clogged their oxygen line. Men fainted. Men died.

The B-24 was a workhorse of specific intent. Its job was to carry bombs long distances. The men aboard were not passengers. They were laborers. They worked for the plane. Their job was to get the aircraft to its target and deliver its payload—usually ten 500- or five 1,000-pound bombs. If they got the plane back home, that was a bonus. The Army had no illusions. More B-24s were made than any other American military aircraft in history for a simple reason: The military expected them to be shot down, blown up, ditched in the sea, or damaged so badly that they crashed on landing and roasted in the flames of their exploding fuel tanks.

They were right. In all, they made 18,428; about 12,000 were lost in combat—nearly 3 out of 4.

Crewmen called it the "Flying Coffin."

Flying it was a wrestling match, especially in combat. Even at minus thirty degrees and wearing only the thin, unlined leather airman's jacket, Thompson returned from missions exhausted and drenched in sweat.

"You have no idea what a difficult thing flying those things was," he said. "The last thing I worried about was being cold. It could be 20 below and I was sweating. I'm not kidding you. I was sweating at 40 below. My shirt was soaking wet. My collar would get frozen with ice. My neck would be raw. . . .

"We did not have power steering in those days," he continued. "It was a physical effort for me just to control it. When we got back from missions I was so exhausted I couldn't get out of my seat for ten minutes. I just had to sit there and relax."[8]

No effort was made to make the planes comfortable. The seats had no padding. They weren't adjustable. The pilot couldn't even wear his parachute during the flight. It wouldn't fit. He had to keep it stowed behind his seat and pray that if he ever needed it he would have the time—and the ability—to get it on and get out before the plane slammed into the ground.

Even getting from one end of the plane to the other was a dangerous dance. Only an eight-inch-wide catwalk ran over the bomb bay doors. Miss a step as the plane bounced and jerked in flight and a man could go crashing through—the aluminum doors only had a one-hundred-pound capacity.

Most of the men had never flown before. Still, they had only a few months to prepare before they were thrown into battle.

Their education began with nine weeks of preflight training, which included four to five hours of academic instruction every day, plus an hour of physical training. Instructors drilled them in mathematics and physics, taught them to use aeronautical maps and charts, forced them to solve simulated operational problems.

After the ground training, pilots began work on their actual flying skills in a small, low-horsepower aircraft. It took two more levels, with heavier and more complex planes, to earn their wings.

Only then, after they were considered pilots, could they begin their training in a combat plane. That phase meant learning not just to handle the plane, but to develop special flying techniques designed for war. They flew at night, at high altitude, and honed their ability to fly in tight V-formation, practicing for the day when they would join three hundred, four hundred, or even one thousand other aircraft on a bombing mission that involved eight to ten hours of wing-to-wing flight.

Training for the 449th suffered several interruptions, as group historian Turner noted.

"The principal difficulties encountered were fivefold: first, the general inexperience of all personnel; second, inadequate training facilities; third, the change of station from Alamogordo to Bruning in the midst of training; fourth, insufficient time for training; and fifth, recurrent bad flying weather at Bruning Army Air Base."[9]

Bruning is an out-of-the-way Nebraska farming village at the edge of the Great Plains, spitting distance from the Kansas border. The Army bought up 1,720 acres in 1942, leveled farmhouses, barns, buildings, and trees, burned crops and prairie grass, and built Bruning Army Air Base. It had what the military wanted most in a flight training facility: lots and lots of flat.

They didn't consider—or didn't care—that Nebraska sits in the nation's "Tornado Alley," and while the thunderstorms and twisters are most common earlier in the year, the fall could bring weather challenges, too.

Nearly one thousand construction laborers and carpenters worked twenty-four hours a day to build the base. When they finished, it had 234 buildings, including hangars, barracks, a post exchange, and a chapel. It had three concrete runways, set in a triangle—one, nine thousand feet long; two, six thousand feet.

They spent just over two months together as a crew in Nebraska when they got the answer to Tony's question: They were headed overseas, via a hopscotch route from Nebraska through Topeka, West Palm Beach, Puerto Rico, Trinidad, and Brazil—to Dakar.

Thanksgiving arrived while they waited in Topeka, Kansas. On December 8, the 717th Squadron, Pompa and Thompson's group, left for West Palm Beach. The same day, the 449th had its first casualties. Fourteen people died when a B-24 piloted by Captain David E. Councill, commander of the 719th Squadron, slammed into a mountain peak south of Marrakesh.

Thompson said that the 449th's commander, Colonel Darr Alkire, was enraged.

"That really got to Colonel Alkire. He was so mad. He didn't care about the guys getting killed. But he lost an airplane and he hadn't even gone into action yet. I'll never forget that," Thompson said. "That was one of the many reasons why everybody hated his guts."[10]

The trip to Grottaglie took one day shy of a month. They lost a second plane in Puerto Rico along the way, and one more in North Africa. They were lucky. All but one man bailed out safely.

Conditions had to be perfect to make the jump across the Atlantic, to the westernmost point of the African continent—Dakar, Senegal. Even the shortest route stretched 1,872 statute miles, just 228 miles less than the combat range of the B-24s. Cutting the load and adding extra fuel tanks let the planes go almost a thousand miles more, but not if wind or weather interfered.

So they waited for the meteorologists to give them the go-ahead, in Natal, Brazil.

"If you look at a map of South America, it's the easternmost point in South America," Thompson explained. "We were there for ten days or so, waiting for the perfect weather. The weather had to be ideal. We could have no headwind. We could have no side wind. Because it was a long flight from there over to Africa. And we sat there doing nothing for a week or ten days, getting drunk every night.

"When they finally called us and said, 'Hey, the weather's right, you're leaving,' it was Christmas Eve—Christmas Eve of 1943."[11]

They spent New Year's Eve in Tunis, again waiting on weather, and crossed the Mediterranean to Grottaglie on January 2.

Tony Pompa wrote home immediately.

Dear Clara:
This time I'm writing to tell you + the folks that I finally got here, I'm "somewhere" in Italy, from now on I guess I'm staying here until I complete my missions, we got here a day before New Year's.

I had planned to write you soon as I got here but we've been pretty busy working on the plane, it's impossible to write

at night because we have no lights, I think we're getting a
lamp today. This place were [sic] *staying in was bombed*
recently so you can imagine how the living conditions are
down here but I still don't mind it very much, mostly because
I know it won't be this bad all time.[12]

Combat missions began the following week. The deaths began a week later. Nine men died first, killed in a glaring example of the squadron's inexperience. A plane above them in the flight formation dropped two bombs on them. Their B-24 ripped apart in the air in a giant fireball.

The next day they lost another. And the day after, another.

"To those who had anticipated two or three missions each week the program for January came as a rude awakening," Turner observed. "During January alone this group completed nineteen (19) missions. . . . As a matter of fact the statement was made at a dinner of Commanding Officers on 30 January that this group and the 450th group flew more sorties together or singly than any group had flown in the same time or period during the entire history of the Army air forces."[13]

They went up about every other day, threading the precarious corridor between fighters and flak. With the fighters, at least, they could fight back. Getting through the exploding fields of flak was more nerve-racking because it depended as much on luck as anything else.

When the antiaircraft guns opened up, puffs of black smoke filled the sky like dark, deadly dandelions. Pilots wrenched their planes through a series of fits and jerks designed to avoid the flak and keep the gunners on the ground guessing. The black smoke, the fliers knew, marked a danger already past. The smoke was the spot where a shell had just exploded. The threat lay in the clear patches between. The trick was to head into the puff of black flak smoke while making the plane bob and cut and weave—but never to make the same move twice, lest the gunners spot the pattern and put a burst right where the plane would be next.

In the words of Ernie Pyle: "The planes have to fly in constant 'evasive action,' which means going right, going left, going up, going down, all the time they are over enemy territory. If they fly in a straight line for as long as 15 seconds, the Germans would pick them off. . . .

"The pilot . . . must never make exactly the same move two days in a row. By constantly turning, climbing, ducking, he makes a calculated hit almost impossible. His worst danger is just flying by chance right into a shell burst."[14]

Even a near miss, though, could have devastating effects as an exploding shell sprayed shards of hot shrapnel indiscriminately around it. As Michael Weber described it: "It is designed to destroy both planes and the people inside them. Sometimes the shrapnel would go in one side of the aircraft and out the other side, hitting nothing in between. Sometimes the shrapnel would pierce the thin skin of the aircraft and bounce around inside a bit. Sometimes, the worst of times, it would go in one side and tear something inside apart. Maybe that something was mechanical, electrical, hydraulic, or human. Shrapnel was indifferent."[15]

It took steely nerves as they steadied the plane over the target, knowing they were vulnerable as they waited for the bombardier to shout, "Bombs away!" Then the captain could yank the controls and run for home.

Tony didn't describe the danger in his letters home.

"Dear Sis," he began one, on January 28, 1944. "Our crew has more missions than others so we're laying around now waiting for them to catch us up, the Col. wants everybody to be even around here. I think its [*sic*] fair enough. I have a picture of our plane + as soon as we are allowed I'll send it to you. I might also be able to send you one of the whole crew beside the plane."[16]

He planned a future with his family, including a church wedding with Dee.

"You asked why I was falling away from my religion but I don't think I'm doing so bad, I told you in the first letter that I had spoken to the Priest here + he told me that everything could be fixed, I've been going to holy Communion every Sunday. That's what mother wants isn't it?? All except for marrying Dee by the church but that has to wait till I come back, I could also have my name fixed back I thought it over + it's best to leave it this way until I go back to the States. Tell my mother all this and let me know if it makes her feel any better."[17]

Three days later, he was dead.

As the month rolled on, the bombers got better at hitting their targets, but the losses kept mounting. January 30 was the 449th's costliest to that point. They lost three planes in a single mission.

Thirty-five planes from the 449th rendezvoused with bombers from the 450th Bombardment Group for an attack on an airdrome at Udine, in northern Italy. They had just dropped their bombs, more than thirty-seven tons of five-hundred-pound bombs, when a horde of Messerschmitts—some thirty to fifty fighters—swarmed the formation.

One B-24 exploded in midair when an ME-109 crashed into it. A second spiraled into the ground. So did a third. Out of more than thirty crewmen aboard the three planes, only seven chutes were seen to open.

That same day, the colonel's plane, the "Maui Maid," named for his wife, smashed into an embankment and had to be scrapped.

The next morning, the last day of January, Alkire took command of another plane, the "Lurchin' Urchin," and picked Tommy Thompson's crew, including Tony, to fly with. Alkire took the left seat. He made Thompson his copilot. Their target was a German-held air base at Aviano.

"Why he picked me I'll never know. And I wish he hadn't," Thompson said, "because I hated that guy's guts. . . . He was an iron ass. He never had a nice word to say to anybody about anything. All he would do is chew your ass out no matter what you did. So it wasn't a pleasant day, you know."[18]

The target sat at the base of the Dolomite Mountains, at the dividing line between Italy and Austria. The "Pale Mountains," as they were once known for their distinctive hue, are basically the foothills of the Alps, about fifty miles north of Venice, at the north end of the Adriatic. The air base, as the planes flew, was almost directly due north of Grottaglie.

As they approached, Thompson steeled himself, waiting for the Messerschmitt fighters. Tail gunners like Tony tensed in the confines of the Plexiglas tails, fingering the trigger on the turret control grip, eyes scanning the sky for the fighters that came up on the rear like packs of wolves.

"One fighter never came in by himself," Thompson explained. "There was always three of them. Each one had six .50-cal. machine guns on their wings. And it looked like a bunch of fireflies, a little blinking light, when the bullets were coming. That was the toughest part. When you've got eighteen machine guns shooting at you, and you've got no place to go. No place to hide."[19]

But the fighters occupied only a fraction of his attention.

"I could only give them a half-a-second glance," he said. "I was busy flying in formation. You can't look at any place except your position in the formation, at the guy ahead of you and the guy alongside. When they came at me, I couldn't help but give a tenth-of-a-second glance and say a little prayer: 'I hope you're a lousy shot.'"[20]

It was a time when the flyboys envied the infantry.

"On the ground you can always dive in a foxhole, you can get behind a tree. You can lay down flat. We couldn't do a single thing. That was the toughest part."[21]

That day, though, not a single German fighter challenged them. There would be no aerial jousting. This would be a jitterbug through a flak field, a dance with Lady Luck.

The sky was clear, visibility unlimited.

They turned toward the target at twenty-two thousand feet. The colonel dropped the Lurchin' Urchin a thousand feet "to surprise the Germans," Thompson said. "He fucked up again."[22]

The antiaircraft guns opened up. Shells exploded all around them. The charges were stacked at fifty-foot intervals, and going off close enough to send violent shocks through the plane.

They released their bombs at 12:58 P.M.

"And right after we dropped our bombs, we got three direct hits," Thompson said, "a direct hit in the tail, direct hit in the nose, and one mid-ship that started a fire."[23]

The last shot had found the B-24's Achilles' heel. To gain range, the bomber had additional fuel tanks built into the midsection. The plane's middle also housed the heart of the oxygen system.

"The third hit was mid-ship," Thompson continued. "Somehow it must've hit the oxygen system because the flames came right through. We were all of us in a split second inhaling flames instead of oxygen. My chest and throat were burned."[24]

From his vantage point on a nearby plane, Second Lieutenant John W. Olson saw the Lurchin' Urchin's death dance.

"Col. Alkire's plane was hit by flak," he explained in the mandatory Missing Air Crewman Report following the mission. "After he dropped his bombs he went into a left bank and then nosed over to the right. He then went into a steep glide, about a forty-five (45) degree angle. It was at least down to two thousand (2,000) feet before I saw any smoke come from the plane. It was his No. 3 engine which had been hit."[25]

From another neighboring plane in the box formation, PFC Eugene W. Briggs watched it, too.

"I was flying in the lower ball position of plane No. 44, Lt. Gifford T. Hemphill, Pilot. Flak began coming up before we reach the target. Just about the time the bombs were dropped the Colonel's ship was hit. He peeled off into a steep right bank. He was hit at about 21,000 feet and dropped probably 9000 feet before pulling out; I saw nine (9) chutes open. Then the ship pulled out it shot up from 600 to 1000 feet in the air; then, stalled out and nosed down and fell straight to the ground and blew up when it hit."[26]

Inside the Lurchin' Urchin, the view was much more chaotic. Flames, fed by fuel and oxygen, flayed by the gale force winds rushing through the open waist gun windows and bomb bay doors, whipped around the inside of the falling plane.

Alkire, Thompson said, had a special slim parachute he could wear as he flew. Other pilots and copilots didn't. The cockpit space was too tight. They had to keep theirs stashed behind their seats.

As the plane dropped, Thompson said, Alkire rushed out.

"He should've been the last guy out," he said. "He was the first guy out. I'm reaching behind my seat trying to find my parachute and he shoved me back in my seat and took off."[27]

Thompson grabbed his parachute and followed. Alkire got out through the bomb bay hatch. Thompson didn't.

"We were battling smoke and flames and right on the verge of passing out," Thompson said. "I was crawling on my hands and knees. We had to crawl from the pilot's compartment back to the radio room, open up a trapdoor in the floor, slide up another door in the entrance to the bomb bay, climb out in the bomb bay, and then jump out.

"That's a lot of time. You never had all that time. So the plane just blew up as I was crawling that way."[28]

Thompson didn't know that Second Lieutenant James Galliher lay locked in the bombardier's position under the nose turret. Galliher had joined the flight at the request of the colonel's bombardier, George Gordon, to get some extra training. Now, as the plane plummeted, Gordon struggled desperately to free Galliher.

"The turret wouldn't turn. The hydraulic system was shot out, and we didn't have power for it. So he was turned sideways, tracking the planes, the bombers that were around us. And he couldn't get it to come back. You had to have it straight back, before you could get out that little door. And he couldn't get it. It wouldn't turn.

"So I told the navigator to go ahead out and I would try to get it. You could . . . down below, there was a little wheel that you could turn. You could turn the turret. So I got down in there trying to turn that thing and then we got . . . I don't know what happened. But it shook us up and threw me over to the side down by the Plexiglas, down at the front, and I looked over and I could see the altimeter as we were going down. It was spinning right along. And I knew we were going down pretty fast. . . . But when we started into a deeper dive, I couldn't move. I could just see the altimeter as I lay there against the side of the plane. And, I could see he would move. And Galliher would move around a little bit, but I couldn't see his face. I had the feeling he had got some shrapnel, but I couldn't tell for sure, because he had his back to us."[29]

Then the plane exploded.

Gordon came to as he fell through the air. He was too low for his chute to open on its own, so he started pulling it out as fast as he could.

"Just as I got it out and I just got straightened around, I hit the ground," he said.[30]

Thompson was just as lucky. The explosion knocked him out, and out of the plane. He came to falling through the air just as Gordon did, but when he pulled his rip cord, he realized "it was only hooked on one side," he said. "So what it did was it pulled the harness right off of me. Fortunately for me, the harness came off and actually looped around my left ankle. . . . As I'm coming down I'm hearing all this—bombs are swishing down all around me, both sides of me. And they would throw me, every time, it knocked me up in the air."[31]

He had barely hit the ground when he was surrounded by more than a dozen German soldiers. An English-speaking officer ran up, pointing his Luger.

"For you," he said, "das war is over!"[32]

For Tony, too.

He had pulled himself out of the tail turret and scrambled forward, toward the camera hatch.

"I spoke to him as he was helping the other waist gunner to open the escape hatch," waist gunner Wayne W. Ross told crash investigators.[33]

Then something went wrong. Tony's chute spilled out. The howling, hurricane-force winds whipping through the interior yanked the shroud and twisted it in a mad tangle in the plane's cables. Tony struggled in the parachute's rigging like a fly in a spiderweb. Then, he stopped.

Ross said he last saw Tony "in the tail lying behind the camera hatch. . . . He was unconscious due to fright caused by his chute opening inside the plane."[34]

He was still there as the plane winged over and exploded into a mountain.

The fire burned for hours, villagers said.

A few days later, the people on Second Street saw something they had never seen before. A Western Union man came riding his bicycle up the rutted dirt path. He stopped at Tony's house. Soon enough, the folks on the street would know what it meant when they saw the telegram carrier coming their way.

CHAPTER SEVEN

Devils in Baggy Pants

When it began, the moon had not yet risen. The sea was pitch-black.

Crowded into the open hold of a landing craft bobbing gently on the dark, calm water of the Mediterranean, Willie could see the dim yellow lights in the windows of the buildings clustered near Anzio Beach. He waited for the telltale crack of machine guns on the shore and the whistling shrieks of incoming artillery to signal that the Nazis were awake and returning fire.

Like most of the paratroopers around him, Willie listened with experienced ears. Most, like him, had changed over the last few months: The knots in their stomachs were different. They were nervous, yes, but no longer with the fear of the unknown. Now they feared what they knew too well.

Seven minutes earlier, two British ships loaded with 798 rockets each had unleashed a screaming barrage at the defending Germans on shore. It lasted five full minutes. The launchers fell silent at precisely 2 A.M., January 22—one week and a handful of hours before Tony Pompa died.

Now, as the onslaught came to an end, Willie and the rest of the 504th Parachute Infantry Regiment stood with their ears ringing, watching as the first squat boats loaded with apprehensive soldiers motored toward the Italian shore. The smell of salt water and diesel mixed with the sharp, acrid smoke from the rockets. A few nervous coughs crackled in the darkness. Some of the pious crossed themselves one last time and mumbled their prayers.

The attack was planned as an end run on the Nazis, after a bloody, months-long deadlock in the frigid, muddy mountains of Italy. Sweeping in at Anzio brought the Allies in far behind enemy lines, where they could break the Nazi defenses and charge in to take Rome.

Or so the plan went.

It would soon be known as one of the costliest military disasters of the war, dragging on for months with the men trapped on a soggy, flat killing field with no real place to hide, totaling almost 67,000 dead and wounded.

More 504th paratroopers would die here than in any other battle in the war, despite their months of experience facing the Germans and their guns.

The 82nd Airborne had been raw and untested for their first jump in Sicily, and shocked and shaken by having their own troops shooting them out of the sky. But the lessons learned in the front-line fighting proved invaluable. They had come face-to-face with the enemy, and with death. As they swept across the Italian island, the ones who would survive discovered the killing instincts that had lain dormant in their genes and honed what was almost a sixth sense for spotting the disturbed dirt or the broken branch where the enemy lay hiding.

It was a brand-new way of fighting for the United States, a test of the men and of their commanders, and Eisenhower watched carefully as the historic experiment of parachuting American soldiers into battle played out. The paratroopers had proved essential in the weeks spent pushing the Germans back to the Italian mainland, and had renewed the hopes of the folks back home that the Nazis could be beaten, but they suffered extraordinary losses. When it was over, the Army moved the men back to Morocco—to lick their wounds, clean their weapons, and learn from their mistakes.

As they regrouped in Africa, Willie was steaming toward them, crossing the ocean for the first time in his life, packed in the cramped quarters of a troopship crammed full with seasick soldiers and heavy with the stench of stale cigarettes and vomit. The weeks of basic training, jump school, and boxing for his company unit in the wooded Georgia hills at Fort Benning were behind him. He even got a chance to visit Silvis one last time, sporting the distinctive Airborne uniform with pants tucked in the tops of his boots, before the orders came directing him to a strange new world where men wore full length cotton robes, women hid behind veils, and Willie saw his first live camels.

The North African desert was a stark and sandy place, especially for someone from Silvis. The base sat along the rocky Atlas Mountains near the small town of Oujda, by the border between French and Spanish Morocco. It was barren and harsh, the ground baked hard as concrete by the sun, and plagued by yellow jackets and hornets. The temperature dropped from 130 degrees in the day to 50 degrees in a matter of hours once the sun set.

"We had picked, on purpose, land that was not in use for grazing or agricultural purposes. We trained in a fiery furnace, where the hot wind carried a fine dust that clogged the nostrils, burned the eyes, and cut into the throat like an abrasive," the head of the 82nd, Brigadier General Matthew Ridgway, wrote. "We trained at first by day, until the men became lean and gaunt from their hard work in the sun. Then we trained at night, when it was cooler, but the troopers found it impossible to sleep in the savage heat of the African day.

"The wind and the terrain were our worst enemies. Even on the rare calm days, jumping was a hazard, for the ground was hard, and covered with loose boulders, from the size of a man's fist to the size of his head."[1]

Sand drifted into their tents, into their clothes, and into their food. Still, the soldiers made the best of it. They traded cigarettes with the local Arabs and offered chocolate to the children who came begging. Willie wrote his sister: "You have probably been wondering why it takes me so long to answer. I move around so much that I get very little chance to write. I'm sorry I can't tell you the name of the town I'm in, but it really is a nice place. I have met a lot of Spanish families and get along with them fine."[2]

He included photographs. In one, now faded black-and-white, a long line of paratroopers, dressed for the desert in white French Foreign Legion caps, make their way along a rocky mountain trail with mules. Another shows Willie in the driver's seat of a motorcycle with a sidecar, looking dashing in his Legion cap and tight double-breasted jacket, surrounded by other young soldiers.

But those photographs were yet to be taken when the 504th got its next call. It came three days before Willie's twentieth birthday, on September 13, 1943.

General Mark Clark's Fifth Army had attacked the Italian mainland at Salerno four days earlier. Clark landed with 125,000 men, but the Germans responded with unexpected strength. By the morning of the 13th, most of the U.S. forces clung to a narrow strip of sand along the shore, on the verge of being pushed back into the sea. Clark summoned a P-38 pilot and gave him an urgent, handwritten message for Ridgway. If Clark didn't get help immediately, it said, the battle would be lost.

Ridgway got the message a little after two. By the time the night spread over the beachhead, help was on the way.

It arrived at 11:35. The beleaguered troops on the beach at Salerno heard the low drone of the C-47 transport planes flying in from the south. Troops on the ground had filled oil cans with gasoline-soaked sand and set them in a T along a stretch of the beach. As the planes neared, they lit them to form a blazing target. Spotting the drop zone, the 1st and 2nd battalions of the 504th spilled out of the planes, and the sky filled with parachutes.

The men on the beach stood in their foxholes and cheered.

It was the 504th's second jump into combat. As they threw themselves through the open doorways, they were relieved that there was no sign of the telltale red tracers streaking up from below. The only lights in the sky came from the full moon and a blanket of stars. Nearly twenty-four hundred men jumped; all but seventy-five landed safely.

In the lore of the 82nd, the jump would forever be known as the "Oil Can Drop."

Within minutes, the 504th's commander, Colonel Reuben Tucker, was rushed to a nearby house to be briefed. The situation was dire. The Germans had swept into the mountain passes facing the beachhead with tanks and artillery. Their infantry had swarmed in over the hills, forcing the Americans back. The men of Company K, 143rd Infantry Regiment, had not had time to retreat. They lay trapped, surrounded by Nazis amid the apple orchards and sunflowers on a hillside near the town of Altavilla Silentina. They needed Tucker and the 504th to get them out.

The paratroopers quickly clambered onto trucks and raced to a spot about eight miles inland, on a flat valley floor by the northern slopes of Mount Soprano. By 3 A.M., just over three hours after the jump light signal had flashed aboard the transport planes, the men of the 504th were in position, dug in, and ready to fight.

After the sun rose, they could see what they faced. Lieutenant Chester Garrison, who kept the battalion's unit journal, wrote: "Fifteen tanks have been sighted to our front . . . six have been knocked out by artillery."[3]

The paratroopers and the Nazis spent the next two days trading jabs as Tucker's men pressed forward. The Germans poured in men and machines, using a web of trails and dry streambeds snaking down through the tree-covered hills. Then they waited, hidden among the trees and crouching in creek beds, to pounce on the advancing Americans.

Nothing stopped the paratroopers. At 3 P.M. on what happened to be Willie's birthday, the 504th began its final advance toward Altavilla to rescue the trapped men of Company K. It was a fantastically hot late summer day. The men dripped sweat as they quick-stepped across the uneven ground. Then, they began to drop.

"The march went across country, ploughed fields, and up a very steep hill," Garrison wrote. "The terrific heat of the day and the stiffness of the walk, together with the excessive weight of the equipment, were too much for the men. They could not keep up with the rate of the march, particularly the mortar platoon, several of whom passed out along the way."[4]

There was no time to stop. They got the troopers who could still move back on their feet, slung the unconscious ones over their shoulders, and kept going.

As they neared their destination, a spray of bullets from two enemy machine guns ripped at the Americans. Then the Germans began raining artillery down on them. The medics scrambled from one wounded paratrooper to the next. Their groans and agonized calls for help echoed all around them.

The shower of shells continued into the night. The paratroopers continued to fall. The next morning, they realized where they were. They had made it to the exact spot where the Germans had decimated the 36th Division and forced the Americans back toward the sea. "Cadavers lay everywhere," Corporal Ross Carter of Company C wrote later. "Having seen only a few corpses in Sicily, it was a horrible experience for us to see dead men, purple and blackened by the intense heat, lying scattered all over the hill."[5]

Shortly after 8 A.M., they lay shrouded by a mountain-air mist, waiting for the Germans to attack again. Shadowy trees in the fog played tricks on their eyes. The coughs and rustling of the uneasy soldiers echoed hollowly through the wet air. Then, out of nowhere, enemy tanks began to pound them. They could hear the terrible thump in the distance as they fired, and waited helplessly in the long seconds as the shells streaked toward them, with no way of knowing if those moments were their last.

Two men in a bazooka position took a direct hit. Another two shells hit a group of men in a cluster of trees, killing six more. As the Americans tried to move out, Nazi machine gun fire tore across the line, and three more men fell dead.

The fighting raged through the day. The artillery fire intensified. A message arrived from the commander of the U.S. VI Corps: Tucker's men were completely surrounded, it said. He should retreat while he still could.

His answer is a now famous testament to the American fighting spirit and the determination that won the war.

"Retreat hell!" Tucker responded. "Send me my 3rd Battalion!"[6]

At a minute after midnight on September 18, Tucker got his wish. The 3rd Battalion was sent rushing up from the beach, to fight its way through the German resistance and reinforce the rest of the 504th. At 3 A.M., a group of determined paratroopers snuck over a leaf-covered path on the moonlit hillside and made contact with the tired, trapped troops who had been fighting through the day.

As the battalions came together and huddled in their hastily dug foxholes, the artillery fell silent. The next morning, the forest lay quiet, but for the occasional light clatter of an American soldier shifting position.

The Germans were gone. The fighting had raged for nearly thirty-six hours straight, but what was left of the Nazi force had slipped away in the darkness sometime during the night, leaving nothing but scattered bodies, trampled leaves, and the freshly churned soil marking the trail of the departing tank treads.

The 504th had been grossly outnumbered, but they had succeeded—the men of Company K were saved. Altavilla and the surrounding territory belonged to the Americans.

But Salerno was only the first step in taking the Italian mainland. The Americans had their sights on Rome, and the paratroopers were needed as foot soldiers—gun-toting ground troops—to help get them there. Between the Americans and their goal, however, stood the Apennines Mountains and a cleverly constructed series of three

Nazi lines that took full advantage of the range's rocky crags, sheer cliffs, and the barely passable trails winding through a tangle of steep mountains and canyons.

Willie would join them there.

The Apennines stretch the length of Italy from the Alps to Sicily, like a knobby spine nearly 850 miles long and 80 miles wide. The mountains' peaks range from 2,000 to nearly 10,000 feet high. The tallest are covered by snow almost year-round. The mountain paths were so narrow that every single bit of the American's supplies had to be carried in by pack mules or, when it got too steep even for the mules, on the backs of men. A nightly chain of cargo bearers scrabbled up and down the mountainsides. On the way up, they brought bullets, mortars, and grenades for fighting, water and K-rations to eat, sulfa drugs and cigarettes for comfort. On the way down, they brought the dead and wounded.

It was a fate the men dreaded.

"A seriously wounded man couldn't live through the terrible, jolting trip," Carter wrote. "We all preferred instant death to a slow croak in horrible pain on jolting stretchers."[7]

To make matters worse, as the 504th and the Allies clawed their way north, the final days of summer gave way to fall, and a bitter chill and unrelenting rain settled over the entire region.

"The land and the weather are both against us," the noted war correspondent Ernie Pyle detailed in one of his dispatches. "It rains and it rains. Vehicles bog down and temporary bridges wash out. . . . The fertile black valleys are knee-deep mud. Thousands of the men have not been dry for weeks. Other thousands lie at night in the high mountains with the temperature below freezing and the thin snow sifting over them."[8]

Compounding their misery, the men still wore their thin summer uniforms, with their winter garb stuck in Sicily. Soon enough, the weather-related casualties surpassed those caused by battle.

The commander of the 3rd Infantry Division, Major General Lucian Truscott, wrote: "Respiratory diseases, fevers of undetermined origin, and jaundice were beginning to take their toll. . . .

"Pneumonia and dysentery were commonplace, and trench foot was endemic in circumstances where men would often go for weeks without changing their soaking socks or remove their boots."[9]

By year's end, the Fifth Army had lost forty thousand men in fighting and fifty thousand more to non-battle injuries and diseases.

The soggy soil and sheer mountains limited the Americans' ability to bring their artillery and armor close to the front lines, and the nearer the men came to the desolate peaks, the more the ground became nothing but rock—a jagged moonscape strewn with broken boulders and shattered, sharp-edged stones.

The Nazis used the terrain to their advantage. They set their machine guns in caves or behind rocks stacked to form pillboxes that were nearly invisible to the approaching Allies. Then they opened up as the British and Americans clawed and stumbled into view. The GIs found cover squeezed cheek to cheek "in little chasms and behind rocks and in half caves," Pyle wrote. "They live like men of prehistoric times, and a club would become them more than a machine gun."[10] There was rarely enough space to lie down, so the men slept sitting up, pressed against any outcropping of rock that would keep them from tumbling off the mountain.

The paratroopers' losses were staggering. A full one out of every three of the 504th's men died in the mountains of Italy. By the end of November, they were worn, weary, and in desperate need of replacements and rest. Their commanders pulled them down from the peaks to eat Thanksgiving turkey in Ciorlano, a tiny village of whitewashed stone houses packed tightly against a hillside north of Naples. They had time to bathe and wash their uniforms for the first time since landing in Salerno. Some even got passes to go into Naples, with strict reminders to wear their Army-issued condoms.

Then they loaded into the backs of trucks and headed off in the rain, back to the front line.

The 2nd Battalion's job was to reinforce the battle-weary men of the 143rd Infantry in a place the military planners called Hill 1205 and the Italians knew as Mount Sammucro. The mountain rose nearly four thousand feet above the German-occupied town of San Pietro Infine, an ancient village of rough-hewn stone homes and cobblestone streets stacked among terraced olive orchards and wild figs.

Until the war, San Pietro had mattered mostly only to the few hundred families that called it their home. Now, though, it stood as the key to the Liri Valley, and a crucial blockade on the road to Rome. Hitler himself issued the orders to hold the town against the Americans. And now, after days of exhausting, unsuccessful efforts, the Americans were massing for an all-out drive to seize it.

Thick clouds blotted out the sky as the paratroopers made their way to the top of Mount Sammucro along "a long, muddy torturous trail"[11] under a steady rain. At one point the only way to continue was by pulling themselves up a long rope. Finally, after more than eleven hours of clawing their way up the mountainside over loose and slipping rocks, they reached the exhausted remnants of the 143rd. They found themselves on a rocky knob where it was impossible to dig a foxhole. They had to stack rocks to shield themselves.

For the next two days, the Germans pummeled the mountaintop with artillery and mortar fire. Nazi snipers hidden among the rocks targeted anyone who seemed to be in command. In a single day, they cut down Company G's captain and lieutenant and killed Company

I's lieutenant as well. Two days later, they got another Company G lieutenant. That night, December 14, the men in the battalion went down to meet some fresh paratroopers transferring to the front line and bring them back. One of the new men was Willie. He had arrived with nearly a company's worth of raw replacements, all stiff and sore from the bone-jarring trip in the backs of trucks jolting over potholes and bomb craters in the road. They got off the trucks at a staging area by a rocky mountain and rested among some olive trees. After months of training and bouncing from base to base, Willie had been assigned to Company F. He had written a letter home to his sister about it the day before.

"Well, Sis," he penned in flowing letters, "after wandering around Africa for a while I find myself now in Italy, hoping to make the best of it. Sis I have finally been attached to an outfit which is the 504 and I supposed [*sic*] this address I have now will be permanently," he told her.

Then, in a note of optimism, he added, "I sure wish I was home for Christmas but I suppose we'll have to finish Hitler before we can enjoy a real Christmas."[12]

Now he was headed into the thick of it for the first time, slogging apprehensively up the moonlit mountainside surrounded by men as green as he was, eyeing the rocks and crags uneasily. They made their way up the mountain as the 2nd Battalion launched an attack to take a hill to the west of Mount Sammucro. The Germans ambushed them as the Americans moved along a ridge. The paratroopers dove for cover in the cracks between the rocks and waited for the Germans to press the attack. It was raining and cold. They sat pinned behind the rocks watching their wounded bleed through the rest of the night and all through the next day.

As the second night draped them in darkness, the paratroopers tried to slip away. The Nazis were waiting. They opened up with mortars and machine guns, grenades and small arms. Paratroopers fell left and right. They had been caught on low ground, on open rock. The major ordered them to fall back, and they scrambled through the hail of bullets screeching off the rocks all around them to make it back to Hill 1205.

By the end of Willie's first forty-eight hours with his new unit, fifteen paratroopers had died and seventy-five lay wounded. He didn't yet know the names of most of the men around him, and he didn't know if any of them would be alive long enough for him to learn.

An even bloodier fight was playing out in the village below them. The 143rd was locked in a full-scale assault on San Pietro. It was a brutal affair. The road into town climbed along a succession of terraces with rock-walled faces, each three to seven feet high. The ground between was a tangle of bare-branched olive trees and burned-out vineyards, cut across by streambeds and gullies.

The Americans had begun the attack precisely at noon on December 15, with sixteen Sherman tanks in the lead. It was a massacre. Nazi anti-tank cannons blew apart three as they came up the road. Land mines halted another four. By mid-afternoon, three-fourths of the Shermans had been crippled or destroyed, and the four surviving tanks clattered back up the road in retreat.

They tried again at 1 A.M., this time with infantry. It was another slaughter. The foot soldiers climbed over the broken terrace walls only to be cut down by sheets of German machine gun fire. A second assault just before dawn shared a similar fate.

"The losses before the town have been heavy," the 143rd's commander, Major General Fred Walker, wrote in his diary. "Many wounded had to be abandoned within enemy lines. . . . This is bad."[13]

They threw men at the tiny village, pounded it with 75mm tank cannons, and poured artillery fire in from the hillsides above. After two days of steady fighting, Americans broke through the German flank and forced the Nazis to retreat. "The silence in San Pietro," by one account, "was almost eerie." Bodies lay everywhere, in green uniforms and gray. San Pietro lay in ruins. It cost the Americans more than 1,200 men—some 150 killed, 800 wounded, and 250 missing.

On the mountain above, the losses for the 504th had been equally devastating. By the morning of December 20, Willie was one of only twenty-eight enlisted men still alive and able to fight in Company F. They only had two officers to lead them. That still made them the biggest company in the battalion. Company D was down to three officers and twenty-four enlisted men, Company E had only four officers and ten enlisted men.

Willie's letter home was right. They weren't done with Hitler. And he wasn't home for Christmas. He spent it shivering in the cold on the mountain, where he could hear the distant voices of carolers drifting up from the valley below. A lucky few support unit soldiers were able to gather for services, and the strains of "Silent Night" carried up to the fighting men above, between the blasts of artillery shells.

The 504th was officially relieved on December 27, but most of the men didn't make it off the mountain until New Year's Eve. They moved to a town about twenty miles south of Venafro where, Corporal Shelby Hord said, "they gave us a bath, sprayed us with DDT, and gave us clean clothes."[14]

They handed out Christmas packages and mail from home, and then the soldiers got another well-deserved break in Naples—resting, relaxing, and cavorting with the locals.

Three weeks later, the R&R ended. The paratroopers loaded onto landing crafts and joined a convoy of 374 ships steaming out across the Mediterranean. The day started with a startlingly clear morning and gave way to a crisp, cloudless night as they traveled. It could have been a pleasure cruise, but for the destination. The men sunned themselves, played cards, wrote letters home, and chatted anxiously about what awaited them.

The original plan called for the 504th to parachute into position on shore just ahead of the main force's landing. But the idea of an airdrop was abandoned out of fear that the planes would alert the Germans to the assault.

So, instead, as the attack began, Willie found himself on the deck of a landing craft, watching the rockets streak through the night sky toward Anzio Beach.

The invasion was no surprise for the Nazis. Its location was. The Americans picked Nero's birthplace, the spot where he reportedly fiddled as Rome burned, now home to a pair of resort towns where Italians had gathered before the war for vacations, to sip cognac and enjoy the sea air. Anzio and Nettuno shared the beachfront and a main road that connected the two towns. Both sat overlooking the water, with the majority of their buildings crowded into a narrow strip within three blocks of the beach.

Three Ranger battalions went ashore first, led by Colonel William O. Darby, who told the mission planners before they set out: "When I run out of the landing craft, I don't want to have to look right or left."[15]

He didn't. When the landing craft's ramp dropped open, Darby charged out, up the beach and into the *Paradiso sul Mare* casino—the "Paradise on the Sea," in English—where he set up his command post. By the time the sun rose, the Rangers were already bringing back prisoners, including four drunken officers in a car on the beach and a group of surprised soldiers who had somehow managed to sleep through the rocket barrage. They had caught the Germans completely off guard, and as the remainder of the invasion force moved steadily ashore, the Nazi response was, in the words of Lieutenant James Megellas, "strangely nonexistent."[16]

Through the night and into the morning, the Americans streamed onto the beach. Willie and the 504th waited in their landing craft, some two hundred men to a boat, crowded shoulder to shoulder with their packs on their backs, their helmets on, and the tips of their guns covered with condoms to protect them from the water. At 9 A.M., it was their turn. The rumbling of the engines shifted to a throaty growl, and the thirteen landing craft carrying the 504th aimed their noses at the beach ahead.

By now, though, the German high command had been alerted. Their phones rang and the words "Case Richard," the signal for an Allied invasion, sounded over the line. They hastily rousted their troops to load onto trains bound for the shore, and sent their planes into the air to repel the invaders.

As the first of the flat-bottomed landing craft carrying the paratroopers grounded on the sandy sea bottom and dropped their loading ramps open, six German Messerschmitt dive-bombers came roaring in from the east with the blinding morning sun at their tails and their machine guns blazing. The line of 7.92mm rounds sent long rooster tails of wet sand slicing toward the boats and the men, and found their targets with the ugly thunk of metal on metal or, worse, the soggy slap of bullet meeting flesh. As the planes came over the boats, they dropped their bombs, then cut back around for another strafing run.

As Ross Carter described it: "The deck of our LCI was crowded with troops standing around waiting to unload into the icy water and make the three hundred yards to the beach. Just as Berkely was reaching for one of Pierson's cigarettes, a dive-bomber came in and hell opened its doors. The bomb missed the bow by five feet or so, but the explosion lifted the boat clear out of the sea and blew a column of oily water into the sky which fell back on the boat and left us oil-coated for several days."[17]

Another bomb made a direct hit on a landing craft carrying the men of G Company and a lone transfer from Company H, PFC Henry E. Ferrari, sent along to serve as an interpreter. "The nose of the craft settled in the water and the stern billowed black smoke," Megellas wrote later. "Its rear was a mass of battered metal, and men could be seen enmeshed in twisted steel. Captain Hyman Schapiro, 3d Battalion medical officer, was one of the men wounded in the blast. He managed to get to the beachhead, where he treated the wounded before leaving for the field hospital. For his gallantry he was awarded the Silver Star."[18]

Under fire, the landing craft Willie was on didn't even wait to reach the beach before it dropped its ramp open. The paratroopers scrambled out through the opening to escape the confines of the boat. They jumped into the water, only to discover in some cases that it was over their heads. Weighted down by their packs and guns, they went straight to the bottom, and desperately held their breath as they fought their way forward in the cold, murky water.

One of the men near Willie, PFC Leo M. Hart, described it: "When I stepped off that thing I went completely underwater. I hit bottom, I followed my nose, straight ahead. The only thought I had was, 'please keep walking straight ahead.' It was just a few steps and I was back [above the surface]."[19]

With the bullets ripping up the sand around them, the landing craft carrying the paratroopers of H Company hit a sandbar, backed off, and ground to a stop a second time near the wreckage of the LCI hit by the Messerschmitt's bomb. "When the LCI made its second landing, it was on a sand bar," Sergeant Donald Zimmerman later told Megellas. "It appeared to be in shallow water, but instead it was deeper just behind the sand bar. I jumped in the water and it was over my head. I was a good swimmer and I managed to get to the sand bar. . . . I lost my helmet and my rifle, but when I got ashore I picked up a discarded rifle. I remember the German planes strafing over us. They made three passes before they left."[20]

Willie and his squad ran up the beach. Between the weight of the one-hundred-pound pack on their backs and the wet sand clawing at their boots, it seemed like they were moving in slow motion. Every step sank in under them. One by one, the men dove behind broken pieces of walls brought down by the rockets, ducked beside abandoned carts and cars. They hunkered, huffing, pressed against whatever piece of cover they had found as the rumble of the Messerschmitts' engines faded into the distance.

Miraculously, none of the men in Willie's squad was hit.

Ferrari wasn't as lucky. The bomb that hit the landing craft he was on left him badly mangled. He died of his wounds a few days later, the first of the 504th's men killed at Anzio.

The rest of the regiment gathered up in a stand of cedars that rose like a cluster of candle wicks just a short distance from the beach. They checked their equipment, regrouped, and reviewed maps for their next assignment. The next morning, they fanned forward to dig in at what would become the dividing line between the Allies and the Nazis for months to come.

The Mussolini Canal had been built by the Italian fascists and named for their leader as part of the massive reclamation effort to convert the low-lying marsh surrounding Anzio into useful, arable land. The levees lining the canal rose ten to twelve feet on each side. A number of bridges crossed the drainage channel, and it was the mission of the 504th to take them—to give the Allies passage as they pressed their attack forward toward Rome and to stop the Nazis from sweeping in to threaten the beachhead.

Recognizing their strategic importance, the Germans had placed their limited forces to defend or destroy the bridges and halt the Allied advance. Private Jim Musa of H Company encountered evidence of their efforts as he neared one of the stone-and-steel structures. "As we approached the bridge," he said, "I noticed an American soldier, probably a Ranger, propped up at the approach with an M-1 rifle on his legs. He had a bullet hole in his head. Why he was left there dead and by whom I never knew."[21]

The 1st Battalion was sent farther north, to take what they called Bridge No. 5 and to dig in to hold it against the anticipated German armored counterattack. The Americans had barely gotten into position when the Nazis hit them with heavy artillery and the first of the waves of infantrymen to come. Sergeant Albert Clark, with Company A, huddled with his squad as the shells fell around them. "We did not have any big guns support," he said. "The end of the first day of their attack, out of our [platoon of] thirty-two men, we had twenty-nine; the next night twenty-seven; the next night nineteen; then the next eleven; and finally down to nine men. Then we started getting a few [of our wounded] back. One day I got three men. One still had a hand in a cast. The next morning, one of them was killed by artillery fire."[22]

The Allies had lost their advantage. The siege had begun.

They had come ashore virtually unopposed. As day one of the assault came to a close, "British Guards officers played bridge and slept in their pyjamas."[23] The battle report for the day showed that 36,000 men, 3,200 vehicles, and tons of supplies—close to 90 percent of the invaders' equipment and personnel—had been brought ashore successfully. The casualties were extraordinarily, and unexpectedly, light: thirteen killed, ninety-seven wounded, and just forty-four captured or missing.

But the first day gave no indication of what was to come. The Germans had few forces in place when the Americans and British landed, but thanks to their network of good communications, roads, and railroads, the Nazis were able to bring an estimated twenty thousand troops from the surrounding area rushing in to block the Allies. By day two, they had doubled that number to more than forty thousand, and by the end of the first week, their ranks have grown to more than seventy thousand soldiers, supported by tanks and heavy artillery.

Darby and his Rangers may not have heard a single shot as they dashed up the beach in that first wave, but their losses mounted drastically as the brutal stalemate dragged on: Of 767 Rangers who came ashore that first night, only six had made it out of Anzio by the time the fighting there ended.

On January 25, three days after landing, Willie and his battalion were sent to take the town of Borgo Piave, a critical crossroads where five highways intersected in a circle at the center of town. Barely a dozen years old, the city was another product of the fascists, a symbol of progress, with a name that conjured an Italian fight song from World War I, "The Legend of the Piave," about repelling foreign invaders. According to the Allies' intelligence report, it was practically a cakewalk. They faced weak troops and no tanks, and no chance of the Nazis bringing in tanks from any place else for at least eight hours.

Company D went first, following a rolling barrage of American artillery—a concentration of shell fire laid down ahead of the troops, then lifted and laid down again a little farther ahead. But as the paratroopers advanced, the Germans realized what the shelling meant. They began laying down their own concentrations, then lifting, to make the paratroopers think it was friendly fire. It worked.

Company D was caught on a flat, open field fifteen hundred yards from the town as the Nazis rained 20mm antiaircraft fire on them.

The Americans broke into a run for the town, with shells exploding around them. Then, the German tanks that weren't supposed to be there rolled in from the north and east. The counterattack split Company D into two parts and cut them and Company E off from the rest of the battalion.

Not expecting to face any armor, the paratroopers had left their antitank weapons behind. The Germans used it to their advantage. They hit the trapped companies hard through the afternoon and into the evening. The Americans' hopes faded as the day dragged into night and the dark fell like a final curtain over the dead and wounded as their blood soaked into the ground. The bullets buzzed around their heads like angry bees. Then, at 8:20 that night, Willie and the men of Company F reached them. They snuck into position on the Nazis' flank and opened up. Their gun muzzles flashed fire in the dark. Tracers streaked down on their targets.

It was the break their brethren needed to escape. As the battered troops of Company D and Company E filtered out to safety, Willie and his comrades kept laying down fire to distract the Nazis. They kept up the fight until two o'clock the next morning, before pulling back to take shelter beyond the steep bank on the west side of the canal.

Only forty men from Company D made it back alive.

On January 29, the Americans tried again. With Willie and the 2nd Battalion in the lead, they hustled to seize one of the bridges spanning the Mussolini Canal before the Germans blew it up. It was the farthest inland yet, and the Nazis were determined to make it as costly as possible. They hid in the villagers' farmhouses and caught the Americans in a deadly cross fire as they crossed the open fields between.

Lieutenant William J. Sweet Jr. was with the 2nd Battalion Headquarters Group, advancing just behind Company E and Company F. "The going was slow," he explained in the company report, "as nearly every house was defended and the enemy small arms fire from the canal banks kept the troops down low in their advance. A system was worked out whereby the troops would advance until fired on from a house or strongpoint, then the tanks would move up, blast the defenders out, to be taken by our troops. The further the advance continued, the more fire was received from the right flank."[24]

E Company broke off to clear the dike along the canal. Dark cattle grazed in the fields, and the men were as likely to land in cowflop as mud when they dove for the ground, and just as likely to care either way. Willie and F Company pressed forward across the marshland until they hit the heaviest strongpoint yet. Instead of inflicting their damage and dropping back as they had before, the Germans held fast, locking Willie and his company in a vicious firefight.

"While F Company was doing this," Sweet reported, "the rest of the battalion was left strung out in a column along the road, and we got our first taste of the Germans' Nebelwerfer, or 'Screaming Meemies.' The entire column was shelled for about ten minutes by this fire and then hit by 88 mm or antiaircraft fire. Several men from D and Headquarters Companies became casualties and the column was spread into the fields."[25]

Both sides knew how important it was for the Americans to take a bridge and give their tanks a crossing over the canal. The Germans were determined to prevent it. They made a stand at what the Allies called Bridge Number 7, until E Company pushed them back. As the Nazis retreated, they blew up the bridge behind them.

Two bridges remained. Willie and F Company finally overwhelmed the Germans at the strongpoint and took twenty-five prisoners, then pushed up the road toward the next bridge. Before they could get to it, the Germans blew up Bridge Number 8.

"Now it was apparent that the enemy had decided to deny us any crossings for armor in the area," Sweet wrote, "so a race started for Bridge Number 9. Before D Company could get well underway, with the tanks, the Germans blew that one, leaving us with no armor crossings of the Mussolini Canal."[26]

It was as far as the 504th would ever get at Anzio. The British had taken Aprilia to the north, and the invasion commander, Major General John P. Lucas, made a fateful decision. Fearing a repeat of Salerno, where the German counteroffensive nearly pushed the Americans back into the sea, Lucas halted the attack and ordered his troops to fortify the beachhead.

Sitting by a fire wearing polished cavalry boots, Lucas gathered a group of war correspondents around him in his villa in Nettuno to explain. As BBC war correspondent Wynford Vaughan-Thomas described it, "He had the round face and the graying mustache of a kindly country solicitor. His voice was low and hardly reached the outer circle of the waiting pressman. They fired their questions at him, above all Question Number 1, 'What *was* our plan on landing and what had happened to it now?'

"The General looked thoughtful. 'Well, gentlemen, there was some suggestion that we should aim at getting to those hills'—he turned to his G2—'What's the name of them, Joe? But the enemy was now strong, far stronger than we had thought.'

"There was a long pause as the firelight played on the waiting audience and flickered up to the dark ceiling. Then the General added quietly, 'I'll tell you what, gentlemen. That German is a mighty tough fighter. Yes, a mighty tough fighter.'"[27]

Thus began the stalemate that would last nearly four more months.

The Allies found themselves stuck on a flat griddle of wet sand and marsh, with the mountains in front and the sea at their backs, and no place to hide but the rain-filled holes they dug. No place was safe.

During the first week of February, the Germans brought in two colossal 280mm railway guns that the Allies soon dubbed "Anzio Annie" and the "Anzio Express." Both could hurl 546-pound shells thirty-one miles—accurately. The Germans kept them hidden in tunnels above the beach until they were ready to use them. Then they rolled them out on the railroad tracks to pound the beachhead with devastating force.

"First you heard a distant, almost discreet cough, away behind the enemy lines, then a slight pause, during which you knew the shell was on its way," said Vaughan-Thomas, settled in with the British forces on the beach. "Fear wound up your guts as if they were on a fisherman's reel. Then came the sickening crump of the explosion and the sound echoed away like a tube train pulling out of the station down a long, black tunnel."[28]

The men built elaborate and extensive foxholes, but the seemingly ceaseless rain and cold made the shelters miserable pits. Water rose above their boot tops, making it impossible to lie down, and they could do little but shiver and curse. They got out whenever they could, but they scurried like crabs to dive in whenever they heard the shells coming.

"It's only the first shell after a lull that gets many casualties," Pyle wrote in one of his dispatches from the beachhead. "After the first one, all the men are in their dugouts."[29]

But even that might not save them. Sometimes the blast caved in the foxhole walls, burying the men alive. Sometimes they didn't make it into the hole quickly enough. Every day, the shelling killed two or three more.

"You know what a direct hit by a shell does to a guy?" said one soldier assigned to collect the dead for burial. "Sometimes all we have is a leg or a hunk of arm."[30]

Life on the beach was a wretched affair. The men were plagued by constant cold, lice, and fear. They might go weeks without a shower or even without changing their underwear. So they doused themselves with delousing powder, whenever they could get some, and made do.

"We used our helmets for everything," Ray McAllister of 45th Division remembered. "I ate out of mine when we got the occasional hot chow. When we had time to shave I shaved from mine. We heated water in it for a bath and, yes, when we were pinned down in a foxhole, we went to the john in it and dumped it over the side of the foxhole during a lull in the fighting."[31]

As if to underscore their determination to hold the beachhead against all odds, the Army built a bakery at the water's edge "turning out luscious, crisp loaves of white bread from its portable ovens at a pace of around twenty-seven thousand pounds a day," Pyle wrote. "Their orders are to keep right on baking through an artillery barrage, but when air raiders come over, they turn out the fires and go to the air-raid shelter."[32]

And despite the conditions in their frigid mud holes, the Allies built on their reputation for resourcefulness. They might be living in Hell, but even damned souls can figure out how to have a little fun. The soldiers caught beetles burrowing in the muck and established a sophisticated racing schedule where men gathered around makeshift tracks to cheer and bet on their favorites. As one British soldier described it: "Runners were plentiful, for beetles seemed to be one of the chief products of the beachhead. Dig a slit trench, leave it for an hour, and the bottom would be black with beetles trying to get out. The system of racing was simple. Various colors were painted on the beetles' backs and the runners were paraded around the ring in jam jars. Just before the 'off,' or I suppose one should say when they came under starters orders, the beetles were placed under one glass jar in the center of the 'course.' This was a circle about six feet in diameter. At the 'off' the jar was raised and the first beetle out of the circle was the winner. A difficulty arose when, for one reason or another, it became necessary to change a beetle's colors in quick time; but one Gunner meeting the problem, assaulted by attaching small flags to the beetles' backs with chewing gum."[33]

Not to be outdone, An American soldier formed his own version of the Kentucky Derby, with mules, donkeys, and horses standing in as the thoroughbreds of the "Anzio Beachhead Racing Association."[34]

The soldiers also discovered that the Italians had buried barrels of wine throughout the area, and in the pauses in the German artillery fire, men could be seen sweeping the zone with mine detectors, listening for the telltale tone signaling the iron bands on the casks.

But they didn't fill all their free time with vices. The 504th's chaplain Delbert Kuehl earned a certain celebrity as a daring, gun-toting minister who dodged bullets and bombshells on the front line with the rest of the paratroopers and would suddenly drop into a foxhole without warning.

"I first met Chaplain Delbert Kuehl when Ray Walker and I were dug in on the Mussolini Canal, manning a .30-caliber light machine gun," PFC James Ward recalled. "On this particular day, shortly before dusk, we observed a soldier moving in our direction. He was carrying an M1. When he arrived at our position, he said, 'we're going to have a prayer meeting.' No one will ever know how much it meant to have our Chaplain there with us. You'd never know where or when Chaplain Kuehl would show up. It seemed like he was always around when you needed him most."[35]

All the chaplains and doctors and medical corpsmen in the 504th were expected to parachute into battle like any other member of the unit. Kuehl was no exception. He had jumped with the men in Sicily and Palermo, and charged the beach at Anzio side by side with the men he ministered to. He was not, however, expected to fight. But long after the war was over, Kuehl made a confession: "I was with four other men by one of the old stone houses on the front when four German fighter bombers which evidently dropped their bombs near the beach and then two came just above treetops on both sides of the road—there were two on each side. The fellows with me jumped in their foxholes as the planes were spitting out machine gun fire along both sides of the main road. I grabbed one of the M1s the fellows had there and got three shots into one plane as he passed—it was stupid. I should have jumped into my foxhole because the machine gun cut a path right beside me and up the house. One fellow who was on the other side of the old house said later that whoever fired at one of the planes hit it and it was smoking badly. I never spoke about that then, as Chaplains are not supposed to be firing at the enemy. I still don't know why I did all that. It was the only time I fired a gun at the enemy."[36]

Mostly, though, the chaplains offered spiritual support for the men and helped them find courage in the Bible. As Easter approached, the ministers gathered small groups of men in the rough stone farmhouses dotting the fields along the canal. It was an oddly tender moment—scruffy, unshaven soldiers laying their helmets on the ground, bowing their heads, and kneeling to pray, but still clutching their carbines as they did.

It was a long way from Our Lady of Guadalupe in Silvis, but Willie said his Our Father with a Catholic chaplain, who wrote to Willie's dad after the service.

"Here, on the Anzio beachhead, like the Christians of old, men must steal away under the cover of darkness into the relative security of a farmhouse where they may worship God and receive the Sacrament," he explained.

"William is well and doing good work," he concluded. He signed it, "Yours in Christ, Father E. J. Kozak."[37]

Willie followed up with a letter—and a request—of his own. In his flowing fountain pen script he wrote his sister Rufina:

Dear Sis,

Writing to let you know that I'm fine and hoping that all of you are in the best of health.

Sis I'm especially writing this letter requesting for a camera with films. I know I'm asking for to [sic] much sis, but if you can try I'll appreciate it very much. Sis if you don't suceed [sic] with the camera, how about sending me those special packages for soldiers overseas. That's the chocolate fanny farmies. Ask the dealer in a candy shop. He'll do the wrapping + sending.

None of his letters revealed his exact location, or what he was going through, but Willie offered cryptic clues of his whereabouts:

You have probably wonder [sic] why I haven't written any sooner or where I'm at. Sis if you follow the newspaper at home day after day, you will probably know where I'm at and what I'm doing.

Say hello to Dad and the rest of the kids. Tell them I'm thinking of them at all times.

By then, life at Anzio had settled into a daily routine of death and desolation. As Ross Carter described it, a "typical day" for the paratroopers "went about like this: Before daylight he is awakened in his hole in the bank by a fall of mortar shells. They shoot out their shrapnel like tentacles feeling just for him and nose into the surrounding dirt like a giant barking hound. After digging ten or fifteen holes around him the enemy mortar man stops probably for breakfast and the joker lies and trembles until daylight. Then he gets out and starts toward a house after some coffee. On the way, he is shot at three times by a sniper in a church tower thee hundred yards away. He dives into the house and makes himself a cup of coffee, but before he can drink it a shell blows off a corner. Just the same he finishes his coffee and starts back to his hole. Halfway across the field he runs into a bevy of screaming-in 88's.

"He is lucky enough to make it to a small ditch that runs through the field. The shells land on all sides and one covers him up with dirt. With his knees knocking, he barrels into his dugout and lies there chain smoking."[38]

The days were miserable—blank slates of rain and gray. At night, though, the beachhead came alive. Shielded by the dark, the men made repairs, replenished supplies, brought in reinforcements, and recovered the bodies that had lain on the battlefield throughout the day. For both sides, it was also time for air raids, artillery bombardment, and patrols across the lines into enemy territory.

The Germans knew that if the invaders made it off the beach, Italy would fall. They threw the remaining might of their crippled air force in the region at cutting off the Allied supply lines. Bomber squadrons from Greece and southern France swung in from over the water with unsettling regularity to unleash their loads of bombs and torpedoes on the cargo ships lined up at the Anzio port. Packs of Luftwaffe fighter-bombers swept over the beach, strafing and scattering flak, showering shrapnel down on the men below.

The men on the beach had a nickname for the plane that dropped the clusters that crackled across the sky. They called it the "Popcorn Man." They scurried for their foxholes as they heard them coming, but some always too late, and the hot metal shards ripped through them and left them howling in pain in the night, waiting for the planes to pull away. Sometimes they lay there stuck all through the night, waiting for the medical corpsmen to clamber exposed across the beach or the flat of the front to try to save those who had survived.

That part was the same on both sides.

"It was sometimes necessary to leave the wounded behind in No Man's Land, because you could not bring them in at night," said German infantryman Joachim Liebschner. "They were screaming, and shouting, or crying for mother. So that you had to plug your ears because you couldn't stand it any longer. But as soon as dawn came and the light was good enough for the other side to see you, all you had to do was wave a little Red Cross flag, go out into No Man's Land, pick up your wounded and cart them back. That Red Cross flag would be respected on either side, and you would be walking past Tommy's fox holes, or he would pass your fox holes ten or fifteen yards from you."[39]

The steady drumbeat of the bombs, the mortars, the artillery, the snipers, and being surrounded by death took its toll. It chipped away at the men's psyches and left some just as wounded as if they'd been hit.

"Some people have had to leave because of nerves, and those who stay like to make fun of their own shakes," Pyle wrote in one of his dispatches home. "The jitters are known as 'Anzio Anxiety' and 'Nettuno Neurosis.' A lieutenant will hold out his hand and purposely make it tremble, and say, 'see, I'm not nervous.' . . . Also, we have the 'Anzio walk,' a new dance in which the performer jumps, jerks, cowers, cringes and twitches his head this way and that, something halfway between the process of dodging shells and just going plain nuts."[40]

The men sent home with "battle fatigue" remained crippled for years, or decades, after. It was not just the breaking—the trembling, whimpering in holes—but having to carry forevermore the fact that they had broken. They had looked into the abyss of their fear and knew exactly where their courage crumbled. And that made every day after shameful, and all the more frightening, because they knew exactly how much they could take—exactly. For those who never experienced it, the fear and the breaking point was somewhere *out there*—and their courage could take them forward. But not these. They had felt its cold breath lurking close in the dark, and they knew it was always close after that.

Oddly enough, Pyle wrote, "comparatively few men *do* crack up. The mystery to me is that there is anybody at all, no matter how strong, who can keep his spirit from breaking in the midst of battle."[41]

But even those who stood steady were not immune. In fact, Pyle saw something worse in the men on the front line who "have that stare."

"A soldier who has been a long time in the line does have a 'look' in his eyes that anyone with practice can discern," he wrote. "It's a look of dullness, eyes that look without seeing, eyes that see without transferring any response to the mind. It's a look that is the display room for the thoughts that are behind it—exhaustion, lack of sleep, tension for too long, weariness that is too great, fear beyond fear, misery to the point of numbness, a look of surpassing indifference to anything anybody can do to you. It's a look I dread to see on men."[42]

And the men at Anzio knew their options were extremely limited.

"The only ways to get away from the guns," said British private Jimmy Reed, "was death, a good wound or leave. Leave was far more difficult to get than the other two."[43]

The paratroopers avoided the beach. They plied the front. There they only worried about machine guns and mortars, land mines and 88s—those extremely accurate antitank and antiaircraft guns that could fire twenty-five armor-piercing rounds a minute. The Germans reserved the heavy shells for the crowded beach. On the front, the paratroopers could get lost among the patchy scrub of the marsh or duck behind the occasional cedar that dotted the plain. And night gave them the cover they needed to spread terror among the Nazis. They painted their faces black and infiltrated the enemy lines, slipping into the German foxholes with their eleven-inch daggers ready, then disappearing silently into the night. Horrified enemy soldiers awoke in the morning to find the bodies of their trench mates lying in deep pools of their own blood, their throats slashed open, eyes frozen open in fear.

It gave the 504th a reputation, and a nickname.

An American infantryman searching for intelligence found a diary in a dead German officer's pocket. It contained a passage that said, "American parachutists—devils in baggy pants—are less than 100 meters from my outpost line. I can't sleep at night. They pop up from nowhere and we never know when or how they will strike next. Seems like the black-hearted devils are everywhere."[44]

When the paratroopers heard about the diary entry, they adopted the designation with pride and began calling themselves the "Devils in Baggy Pants."

Sixty-one days after landing, the weary, ragged remnants of the paratrooper battalions got orders to withdraw. They boarded steam trains that left long streaks of black smoke against the sky as they chugged south to Naples. They spent just over two weeks there, doing what soldiers do after spending too long in battle and too long without women.

Then, on April 10, they marched proudly through the center of the Italian town to the waterfront and up the gangplank of a British liner called the *Capetown Castle*. Nazi radio broadcasts warned that they were being stalked by U-boats that would never let them reach their destination. But the only danger they encountered came twelve days later, as they caught sight of the red roofs of the houses and buildings of Liverpool, brilliant under the sun of a bright spring day. The 82nd Airborne band stood in formation on shore, playing "We're All American and proud to be . . ." Smiling young ladies crowded the wharf alongside them, waving hello. As the paratroopers all rushed to the same side of the ship to wave back, the liner listed dangerously under the shifting weight, threatening to capsize.

The captain hastily issued a stern warning that all the men would be sent belowdecks if they didn't spread out. They did, order was restored, and the ship proceeded to dock.

Once the lines were secured, the paratroopers hoisted up their barracks bags and personal belongings and stepped happily onto English soil. They boarded a train to the small city of Thurnby, near the heart of the country, halfway between Liverpool and London. There, they settled into tidy rows of tan tents with five cots each, clustered by neatly graveled Company streets. The camp had proper latrines and a large mess hall where cooks served up freshly made hot meals.

After what they had been through, their new home seemed like paradise.

Back in Italy, though, the fighting at Anzio dragged on.

The goal remained Rome.

A month after the 504th landed in England, the entire U.S. 36th Infantry Division landed at Anzio. The next morning, 150,000 Allied fighters threw themselves at the Germans. The attack began with a forty-five-minute artillery barrage, followed by waves of armor and infantry. Overhead, thick flights of Allied aircraft rained bombs on the Nazis.

It took two days to break the German defenses, but on May 25 the Americans took the Nazi stronghold at Cisterna and began the march to Rome.

The Americans liberated the Eternal City on June 4. Lieutenant General Mark Clark had his coveted prize. It had taken more than four months, and cost them 7,000 Allied dead, 36,000 wounded or missing, along with 44,000 non-battle casualties. The 504th lost more men there than in any other battle of the war.

But by then, hardly anyone noticed—the Allies' sights were set on what would be the biggest amphibious invasion the world had ever seen, involving nearly 2 million soldiers, sailors, and airmen, more than five thousand ships, and more than a thousand planes. It was called D-Day, and would be forever remembered as one of the most horrifically deadly assaults in history. Willie's dear friend Luz Segura was already in the British countryside, gearing up for the massive, still-secret invasion.

On the morning of June 6, 1944, the first wave of landing craft in the invasion force dropped open their ramps—only to have the infantrymen on board raked by withering German machine gun fire.

Miraculously, none of the men from Hero Street would fall there. Recognizing the price they had paid at Anzio, the Army held Willie's unit back. Luz went ashore after the beaches had been secured, to begin the Allied advance across Europe.

But it wouldn't be long before the Western Union man returned to Hero Street, like death's deliveryman, carrying a telegram no one wanted to read.

CHAPTER EIGHT

MORE TEARS ON HERO STREET

A continent away from the Normandy beaches, in the thick jungle of Burma, Frank Sandoval's engineer battalion remained locked in a fierce siege. As the D-Day invasion crashed ashore in France, he had three hellish weeks left to live.

The engineers had not come to fight. They had come to build a road. But this was a road-building job like no other. They had been called on to carve a jagged 465-mile strip through dense tropical forest, over muddy mountains, and across monsoon-swollen rivers connecting India and China, in the most primitive conditions.

It was a crucial part of America's war strategy—in a theater that few back home had ever heard of, or ever would. They called it CBI—China, Burma, India—a geographic umbrella term that gives little hint of the challenges and stakes of the construction project, guerrilla warfare, and unprecedented aerial missions it included.

The work combined bulldozers and elephants, mules and men,

in a forest thick with deadly snakes, bloodsucking leeches, man-eating tigers—and Japanese. To get from the starting point in Ledo, India, to the end in Kunming, China, they had to climb up from the steamy jungle floor, across rivers that rose forty-five feet in monsoon season, and over ten-thousand-foot-tall, snowcapped Himalayan peaks.

Fewer than half the workers would see the road reach the end.

It was, in the words of the man in charge of the project, Major General Lewis A. Pick, "the toughest job ever given to U.S. Army Engineers in wartime."[1] But when someone told him it couldn't be done, Pick answered it would be, "rain, mud, and malaria be damned."[2]

Pick set his men to work round-the-clock, seven days a week, in eight-hour shifts, setting a breakneck pace of more than a mile a day.

Chinese Army engineers went first, marking a path through the jungle. Then came Americans with bulldozers, roughing out the way. Aviation engineers followed, clearing a hundred-foot-wide right-of-way. Behind them came the graders, and, lastly, a battalion laid down the gravel for the road surface.

Engineers moved 13,500,000 cubic yards of earth for the road, some 100,000 each mile. It was enough soil, the *New York Times* estimated, "to build a solid dirt wall three feet wide and ten feet high from New York to San Francisco."[3]

Sometimes, even the heavy construction equipment wasn't enough to clear the way.

As one of Frank's friends, Charlie Monroe, described it: "Some of the trees were so large around the bottom four men hand in hand could hardly reach around them. In order to get them down we would in some cases use one or two cases of TNT to cut them off at the stump."[4]

Elephants helped.

A British officer nicknamed "Elephant Bill" handled the giant beasts, which had been trained for use in the Burmese teak industry before the war. As a *Life* magazine article explained: "His elephants are the light cranes and mobile winches of front-line screen troops. . . . To drive piles, the elephant simply stomps down on a log with his feet. Culverts are built much the same way. Wearing chain harness, the elephants haul logs to the bridge or culvert site. Then it is a question of pushing the log into the right place."[5]

Burma posed challenges that required innovative engineering solutions. And Burma tested men.

There were the rock and mud slides that undid days of work as they blocked the road, the underground springs that weakened the roadbed, and the rain. The monsoon season could bring 150 inches of rain. It turned the ground into virtually impassable masses of mud that swallowed vehicles up to their axles and turned every walking step into an exhausting slog.

When the rains came, rivers rose as much as forty-five feet above their dry season height in just a few days, making traditional bridges useless. So Pick devised a novel way of anchoring floating bridges that could adjust to the quickly changing level.

There was no escaping the torrential downpours. And there was no escaping the swarms of biting black flies and ants, infectious mites and ticks, malaria-carrying mosquitoes, or the bloodthirsty leeches.

They slithered into men's beds at night and, as Colonel Nevin Wetzel noted, "because of all the dead, the leeches were thick along the trail and on the leaves of bushes lining the trail, it appeared the bushes were being touched by a slight breeze, until you noticed that the leaves did not move—only the leeches."[6]

The men began the day by pulling off leeches filled fat with their blood. They quickly learned to burn them with the tips of their cigarettes to make them drop off. Yanking them would rip their heads off beneath the skin and cause infections and painful, slow-healing "Naga sores" that would eat the flesh away through to the bone.

"It got so that I began every morning with an examination to see how many leeches had been living off me through the night. Once there were nine, swelled to the size of half sausages with my blood," Captain Fred O. Lyons explained. "Some of the boys got them into their ears and noses, and then the medics made use of a special technique. It seems a leech will reach down to put its tail in water that's near, so the medics would hold a cupful of water under a leech sufferer's nose or ear. As the leech reached down, the medic would tie a loop of string to the tail and pull tight. Then he would touch the end of a burning cigarette to the leech, and it would immediately come loose."[7]

And the men soon learned to recognize the signs of the panicked mules carrying their equipment for what they were: a warning of tigers lurking nearby.

Still, the engineers worked at a pace that put them just behind a bold band of commandos clearing the way of Japanese defenders. The construction crews often came across their handiwork by the side of the freshly cut road—the rotting carcasses of recently killed enemy and, once, a skeleton still poised neatly at the wheel of a Japanese jeep.

The plan originally envisioned the commandos as an elite unit of handpicked troops. They wound up with a ragtag group of adventurers, misfits, and castoffs unloaded from other units—about three thousand in total—willing to accept Roosevelt's call for volunteers for a "dangerous and hazardous mission" in an undisclosed location.

Even as they came together, "secrecy was the watchword," Captain Lyons remembered. "I was confined to a hotel along with the men and not allowed even to walk around the block or telephone my home, just 200 miles away. Other men who had volunteered for the 'dangerous and hazardous secret mission' were pouring into other hotels: cavalrymen from Jamaica, engineers from Puerto Rico, riflemen from Panama, radio experts from Washington. They had no more information than I on where we were going or what we were to do."[8]

In a scene out of a spy novel, he continued, "the next morning we boarded two trains with curtains drawn," with no idea where they were headed.

Code-named GALAHAD, the group assembled in India for physical conditioning and to train in an array of lethal skills designed precisely for jungle warfare: long-range penetration tactics, scouting and patrolling, stream crossing, weapons, demolitions, camouflage, small-unit attacks on entrenchments, evacuation of wounded, and what was then a novel technique—supply by airdrop.

They were led by a charismatic and determined West Point graduate who had studied Japanese and had been in Burma when the Japanese invaded, Brigadier General Frank D. Merrill.

Officially, they were called the "5307th Combined Unit (provisional)," but they are better known by a simpler name: Merrill's Marauders. And they were everything to be expected of a band of thrill-seekers and disciplinary problems other commanders were all too happy to get rid of.

In fact, military historian David W. Hogan noted that they "soon earned a reputation as an unruly outfit. A British officer, who had been invited to GALAHAD'S camp for a quiet Christmas evening, noted men wildly firing their guns into the air in celebration and remarked, 'I can't help wondering what it's like when you are not having a quiet occasion.'"[9]

If the engineers' job was hellish, theirs was abominable. Both were crucial.

Japan launched all-out war on China in 1937 and by 1942 held much of that nation's east. They still faced resistance from Chiang Kai-shek's forces there. When the Japanese invaded Burma, however, they took the Burma Road, cutting off the last overland supply route for the Chinese.

To keep the pressure on the Japanese, the Americans set out to build another route, from Ledo, India, to connect with the old Burma Road in the north of the country.

Enter the engineers, and Frank.

They were workers, not fighters. Few had ever fired a gun before boot camp, and most had not fired one since. The engineers came by troopship to Bombay on a converted luxury liner, the *Mariposa*, pressed into wartime service. The seas were rough much of the time on the crossing. Frank got seasick.

They arrived October 12, 1943, then traveled by rail and truck to Assam, India.

"We traveled by train to the interior of India and many many times the train would have to stop to let someone remove a starving person from the tracks," Frank's friend Charlie Monroe recalled in a letter. "The boxcars were like cattle cars, and had wooden benches. Short of walking we moved at a snail's pace because some mountain areas we [*sic*] so steep the train would hardly go."

Everywhere, it seemed, they were surrounded by masses of poor pleading for handouts.

"Brother you should see these people," Frank told his brother Joe a few days after landing, "well you know how Second Street looks, well this place looks worst [*sic*]. From port we travel by rail to this camp and along the road there were beggars or salesman selling rings, knifes [*sic*], wallets and many other things.

"You should see the beggars," he continued, "they ask for anything that can be eaten, they even take the bread that is left in our mess kits."[10]

They set up camp there, in the land of the Naga, a tribe of head-hunters. They were friendly enough with the Americans, but still practiced their craft with deadly competence. They proved it during an ugly incident involving two men from Frank's battalion who had found a young Naga girl in the jungle and took turns raping her. Her brethren from the tribe caught the second one still in the act—and beheaded him on the spot.

Generally, though, things seemed just short of a vacation.

"In November 1943 life for the 209th Engineer Combat Battalion was posh by Army standards. Camped in the Naga Hills of northern India, six thousand feet above sea level, we actually had wooden floors for our tents and kerosene lamps," engineer Lloyd L. Kessler recalled. "There were movies nearly every week. Rumors circulated about Hollywood entertainers coming to visit us in India. I even saw one celebrity waiting in the mess line ahead of me—Major Melvyn Douglas, the American actor, in dress uniform, mess kit in hand, apparently unaware that officers ate separately."

Soon, though, it was time to do what they had been brought for. They moved ninety miles east, Kessler added, "going from cool mountains to hot, humid lowlands."[11]

Frank and Charlie set to road building, "making it wider and putting in drain lines (culverts) which was very hard work, also widening the sharp turns," Monroe explained. "Many of us had our first experience in operating heavy equipment, bulldozers, road graders, rock crushers and heavy dump trucks."

They also teamed with Kessler's company to build a 960-foot span across the Tarung River. One unit set up a sawmill to provide lumber. The teams at the bridge site toppled trees to shape and fashion into supporting columns, then linked them with steel girders and topped them with the timber planking.

Sensing its significance, the Japanese planted mines in the road to stop the American advance, and stationed snipers to pick off bulldozer drivers.

"It's bad enough that the rain washes away our roadbeds and the jungle rot effects [*sic*] us all," one road builder wrote in his diary, "we have to constantly worry of enemy fire. We're told the Chinese forces under General Stilwell's command protect our flank. Although this may be true I've seen none of them for months."[12]

Soon, too, jungle diseases and dangers began to take their toll.

"Malaria has effected [*sic*] many, and it is almost impossible to control because of the insects that feed on us daily," the diarist commented. "Leeches are everywhere. A few days ago Len fell when a roadbed collapsed. After we pulled him out of the mud he had over 20 leeches covering his body. I don't know how he's doing."

As Frank and the engineers hacked their way through the jungle below, the United States continued to provide vital supplies to the Chinese by air. The Air Transport Command flew over "The Hump"— their name for the freezing, thin-aired heights of the Himalayas—while the American Volunteer Group, a rambunctious assortment of boisterous and bold mercenary pilots, jousted with Japanese fighters with infuriating success.

"Though they only existed for seven months before being absorbed into CBI, the 113 pilots and 55 planes of the American Volunteer Group would not only shoot down 299 Japanese aircraft (with 153 more 'probable kills'); they would lose just four pilots in combat," the writer Donovan Webster noted in his magnificently detailed account, *The Burma Road.*[13]

They called themselves the "Flying Tigers," flew in cowboy boots, drank bootleg whiskey, and had been spotted riding water buffalo through the streets of Rangoon after a night of drinking. And they mercilessly harassed the Japanese.

They showered Imperial Army camps with homemade pipe bombs and Molotov cocktails they fashioned from gasoline-filled whiskey bottles, flinging them from their cockpit windows as they flew over just above the treetops.

"To deceive the enemy into thinking the AVG had countless aircraft, the Americans repainted their propellers new colors every week," Webster wrote.[14]

It worked.

"By early 1942," Webster continued, "the Japanese vowed to destroy 'all 200 planes' possessed by the Flying Tigers, despite the AVG having only 29 aircraft in commission at the time."[15]

The Hump pilots were equally daring and equally flamboyant. They kept leopards and baboons as pets, Webster noted, and "cultivated a rumpled but specific style, in which they wore their officer's hats with the crowns crushed flat, and always kept their .45-caliber pistols shoulder holstered beneath their left armpits."[16]

They traded beer and whiskey with soldiers at a nearby British motor pool, who let them take vehicles of their choosing. The pilots picked one-cylinder military motorcycles, and "before long, every plane crew had their own bike, which they proceeded to paint in various colors like a flying circus," First Lieutenant John Walker Russell recalled in his memoirs. "On trips to other fields, we loaded the bike on board and had our own transportation to wherever we wanted to go on the ground."[17]

Inevitably, the combination of heavy drinking and hard driving led to the obvious conclusion.

"The end result of this was two racing bikes crashing into and killing a sacred cow and hospitalizing two pilots," Russell concluded.[18]

The pilots cut a hair-raising path over the world's tallest mountain range, buffeted by turbulence and freak typhoon-strength gusts so fierce they were losing an average of eight planes a month. In all, the ATC lost nearly six hundred planes and one thousand men.

Nonetheless, they succeeded in delivering a lifesaving three thousand tons of needed supplies to the Chinese every month.

Eventually reconstituted as the Tenth Air Force, those dashing daredevils lent air support for the engineers as well and dropped crucial supplies to Merrill's men deep in the jungle. Those missions carried their own special risks.

Coming across enemy-held territory naturally opened the unarmed planes up to ground fire and Japanese fighters. If they were forced to bail out, the dangers they faced included much more than just the enemy. As their jungle survival manual cautioned:

In just about ninety-nine cases out of a hundred, jungle animals will be just as frightened of you as you are of them. They will hear you long before you can see them and in most cases they will do their best to keep out of your path. If you are traveling alone and want some form of protection at night in a particular area where you feel large animals are present, build a fire and pile on bamboos. They will go off like gunshots and make enough noise to scare away any animals that may be nearby. In an emergency, a shot from your signal pistol will scare off an angry elephant or a tiger.[19]

A downed airman also needed to be wary of natives. The Japanese offered head hunters 300 rupees for an American head.

They risked dysentery from drinking contaminated water, malaria from mosquitoes, death at the hands of the Japanese or their henchmen. One thing they didn't have to worry about was food.

"Natural food is plentiful in most jungles if you know where to look for it and are able to distinguish between the edible and the poisonous," the survival manual stated, and offered a simple guideline: "ANYTHING THAT YOU SEE MONKEYS EAT, YOU CAN EAT."

Still, nothing compared to the brutally arduous and perilous mission of the Marauders.

These Long Range Penetration Teams pushed through the thickest and most uninhabitable backcountry and swamps to catch the Japanese in murderously efficient ambushes.

They proved it in their very first mission. "Casualties had been light," reported historian Gary J. Bjorge, "only eight men had been killed and thirty-seven wounded during the fighting in which an estimated 800 Japanese had died."[20]

Merrill's troops didn't always have the advantage of surprise, but their fierceness made up for it. Once, a Marauder company huddled through the night, waiting for the Japanese attack they knew was coming.

"We knew it was coming," Marauder Captain Lyons recalled, "for all night long on the road we could hear the bang of truck tail gates and the thud of feet landing on the ground. Every bang meant another truckload of Jap soldiers unloading.

"In the morning they struck. I had heard of Banzai charges before, and now I was in the middle of one. . . . There's not much expression to a Japanese face, but I could plainly see the strained look about them that turned to shock and surprise as our machine-gun fire hit. One Jap's rifle seemed to fly like a spear as he fell. Another sank to the ground, hit in the stomach.

"Jap bodies were piled so deep after the fourth wave had been cut down that, during a lull in the fighting, Cadamo had to sneak out and kick some of them out of the way to clear the range for his gun. In front of another gun I counted bodies seven deep."[21]

What the Japanese couldn't do, though, the jungle did. The Marauders, drinking muddy water from elephant tracks and contaminated river water, soon fell victim to vicious amoebic dysentery.

By the time they got to what would be their most important, and final, battle, the men of the 5307th were disease-ridden and exhausted, and desperately in need of a rest. They didn't get it.

Instead, they got orders to take the Japanese airfield at Myitkyina. It was an important prize. It not only gave the Allies a base from which to fly missions over Burma and ferry munitions to the Chinese, it took away the base the Japanese used to disrupt those missions.

Victory was easy. Or so it seemed. The attack the morning of May 17 caught the Japanese completely by surprise. The airfield fell quickly.

But "Mitch" was the third-largest city in northern Burma, with houses, buildings, a railroad station, a hospital, and a movie theater. Roads towered a story or more above soggy rice paddies. As the Japanese retreated to these natural defenses, the Allies found themselves locked in door-to-door fighting—an urban battle as foreign to the Marauders and their Kachin allies as the jungle would be to a GI yanked out of France and dropped into Burma.

The battle turned into a debilitating siege, with the Allies pushed back into the thick of the tropical brush surrounding the city. But the Marauders were in no shape for an extended fight. The ravages of dysentery were so severe that some of them cut holes in their pants so their diarrhea didn't interfere with their shooting.

By the week after the attack on the airfield, exhausted Marauders fell asleep as they fought.

"By 25 May the Marauders were losing 75 to 100 men daily to malaria, dysentery, and scrub typhus. Merrill himself was evacuated after a second heart attack. Morale plummeted even further when desperate staff officers, trying to hold down the rate of evacuation, pressed into service sick or wounded troops who could still walk."[22]

The Marauders called for reinforcements. The only ones available, despite their lack of combat capabilities, much less any jungle-fighting skills, were the engineers.

"At 4 A.M. we were told to get ready to load on the plane and move into combat which was near Myitkyina," Charlie Monroe recalled.

They arrived as the monsoons began.

"Remember the film *Burma* that Errol Flynn played in? This is the area," he continued. "General Stillwell was commander of the Chinese troops that we were to join up with. We were told to move toward the front lines. No one wanted to move, because we could hear the guns. We knew this was not a training mission but the real thing. It was more jungle, rain, and mud."

From then on, the Japanese assault continued relentlessly. In a letter to his former commander at the translator training school "from somewhere inside Burma," Technical Sergeant Edward Mitsukado, a Nisei interpreter with the 5307th, said:

"Fighting out here is heavy and goes on day and night. You can hear the machine guns, rifles, and big guns all through the hours. You go to sleep hearing them and wake up with the din still in your ears. Occasionally the Japanese throw their big shells over this way, and the whistling shells make you start thinking and wishing for a haven like Savage. Tsubota and I have a dugout that gives us good security. You can stand in it and still be below the surface. I had to stop Tsubota from digging any deeper as we struck water. At nights the firing, the tracers, flares, and the fires make one think of a big New Year's celebration in Chinatown."[23]

The untested engineers faced a battle-hardened and stealthy enemy, willing to fight to the death.

"We had been trained to build, destroy, and fight, but few of us were prepared to do all three," Lloyd Kessler recalled. "I still remembered how to clean my M-1 rifle, but I had not shot at anything except a target since basic training."[24]

He didn't have long to wait.

One night shortly after arriving, the Japanese attacked.

"Whatever sleep we might have gotten was interrupted at 2300 hours by a volley of rifle fire," Kessler continued. "Orange tracers cut through the darkness. One of our machine guns opened up, answered by the rapid chatter of a Japanese light machine gun. Flares bathed the area in bright light. I saw the Japanese coming toward us—silently, not a banzai attack but slowly and deliberately, as though they expected little opposition. I held my rifle with the sling wrapped around my arm, just as I had learned in boot camp, knelt, and waited until I saw them clearly. I started firing and kept firing until there were no more Japanese in front of me. They stopped shooting flares. I stared into the darkness, but all I could see or hear was the whimpering and groaning of the wounded. Our medics were busy that night."[25]

The bloody back-and-forth continued that way until June 13, Kessler said, when he got his "introduction to the horrors of short-range mortar fire."[26]

The mortar attacks came in a concentrated frenzy—shells exploding, a hail of rifle fire from all sides, the deadly spray from a machine-gun or two. Men screamed. Men died. Men shook in their foxholes and called out for their moms.

But as the days wore on, the engineers grew accustomed, and grew experienced.

"As the days went by, the fright was still there but not as much," Monroe remembered. "Our first contact with the Japs was very hard to take and especially stay put. I guess we all wanted to run. This is what I call facing the most difficult time in my life."[27]

The fight would last through August. But it ended for Frank three weeks after the invasion in Normandy.

Outnumbered and outgunned, the Americans were ringed by Japanese soldiers—pummeled brutally by terrifyingly accurate mortar fire by day and locked in savage hand-to-hand fighting with infiltrators by night. Weakened by dysentery, on the point of starvation, and deluged by the driving monsoon rains, men drowned in their foxholes.

"All food, ammunition, medical supplies, and other essential material was dropped to us by plane," Monroe said. "The only time we got meat was only [sic] came across a buffalo and kill [sic] it. Sometimes we would carry to [sic] meet [sic] in our pocket all day before we had a chance to cook it. We had canned heat to cook with."[28]

On June 29, tangled in yet another firefight, Frank's luck ran out. At least, his chaplain wrote later, it was quick. His body was buried in India, to await the end of the war. The chaplain read John 14:1–8 over his grave: "Let not your heart be troubled . . ."

"There was so much going on in the combat area that is not easy to talk about or even wright [sic] about, I hope you understand," Monroe said in a letter to Frank's mom. "I really don't remember the number from our company 'C' that died there."[29]

The price had been high.

By the time Myitkyina finally fell on August 3, the fight had cost the 209th 71 killed and 179 wounded. The Stilwell Road, as the 1,079-mile Ledo–Burma Road connection later came to be known, opened the following February, long after it had any real value for the war effort.

By the time it was completed, 624 engineers had been killed in combat, 63 had died of typhus, 11 of malaria, 44 in road accidents, 173 in aircraft accidents, and 53 drowned. Total Ledo road fatalities: 1133.

That's almost one per mile.

"At war's end, the battalion was one of the most decorated in the CBI Theatre," according to the 209th's unit history. "Their awards included one Distinguished Service Cross, four Silver Stars, 33 Bronze Stars and 181 Purple Hearts."[30]

One of them was Frank's.

On July 16, the Western Union man rode his bicycle up Second Street. He stopped at Frank's house. At the end of the street, Frank's sister Georgia was stepping off a bus, coming back from the movies. She heard her mother Angelina's wails from a block away.

It wouldn't be long before Angelina would cry again.

CHAPTER NINE

THE BLOODY BOCAGE

The summer of '44 was in many ways the beginning of the end. The Allies spread across France and Italy and pushed into Belgium, seemingly unstoppable as they liberated increasingly vast chunks of Europe from the Nazis.

But they were hard-won gains. The men moved at a deadly crawl for most of June and July, over heavily defended and unexpectedly challenging terrain that caused huge losses for the Americans—roughly one death for every yard gained—and Slugger, Joe, and Claro found themselves in the thick of it.

As one member of Claro's unit described it later: "Of the 12 company commanders who led companies across the canal, 8 of them were casualties by the end of the week. Co. C of the 120th lost 3 co. commanders in one four-hour stretch. The 30th Division suffered 3,934 casualties, almost 40% of its strength in that 11-day battle to

St-Lo. The toll on front line platoons like I was in was even higher—close to 75% according to one surviving officer."[1]

That wasn't the worst of it. The worst came later, and would earn Claro's regiment a Presidential Unit Citation.

Slugger came ashore three days after D-Day, as part of the storied 2nd Armored Division—aka "Hell on Wheels."

"In the boats, there was about a thousand guys," he said.

They offloaded at Utah Beach, the westernmost of the landing zones. Even though, by then, the beach was officially secure, it was far from safe.

"The day that we were there," Slugger said, "they bombed the heck out of us. They strafed us and they went berserk. . . . And then when they opened up the stairs to get out, where were we going to go? There was an ocean out there."

He manned a 40mm antiaircraft gun, commonly known as a Bofors gun. To call it formidable is an understatement.

Developed in Sweden and built for the U.S. military by Chrysler, the gun fired two-pound exploding projectiles at the rate of 120 a minute. Plus, it had an advanced sighting system that could be "adjusted" for lead with a manual computer, significantly increasing its accuracy.

The first ones mounted on U.S. naval ships as they came off the assembly line earned credit for helping the United States claim its first naval victory over Japan, at the Battle of Midway.

The exploding shells proved especially effective against kamikaze attacks, capable of literally tearing the planes apart in midair, before they could hit the ships. Together with their rapid-fire capability and stunning accuracy, the Bofors made mincemeat of the Japanese Zeros.

In one battle in October, a mysterious new U.S. ship known to the public only as "Battleship X" blew thirty-two kamikaze aircraft out of the sky in thirty minutes—better than one a minute—even though it had never been test fired and its gunners were inexperienced reservists. At one point, even mess hands fired it, at their request.

In Slugger's hands, the Chrysler-built Bofors could provide ground cover for advancing infantry and although generally the practical maximum ceiling was closer to 12,500 feet, it could take out enemy aircraft flying at almost twice that.

It was more than an attack weapon. More than once, it saved his life.

"One time, threes Stukas came and bombed us," he said. "They were a funny-looking plane and they made a funny noise. They strafed us and bombed us."

The Bofors proved itself.

"We shot two of them down and the other one went away toward the German side, smoking."

The success of D-Day had given the Allies a precious toehold on the continent, a tiny chink in the German armor, for funneling in men and materiel. The frantic buildup soon clogged the landing zones so much that officials sometimes had to halt ground operations to permit air traffic.

Taking the beaches had been costly. The Allies suffered more than 12,000 casualties, most within the first few hours of the D-Day landing. The Americans fared the worst—more than 6,600 dead and wounded, including 2,500 at Omaha Beach alone and another 2,500 among the airborne.

The new arrivals still found the wounded forming long lines waiting to be transported to hospitals in England.

The beachhead, however, stood under firm Allied control by the time Slugger got there, and the torrent of arriving equipment and troops continued unabated. By the end of June almost a million men, half a million tons of supplies, and more than 150,000 vehicles had poured in. And more were coming.

But extending their drive inland was falling far behind plans. The commanders had expected to take most of Normandy within the month. Instead, the Allies remained confined to an area less than one-fifth that, in a stretch about fifty miles long by anywhere from twenty to as little as five miles deep.

They found themselves hampered by determined German defenders, bogged down on marshy lowlands that made movement difficult, and hobbled by near constant downpours that turned the rich French soil to a nearly impassable mire. It was, in fact, the wettest early summer on record since 1900.

"The frequent rains that fell intermittently daily didn't help matters much in our cramped and often-muddy foxholes we dug in the ground at the base of the 10-foot high hedgerows," Don Marsh, a 2nd Armored wireman, recalled. "We had the choice of attempting to cover the entrance to our hole in the ground with our raincoats or wearing them to try to keep our smelly gas impregnated clothing from becoming more caked with mud—neither option worked well. Even the damn mud was unfriendly."[2]

Worse, though, was the *bocage*.

The ancient network of hedgerows cut the countryside into a Mad Hatter's quilt of irregular patches and turned the ground in between into death traps.

Half-earth, half-hedge, the man-made enclosures formed substantial barricades to foot soldiers and tanks. The dirt base ranged from four to ten feet thick, with steep banks anywhere from three to fifteen feet tall. Atop that grew a tangle of small trees and brush that could be nearly as thick and just as tall as the foundation. They served as boundaries and fences around small and unevenly shaped plots of pasture and farmland, with no apparent rhyme or reason to their design.

The First Army's commanding general, Omar Bradley, called it the "damndest country I've seen."[3]

And the hedgerows were endless. One combat engineer commander estimated that in just a mile-and-a-half an attacking tank company would come across roughly thirty-four separate hedgerows. One report noted that an aerial photograph of a "typical section of Normandy" eight miles square showed more than 3,900 of the hedged enclosures.

"The Germans have used these barriers well. They put snipers in the trees. They dig deep trenches behind the hedgerows and cover them with timber, so that it is almost impossible for artillery to get at them," Ernie Pyle explained to the folks back home. "Sometimes they will prop up machine guns with strings attached, so they can fire over the hedge without getting out of their holes."[4]

The Nazis laced the fields and thickets with booby traps, and once the Americans broke through that hedgerow into the open ground in between, they'd find themselves caught in a vicious cross fire of German rifles and heavy machine guns.

A 1944 Army "Combat Lesson" training article warned: "The German soldiers had been given orders to stay in their positions and, unless you rooted them out, they would stay, even though your attack had passed by or over them. Some of their snipers stayed hidden for 2 to 5 days after a position had been taken and then popped up suddenly with a rifle or AT grenade launcher to take the shot for which they had been waiting.[5]

"We found fire crackers with slow burning fuses left by snipers and AT gun crews in their old positions when they moved. These exploded at irregular intervals, giving the impression that the position was still occupied by enemy forces."

Eventually, as the Americans continued their push, the Germans would drop back, only to dig in at the next field and do the same thing all over again.

Tanks were little help. Going up the steep banks of the hedgerow exposed their vulnerable undersides, which the Germans were only too willing to exploit.

Even after the Americans developed more effective strategies, using explosives and modified tanks—"Rhinos"—that allowed them to push through the hedgerows instead of over them, progress through the *bocage* remained frustratingly slow and lethal. In a mere fifteen days, the 30th Infantry Division lost 3,934 men; the 29th, 3,706; the 35th, 2,437.

Allied leaders began to fear a repeat of the lengthy, debilitating trench warfare of World War I.

They needed better mobility.

They needed Saint-Lô.

Originally a fortified Gaulish settlement, the city had been sacked by Vikings and English, ravaged by plague, seized by Huguenots, and partly destroyed by soldiers of the crown. But it had never seen the level of destruction about to be visited upon it.

The town itself held little value for the Allies; it sat on low ground surrounded by hills. But it sat at the juncture of a web of main roads leading in every direction. Those routes, and the hills, gave the Americans a necessary jumping-off point for the next phase of the war—the "Breakout."

The 2nd Armored, and Slugger, played a vital role. Dislodging the Germans involved coordinated concentrations of artillery laid down in a grid a hundred yards to a side and a flood of foot soldiers.

One zone alone counted twenty thousand American shells fired on the first day; another, thirteen thousand.

As they approached their objective, one company found "patches of forest on the hill were dense, but had been riddled by artillery fire so effectively that hardly a tree was untouched. . . . Considerable opposition had been anticipated in the woods, but they had been so thoroughly smoked and burned with white phosphorus shells and raked with artillery fire, that the enemy had withdrawn all but scattered elements from the area."[6]

It was hardly a one-sided fight. The Germans unleashed barrage after barrage from an estimated twenty-four 105mm gun howitzers, twelve 150mm howitzers, one battery of 150mm Nebelwerfers, and two batteries of 88mm guns.

In the middle of it all, sat Saint-Lô.

The battle raged for twelve days. On July 19, the Americans wiped out the last pockets of enemy resistance and called Saint-Lô their own. The devastation was so complete that the playwright Samuel Beckett, reporting for Irish radio, called it the "Capital of the Ruins."

Second Lieutenant David Garth painted a detailed picture of wartime destruction.

"St-Lo, as the Americans found it, was a shell of the former town, a place of gaunt walls and sprawling heaps of crumbled masonry. The twisted shapes of vehicles lay among piles of rubble. It was as though the whole bitter Normandy campaign had been summed up in this one spot. What had not been bombed out by American air attacks was blasted and rent by artillery, and the destruction was not ended. The enemy shells that came hurtling into St-Lo during 18–19 July smashed the ruins into further chaos."[7]

Another American soldier looked out over the piles of rubble and shattered shells of buildings and hissed, "We sure liberated the hell out of this place."

But Saint-Lô was merely a prelude. The Allies had spent nearly six weeks getting barely twenty-five miles off the beachhead. Now they were ready to break out. Five days after taking Saint-Lô, the Americans launched Operation Cobra, the drive to push the Nazis from France.

The stakes were high.

"Cobra thus assumed vast importance in my mind," Lieutenant General Bradley later commented. "If it succeeded, I was certain it would give everybody a much-needed shot in the arm. It would help eliminate the back-stabbing. It would put such momentum in the war that the very speed of it would heal the seams in our rupturing alliance. Conversely, if it failed, it could develop into much more than another military setback. It could bring on dangerous open warfare in the alliance that might lead to Monty's relief and perhaps Ike's and my own."[8]

It was scheduled to begin on July 21. Claro had just arrived.

Even though he had enlisted almost two years before, his efforts to join the Army Air Corps had delayed his final assignment to an infantry unit. On February 20, 1944, he explained the delay in a letter to Frank Sandoval: "I failed to make Air Cadets in the Air Corps on the [sic] account of my eyes. This left me with a sort of bitter feeling and consequently I decided to go back to the old outfit. I am reporting there on the 28th of this month. I guess the Infantry is my first and only love and I am returning to it."

He came, via troopship to Naples, Italy, as Slugger fired away at Nazis outside Saint-Lô. Claro quickly joined the replacements replenishing the front-line ranks of the 120th Infantry Regiment. It was part of the 30th Infantry Division—"Old Hickory," named in honor of Andrew Jackson, the bold and fearsome Indian fighter, Army general, and seventh president. Claro carried a .30-caliber MI Garand in his hands and a romantic vision in his heart.

"There is something about the foot-soldier that I like," he continued to Frank. "There is nothing glamorous about his work. Yet, it is very important and the newspapers can't lie about the work he is doing on [*sic*] the various theaters of operations. He takes a lot [*sic*] hard beatings. His bed might be [*sic*] muddy foxhole or a bomb crater, but that is his home for the night. Yes, he takes a lot. Somehow I want to share that with him. I want to be with him when it is all over. I want to come back with him when it is all over and there will be no more camps. I want to be with him when he goes home for good.

"My love in the U.S. Army is the infantry."

His introduction to the tragic reality came in Cobra.

The Americans massed more than two hundred thousand men for the attack, with Claro and the 120th in front. Bad weather delayed the start for three days. It finally began on July 24. The battle plan called for the infantrymen to wait as 1,586 Eighth Air Force heavy bombers from England pounded the German defenders, then attack.

Two days in a row, though, the red smoke fired to mark enemy positions drifted back over them. Claro and the others huddled helplessly as the bombers—maintaining strict radio silence and unable to be warned away—carpet bombed them with more than 3,300 tons of explosives. Nearly one thousand were wounded, nearly two hundred killed—sixty of them buried alive by the tons of dirt thrown up by the bombs, their bodies discovered later.

One of Bradley's aides, Major Chester Hansen, kept one of the most detailed diaries of the war ever—more than three hundred pages in all. His description of what happened reveals the surprise of the men on the ground.

"Soon the heavies came in, we heard them long before seeing them. Heavy roar up above the clouds which were now about 8000 feet with small patches of blue beginning to show through. Ground grunted and heaved as the first cascade of bombs came down, horrible noise and the shuddering thunder that makes the sound of a bomb so different from that of artillery. Suddenly when the next flight came over there was a sharp deadly screaming whistle. . . . We dove to the ground. . . . The ground shook and 500 yards in front the angry black spirals of dirt boiled out of the ground. Doughboys on the road had taken cover in ditches."[9]

By the time the bombing stopped, the 30th Division had lost more than 150 men—25 dead and 131 wounded. The 120th Regiment's 2nd Battalion, Claro's battalion, had been in the open, ready to lead the attack. It suffered the majority of the losses.

Bradley exploded in rage, demanding to know what had gone wrong. The operation, however, had to continue. He rescheduled the aerial bombardment for the following morning.

The next day was even worse.

Again, artillery batteries fired the red smoke. Again, a breeze lifted the marking clouds and sent them rolling toward the Americans. And again, the bombers unleashed their payloads onto their own troops.

The men had prepared better this time, digging foxholes instead of waiting in the open. It was no use. The 120th's regimental history describes how the men's initial awe gave way as the bombs crashed on top of them: "Huge flights of planes [arrived] in seemingly endless numbers. . . . Fascinated, we stood and watched this mighty drama. . . . Then came that awful rush of wind—that awful sound like the 'rattling of seeds in a dry gourd,'. . . . The earth trembled and shook. Whole hedgerows disappeared and entire platoons were struck, huge geysers of earth erupted and subsided leaving gaping craters."[10]

On the ground near Claro, waves of explosive blasts knocked Lieutenant Charles Scheffel off his feet.

"On my left, a crashing boom slammed me against the side of my foxhole and bounced me off the quaking ground. Pain knifed into my ears and squeezed air out of my lungs. I sucked in dirt and choked trying to breathe. Spitting, I opened my mouth against the deafening roar. Mother of God, they were going to kill us all. . . . I prayed somebody somewhere was on the horn telling these guys what they were doing to us down here."[11]

The death toll was even higher than it had been the day before. The 30th Infantry Division casualties came to 61 killed, 374 wounded, and 60 missing, presumed buried alive in their foxholes. The dead included Lieutenant General Lesley J. McNair, the highest ranking officer killed in the European theater during the war.

Bradley's description revealed his horror over the incident.

"A bomb landed squarely on McNair in a slit trench and threw his body sixty feet and mangled it beyond recognition except for the three stars on his collar."[12]

The mission, however, went on. The remnants of the 120th, along with the rest of the 30th Division, charged forward to attack the equally battered and shell-shocked Nazis. Within two days, the foot soldiers had advanced more than six-and-a-half miles and opened the way for the armored assault that would complete the breakthrough.

The Americans drove forward at a stunning pace—twelve more miles by the 28th, then on to take Coutance, Cerences, Villebaudon, and, despite the Nazi commanders' insistence that it be held at all costs, Avranches. On the 31st of July, Granville fell.

Cobra had ended. The Nazis had lost Normandy. The road to Paris had been opened.

An intercepted telephone conversation between Field Marshal Gunther von Kluge, commander in chief of the German's western forces, and Berlin, described the tenuousness of his situation.

"Every movement of the enemy is prepared and protected by its air force. Losses in men and equipment are extraordinary. The morale of the troops has suffered very heavily under constant murderous enemy fire, especially, since all infantry units consist of only haphazard groups which do not form a strongly coordinated force any longer. In the rear areas of the front, terrorists, feeling end approaching, grow steadily bolder."[13]

By August 4, seven divisions of General George S. Patton's Third Army had streamed across the Pontabault Bridge into Brittany.

That same day, unbeknownst to the Americans, Nazi police raided the secret annex of a building five hundred miles away, in Amsterdam. They arrested eight people. One of them was a fifteen-year-old girl named Anne Frank.

At the time, the Americans didn't know about Anne Frank, and they didn't know of the existence of the concentration camps like the one at Bergen-Belsen where she was sent, and where she would die.

In France, though, the Germans were in disarray. Their defenses shattered and communications destroyed, they fell into uncoordinated clusters, with no way for their commanders to get a true grasp of the situation.

"It's a madhouse here," von Kluge complained.[14]

The Americans had taken twenty thousand prisoners in the last six days of July who, one G-2 report noted, were "so happy to be captured that all they could do was giggle."[15]

Hitler was livid. He ordered von Kluge to launch "an immediate counterattack."[16]

As he did, Joe Sandoval was arriving from England and being rushed forward to join the 41st Armored Infantry Regiment. The men of the 41st carried rifles, but they were part of the 2nd Armored, traveling with, or on, the Hell on Wheels tanks. He joined them right where Hitler ordered his commanders to "annihilate" the enemy.

The spot Hitler chose was a place of crags and streams, caves, forests—and legends. Here, it was said, was the final resting place of King Arthur and Lady Guinevere, where Merlin had brought them back to life to share their love anew. Here, amid the deep, thick poplars and beeches of the Mortain Forest lies *La Fosse Arthour* and the tallest waterfall in France. Here, Hitler demanded, the Allies must be stopped.

The Mortain Counterattack, as the Americans called it, began August 7, led by three Panzer tank divisions. They struck shortly after midnight, shrouded by darkness and a thick fog, directly at Claro's position.

The attack wasn't much of a surprise. A French villager alerted the Americans about the German tanks massing outside Mortain the day before the attack. Once darkness fell, the Nazis made no effort to disguise the increasing clatter of their tank tracks as they moved into place.

When the actual attack began, the 2nd SS Panzers swarmed

around Hill 317, where the 120th Regiment's 2nd Battalion, including a still green Claro, had taken up hasty defensive positions.

The only way to keep them from overrunning the 120th was to call in an artillery strike that fell so close that the shells exploded within yards of Claro. It worked. The Germans fell back, but when the sun came up the Americans realized they were surrounded. The siege, which would earn Claro's company the title the "Lost Battalion," had begun.

For six days, the Panzers launched assault after assault. Time and again the Americans repulsed them with artillery strikes. By midnight of the second day, Claro and the rest of E Company were out of water and dangerously low on ammunition. They had only a few mortar shells left and one bazooka with nine rounds. Medical supplies were running out.

By August 9, Major Ralph A. Kerley remembered, "attempts by the regiment and the remainder of the division to relieve the battalion had failed. The first gnawing pains of hunger and thirst were appearing. The ammunition supply had dwindled to practically nothing."[17]

Worse, he continued, the men had a constant grotesque reminder of the fate awaiting them if they failed: "Several of the severely wounded died during the night. The bodies of the dead, both our own and the enemy, were deteriorating fast in the warm August sun, and the stench on the Hill was nauseating."[18]

Somehow, the Germans knew.

At six o'clock that evening, a German officer appeared, carrying a white flag. He offered the Americans a chance to surrender. If they didn't, at 8 P.M., "the battalion would be blown to bits."[19]

E Company's commander gave a terse reply, according to later reports: "Some sources quote E Company Commander as saying that he would not surrender until the last round of ammunition had been fired and the last bayonet broken off in a German belly. Actually the reply wasn't quite so dramatic. It was short, to the point, and very unprintable!"[20] The German officer kept his word. At 8:15, they attacked. Claro and the rest of the men were so low on ammunition, they barely fired. As the flood of Germans surged onto the hill, the commander had a surprise planned.

He had told his men to dig into holes and protect themselves. When the Germans penetrated their position, he called in an artillery strike on his own position.

For the third time in two weeks, American shells pounded Claro's unit, and the men could do nothing but hunker down and wait for it to end. When it did, the Germans had been repulsed. The Americans still held the hill.

They held out for two more days. On the 11th, the Germans began to retreat.

"Our artillery plastered every available route of withdrawal and was very effective," Kerley recalled, "as was evidenced by the screams and hysterical cries of the enemy."[21]

The next day, relief finally arrived. Soldiers from the 320th made contact with some of the men on the hill. They brought food, ammunition, and water. By 1 P.M., the "Lost Battalion," as the media dubbed them, was lost no more.

Their bravery in standing off the enemy came at a high price. Of the 647 men who went up the hill, only 370 walked away. It also earned them a Presidential Unit Citation.

Claro wrote home after it was over, his artist's eye and sensibilities showing through: "Second Street is really not much—just mud and ruts. But, right now, to me it is the greatest street in the world."

CHAPTER TEN

A Bridge Too Far

On the brilliant blue morning of August 25, 1944, champagne corks popped and cheering crowds spilled into the streets of Paris to welcome the advancing tanks of the Allied forces coming to liberate them from the Germans.

The writer Anais Nin's reaction captured the elation of her countrymen: "JOY. JOY. JOY. JOY. JOY. JOY. JOY. JOY. JOY.

"Such joy, such happiness at the hope of war ending. Happiness in unison with the world. Delirious happiness.

"At such times we are overwhelmed by a collective joy. We feel like shouting, demonstrating in the street. A joy you share with the whole world is almost too great for one human being. One is stunned before catastrophe, one is stunned by happiness, by peace, by the knowledge of millions of people free from pain and death."[1]

The Parisians showered the French and American soldiers with kisses and flowers, waved the Tricolors they had kept carefully hidden awaiting this day, and wept in joy—with no idea how close they had come to seeing their beautiful city burned to the ground on Hitler's orders.

The Führer had taken increasingly direct control of his armies, issuing directives that seemed divorced from the reality of the situation on the ground. He remained determined beyond reason to hold the Allies at Avranches and insisted that his commanders hold positions "to the last man, to the last cartridge."[2]

He personally ordered the counterattack at Mortain and stubbornly resisted the suggestions of his commanders that they withdraw and regroup to make a stand another day.

The result cost him tens of thousands of men, so many that the Allies lost count.

"From 13 through 17 August it was possible to count them accurately—British and Canadians reported daily figures in excess of a total of 6,000," Army historian Martin Blumenson noted, "the First U.S. Army 2,500 for 15 August alone."[3]

After that, so many Germans laid down their arms, the Allies could only guess at the numbers. The First Army figured more than 9,000 surrendered on August 21 alone. In all, the Allies estimated they took some 50,000 prisoners.

Another 10,000 or more Germans lay dead on the battlefield.

It developed as the Germans battled unsuccessfully to take Hill 317, where Claro and the remnants of the 120th Infantry's 2nd Battalion refused to surrender. Bradley sent his rapidly advancing forces to envelop the Nazis. Aided by Canadian troops near Falaise, the Americans had nearly encircled the Germans by August 17. Rather than accept blame for the disaster his efforts had come to, Hitler replaced von Kluge as commander, west. He sent Field Marshal Walther Model to take over.

Hitler also finally permitted his armies to retreat, but ordered them to slow the Allied advance by leveling everything useful in their path. "Not one locomotive, bridge, power station, or repair shop shall fall into enemy hands undestroyed," he ordered.

Von Kluge responded by committing suicide. He swallowed potassium cyanide hours after handing command to Model. In his final note to Hitler, he foresaw the bleak future, and called on the Führer to stop the bloodshed.

"When you receive these lines, I shall be no more," he began. He defended his actions and told Hitler the folly of trying to hold Avranches.[4]

A little later, he continued: "The German people have suffered so unspeakably that it is time to bring the horror to a close. I have steadfastly stood in awe of your greatness, your bearing in this gigantic struggle, and your iron will. . . . If Fate is stronger than your will and your genius, that is Destiny. You have made an honorable and tremendous fight. History will testify this for you. Show now that greatness that will be necessary if it comes to the point of ending a struggle which has become hopeless."[5]

For major portions of the Panzer forces and Seventh Army elements caught in the tightening Allied noose, the war was already over.

"It was as if an avenging angel had swept the area bent on destroying all things German," a Twelfth Army Group observer reported after witnessing the carnage.

"I stood on a lane, surrounded by 20 or 30 dead horses or parts of horses, most of them still hitched to their wagons and carts. . . . As far as my eye could reach (about 200 yards) on every line of sight, there were . . . vehicles, wagons, tanks, guns, prime movers, sedans, rolling kitchens, etc., in various stages of destruction. . . .

"I stepped over hundreds of rifles in the mud and saw hundreds more stacked along sheds. . . .

"I left this area rather regretting I'd seen it. . . . Under such conditions there are no supermen—all men become rabbits looking for a hole."[6]

The German counterpunch was broken. The Nazis fled wholesale, dropping their rifles by the road in their mad dash toward the fatherland.

The Allies turned their aim to Paris. So did Hitler's fury.

"In history the loss of Paris always means the loss of France," he commanded, ". . . Paris must not fall into the hands of the enemy except as a field of ruins."[7]

Losing the French capital, Hitler insisted, would cost him not only France, but the launching base for his vindictive V-2 assaults on London.

His generals had other ideas.

When Dietrich von Choltitz, the Nazi commander of Paris, received the order, he realized that he was being ordered not only to reduce Paris to rubble, but to die defending it. He called Model, insisting Hitler was out of touch. Defending the city was impossible. His troops were almost out of rations.

Model ignored him.

Choltitz may have already decided to ignore Hitler's order, but he told Model's chief of staff he was ready to follow through. He had placed three tons of explosives inside the Cathedral of Notre Dame, another two in the Invalides, and one more in the Palais Bourbon. In addition, he stated that, "he was ready to level the Arc de Triomphe to clear a field of fire, that he was prepared to destroy the Opéra and the Madeleine, and that he was planning to dynamite the Tour Eiffel and use it as a wire entanglement to block the Seine."[8]

Boxing began early for the Second Street-ers. Al Sandoval had gloves on (probably Willie's) before he was big enough to step into a ring. *Alfonse M. Sandoval*

Angelina Sandoval's tears seemed constant after Joe and Frank died.
Tanilo H. Sandoval and Georgia Herrera

Claro Soliz (back row, far right) loved playing on the local Mexican baseball teams.
Guadalupe L. Soliz

ABOVE LEFT: Claro wanted to fly, but when he wasn't accepted in the Army Air Corps he embraced the infantry with new vigor.

Guadalupe L. Soliz

ABOVE RIGHT: Eduviges (center, back) and Angelina (left) pose with an unidentified woman and their growing clan of U.S.-born children.

Tanilo H. Sandoval and Georgia Herrera

RIGHT: Eduviges holds Willie's sons, Mike and Hank, around the time of Willie's death.

Tanilo H. Sandoval and Georgia Herrera

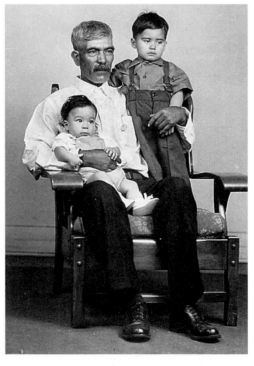

Elliott Thompson with his wife, Dolly.

Sherrie Neilson

Frank and Joe Sandoval (back row, in overalls) joined the growing hordes of Mexican-American children growing up in the rail yards.

Tanilo H. Sandoval and Georgia Herrera

Frank Sandoval (front row, far right) wore the serious look of a young soldier as he posed with members of his unit in dress greens.

Tanilo H. Sandoval and Georgia Herrera

Frank Sandoval in happier, and fancier, civilian times.

Tanilo H. Sandoval and Georgia Herrera

Frank Sandoval in his basic training graduation photo.

Tanilo H. Sandoval and Georgia Herrera

Frank Sandoval, in front with the garbage can, even found a way to smile on KP duty.

Tanilo H. Sandoval and Georgia Herrera

George Gordon with his wife, Helen. After he returned from the war he was plagued by nightmares for the rest of his life.

Helen J. Gordon

Flags, uniforms, and pride marked the Hero Street dedication ceremony.

Joseph A. Terronez

ABOVE: Joe Gomez seemed young for his years when he first put on his uniform and headed off to Germany for a tour in the peacetime occupation army.

Alvina A. Tafalla

RIGHT: On the day of his mother's funeral, Joe Gomez and his brother Buddy still had bandages on their foreheads covering the injuries they received in the car accident that killed her. *Alvina A. Tafalla*

A young Terry Garza Gomez holds the Silver Star and Purple Heart her husband, Joe, earned fighting the Chinese and North Koreans in the Korean War.

Alvina A. Tafalla

Joe Sandoval posed for a portrait in his U.S. Army dress uniform.

Tanilo H. Sandoval and Georgia Herrera

Johnny Munos wore a deliriously happy smile the day of his wedding to Marion Beserra.

Mary M. Ramirez

The orchestra in "La Yarda," with Willie's brother Ruben sitting in the very front middle.
Alfonse M. Sandoval

Children and adults alike worked in the fields "topping" onions, getting paid by the acre as they brought in bushel after bushel.
Alfonse M. Sandoval

Peter, third from the right in his airborne uniform with the distinctive trouser legs bunched in his boots, posed with a group of friends from his unit.   *Rufina Guerrero*

Peter, in his dress greens, posed on a sprawling parade field.

Rufina Guerrero

Peter, left, posed in a parade uniform at camp.   *Rufina Guerrero*

The first five of Jose and Carmen Sandoval's children, including Willie standing at the far right and baby Al dressed in white, posed outside their home in the rail yard. *Alfonse M. Sandoval*

Johnny Munos, home on leave before he was sent overseas. He got his wish to have his last leave extended. It cost him his life. While the rest of his unit headed to Germany, Johnny ended up in Korea. *Mary M. Ramirez*

Terry Garza Gomez holding her new-born daughter Linda, born shortly before Joe shipped out to Korea.

Alvina A. Tafalla

ABOVE: Willie wore a suit and tie to pose for his senior year school picture. *Alfonse M. Sandoval*

LEFT: Willie in his cap and gown for his high school graduation ceremony. *Alfonse M. Sandoval*

Dashing, debonair, and devil-may-care in a legionnaire's cap on a motorcycle with a sidecar, Willie looked like he was off on an adventure in the desert of North Africa. *Mary Garza*

Willie bites into some picnic fare during a chilly gathering on Billy Goat Hill. The older Second Street teens used the gatherings for fun and as send-offs once they started getting their draft notices.

Rufina Guerrero

Willie, second from right, clowning with work friends. *Alfonse M. Sandoval*

Willie, center, looked grim at his mother's funeral. *Alfonse M. Sandoval*

Willie, in uniform, shakes hands with an unidentified friend. *Alfonse M. Sandoval*

Willie, home on leave in the distinctive paratrooper uniform, not knowing that he would never see Second Street again. *Alfonse M. Sandoval*

Willie, middle row, second from right, with his airborne boxing squad.

Alfonse M. Sandoval

TOP LEFT: Willie's mother, Carmen. *Alfonse M. Sandoval*

TOP RIGHT: Claro Soliz had an artist's eye and a poet's way of looking at the world.

Guadalupe L. Soliz

RIGHT: A young Luz "Slugger" Segura took the job he was assigned on a field artillery team, and wound up chasing Germans across Europe and through the bitter cold of the Battle of the Bulge.

Robert Segura

LEFT: He was Tony Pompa to the people who knew him on Second Street, but to the Army Air Corps he was known by the fake name he enlisted under, Tony P. Lopez.

Joseph A. Terronez

BELOW: In 1928, the workers in the Silvis railroad yards were a mix of men from a host of backgrounds, with whites, blacks, and Mexicans working side by side to keep the expanding railroad running.

Rufina Guerrero

THE WHITE HOUSE

WASHINGTON

October 21, 1971

Dear Friends:

It was particularly inspiring for me to learn
about Hero Street, and I can well understand
the mixed emotions of pride, patriotism and
gratitude that have brought you to honor your
men from Silvis who have served our nation
so well over the years.

A spirit of love for America is alive in millions of hearts across this land, but it is doing
especially well on Hero Street. The people of
your town have made great sacrifices for our
nation, and I join your pledge to those who have
died in our service that we shall never lose
sight of the principles of justice and freedom
for which they so gallantly fought and gave
their lives.

With my warm wishes to each of you,

Sincerely,

Richard Nixon

The Friends of Hero Street
c/o Honorable Tom Railsback
House of Representatives
Washington, D. C.

TOP LEFT: Joe Terronez and the folks who wanted to build the Hero Street Memorial
Park resorted to a variety of means to raise the funds necessary to complete the project,
including selling tacos and holding dances.   *Joseph A. Terronez*

ABOVE: None other than the president of the United States, Richard M. Nixon, con-
gratulated the people of Silvis for the sacrifice that made Hero Street a reality.
                                                                 Joseph A. Terronez

His true sentiments may have come out in a sarcastic dinner comment: "Ever since our enemies have refused to listen to and obey our Fuehrer, the whole war has gone badly."[9]

Nonetheless, whether he feared Hitler's wrath if he fled Paris, or because he felt duty-bound to stand his ground even if he didn't permit the destruction of the city, Choltitz remained, and refused to surrender. In fact, the Germans put up strong defenses at various points on the routes into the city.

The Americans could have easily charged in and overwhelmed the Nazis, but they were concerned that a head-on battle within the city would lead to exactly the kind of destruction Choltitz was attempting to avoid. Plus, there was a political consideration, as Bradley noted: "Any number of American divisions could more easily have spearheaded our march into Paris. But to help the French recapture their pride after four years of occupation, I chose a French force with the tricolor on their Shermans."[10]

Slugger and Joe Sandoval, in fact, had come well within striking distance of the city when the orders came to hold up. They stopped across the Seine River from the City of Lights and waited for the go-ahead to move in. At dawn on August 24, as the two Second Streeters cursed the downpour soaking them, French general Philippe Leclerc launched his attack.

Three spearheads of the French 2nd Armored Division soon ran into mines, artillery fire, and a close-range fire fight that lasted four hours. The strong opposition from the Germans faded quickly during the night, and by the following morning they offered little impediment to Leclerc's advance. Still, the Americans, frustrated that the French general had not achieved his objectives on the 24th, decided to charge in on August 25. By noon, encountering no resistance, they reached Notre Dame. The biggest obstacle to their approach came from the enormous crowds of jubilant Parisians filling the streets.

At almost the exact same time the Americans reached Notre Dame, the French surrounded Choltitz's headquarters at the Hotel Meurice. As Choltitz described it, a young French lieutenant charged into his room and demanded, "Do you speak German?"[11]

"Probably better than you," the general replied.

Choltitz was taken to meet Leclerc at the Prefecture of Police. There, he signed a formal surrender. A color film captured the immediate aftermath, as Leclerc sat in the front of a Free French jeep. Choltitz, appearing dejected, slumps in the seat behind him.

The celebrations of the French only grew larger.

"I had thought that for me there could never again be any elation in war," Ernie Pyle commented. "But I had reckoned without the liberation of Paris—I had reckoned without remembering that I might be a part of this richly historic day."[12]

All of them were showered with cheers, hugs, and kisses. The French offered champagne, they offered baths and beds. Most of all, though, and most humbling for the soldiers, they offered their sincere and profound gratitude.

Ed Ball, the Associated Press correspondent, felt words escape him: "Describing Paris in words today is like trying to paint a desert sunset in black and white."[13]

At 7 P.M. the following day, August 26, General Charles de Gaulle, the leader of the Free French, returned to the city he had been forced to abandon almost four years earlier. Leading a column of sharply marching French soldiers, he paraded down the Champs-Élysées, past the wildly adoring crowds of Parisians packed as many as twenty deep on each side.

Later, in a radio broadcast from the Hotel de Ville, he said: "Paris!

Outraged Paris! Broken Paris! Martyred Paris, but liberated Paris! Liberated by the people of Paris with help from the armies of France, with the help and support of the whole of France, of France which is fighting, of the only France, the real France, eternal France."[14]

His speech was short and passionate. It concluded with words that had extra meaning that day, for a city saved from destruction, and a country freed from oppression: "*Vive la France!*"

Slugger and Joe remained at the Seine until after DeGaulle's French forces entered Paris. But the hugs and kisses were still in abundant supply as they headed past the shops along the Champs-Élysées toward the Arc de Triomphe. It made a lasting impression on Slugger.

"You should have seen the girls!" he said. "That's one of the reasons we were mad they made us wait. We hadn't seen a girl in so long."

As the people of Paris welcomed Slugger and Joe, a troopship carrying Peter Masias and the 17th Airborne Division docked across the English Channel in Liverpool, as far away from Second Street as he had ever been. The toll of D-Day and the battle for Europe had forced America to pull more of its reserves into the fight. After months of extensive training in the United States, the youngest of the airborne divisions was finally shifting into position to join the fight. The move put Peter and Willie Sandoval at bases just miles apart, dancing with British schoolgirls by night and training for a still-secret mission by day.

It was a time for optimism. All across America, the song "I'll Be Home for Christmas" began to sound like more than wishful thinking. The Allies had swept across France and rushed toward Belgium, overwhelming the retreating Germans as they went.

Emboldened by their success, British Field Marshal Bernard Montgomery hatched a plan that was practically brazen in its magnitude, involving the greatest airborne assault in history, before or after. It called for nearly thirty-five thousand men—in broad day-light. (In fact, it was so audacious that when the battle plan fell into the hands of the opposing Nazi commander on the first day of the attack, he considered it so unbelievable that he suspected it was a fake planted to throw him off, so he ignored it!)

Montgomery insisted it would end the war by Christmas. It didn't. His ill-conceived and overly ambitious plan, code-named Operation Market Garden, crumbled into one of the biggest disasters of the war. In just nine days, nearly half the Allied force—seventeen thousand men—would be dead or wounded, and Montgomery would be scrambling to save isolated pockets of survivors.

It began on the morning of Sunday, September 17, when the engines on 1,051 C-47 transport planes roared to life. The paratroopers finished a breakfast of hot cakes and syrup, fried chicken with all the trimmings, coffee and hot apple pie.

By then the men of the 504th had been kept isolated, in warehouses, for three days. Officers went over mission objectives. They studied sand maps and identified landing zones and targets. The enlisted men merely waited.

"We were sleeping at the base on the floors," said then Private Leo Hart.[15]

To keep them entertained, he said, "they had movies going all the time."

The men got a real kick out of one war movie starring Errol Flynn. "He was leading this patrol against the Japanese. And he pulled out of his pocket this eight-inch-long oblong object and he was talking in it, and everybody burst out laughing. . . . If we had had something like that, my God!"

The paratroopers kept waiting for the mission to be called off, as three previous ones had been. It wasn't. The gloomy overcast day of rain and drizzle on Saturday gave way to a sparkling bright Sunday. After breakfast, chaplains offered religious services for all denominations.

The men checked their equipment one last time, divided into twenty-man sticks, boarded the planes, and, at 9 A.M., the Market part of the operation lifted off.

"The tremendous air column was over a hundred miles long and contained 1544 aircraft with 478 gliders. 1113 bombers were in the air, and 1240 fighters, all in support of Operation Market."[16]

The 17th was held in reserve. Peter would wait in England as the war raged on.

But not Willie. The 504th's job was to seize several bridges, including the longest span in Europe, across the Maas River. Field Marshal Montgomery's plan envisioned an air and ground assault to flood with men the Dutch zone abutting Germany, sweep around the north end of the Siegfried Line, cross the Rhine into Germany, and end the war before Christmas.

The 82nd Airborne's drop zone lay fifty-seven miles behind enemy lines. To get there, they had to fly a route the bomber pilots had nicknamed "Flak Alley" for the treacherous antiaircraft barrages along the way. For the men in Willie's company, even the target's name seemed ominous: Grave.

At precisely 1:01 P.M., the sky over the sun-dappled fields of Holland filled with tens of thousands of blossoming parachutes, and within seconds, it was filled with the bright streaks of German tracers and the black puffs of antiaircraft fire.

Bullets tore through the paratroopers' canopies as they floated down. Men were shot to pieces as they drifted helplessly. Planes fell in flames from the sky. Crippled gliders slammed into the ground, where the tons of heavy military equipment they carried—jeeps, antiaircraft guns, and artillery—broke free of their tethers and crushed the men on board.

Willie and Leo Hart jumped twelve minutes later, after the sky had become a deadly gauntlet of exploding flak, hot shards of shrapnel, searing tracers, and machine gun and rifle fire.

"Everything just came at us—Messerschmitts, artillery, antiaircraft," Hart said. "It became one miserable Fourth of July right there."

The pilots flew under strict orders to follow their designated course, no matter what. So, as the Germans pockmarked their planes and knocked out engines, the airmen fought to keep the C-47s under control until all the paratroopers had cleared. They found the safest corridor beneath the flak, skirting just a few hundred feet above the enemy.

"I would think we left that C-47, I left that plane, at around four hundred feet," Hart said.

Willie and Leo Hart landed just north of their target and quickly shot their way through the first pockets of German defenders. Their goal: the Grave Bridge. They made it to the top of a dike fronting the bridge and found themselves facing a determined 20mm antiaircraft gun crew. Every time one of the paratroopers poked his head up, he became a target.

Even after they cleared out that gun crew, the bridge remained heavily defended.

"We were maybe sixty yards from the bridge and everything started to fire," Hart said. "There was a German machine gun nest on the opposite shore, on the Grave side, up the river from the bridge. And they were firing immediately into the bridge. And that meant I was not going to try to cross that bridge."

Lieutenant Martin Middleton, Company F's commanding officer, thought otherwise. He led his men across the bridge—double time, single file.

"I was following right behind Lt. Middleton for a while," Joseph Watts Jr., recalled. "Bullets and fragments were buzzing all around us—then I saw him get hit in the hand by a ricochet off a girder. We bandaged it. He said it hurt but he didn't need my help. The Lieutenant already had been issued four Purple Hearts, the latest from Anzio. Therefore, I put more space between us, I ran ahead. If he was the target, I didn't want to be too close to him."[17]

They made it. They took out the machine gun nest. The first bridge was theirs.

"All initial missions of 504 were accomplished by 1930," the 82nd Airborne Division's commanding officer, Major General James W. Gavin, reported.[18]

As Company F moved into Grave, they found that the Germans had retreated.

"When we went into the town, the people gathered and a lot of the women had no hair," Hart said. "So we naturally want to know, and we were told that they were the women who associated with the German soldiers while the Nazis occupied the town. . . .

"I think we were four nights in the town. The Germans pushed us out. And I'll be damned if there wasn't more women who had their head shaved—because they associated with the Americans!"[19]

Other units in the 82nd Airborne weren't so lucky. Their field radios proved useless, leaving them unable to communicate with one another; and instead of lightly manned German positions staffed by poorly trained conscripts, they found themselves facing thousands of battle-hardened SS Panzer troops.

Then the weather turned against them, preventing the arrival of the second wave of paratroopers. Montgomery's battle plan bogged down. Casualties mounted. Three days after landing, they were locked in a bloody standstill. Willie's unit was called in to help break the impasse—in one of the most courageous assaults of the war, a bloodbath that came to be known as the Waal River Crossing.

CBS war correspondent Bill Downs described it as "a single, isolated battle that ranks in magnificence and courage with Guam, Tarawa, Omaha Beach . . . a story that should be told to the blowing of bugles and the beating of drums for the men whose bravery made the capture of this crossing over the Waal River possible."[20]

The goal was the railroad and road bridges crossing the river into Nijmegen. Gavin came up with the idea of sending his men across the river in boats, then attacking the Germans from the rear. From the outset, the plan seemed insane.

"When we were briefed for the assault crossing, we took it as a joke," Lieutenant John Holabird, one of the engineers assigned to the mission, recalled. "We couldn't believe anyone could be serious about it. I saw that huge railroad bridge looking right down on us. Suddenly, it came across that this was not a joke; that we were going to paddle those flimsy boats across, and at that moment, I would have liked to have been any place in the world, except there."[21]

It wasn't just the twelve-hundred-foot width of the swift-moving river. The Germans had the far bank heavily fortified. From where they stood, the paratroopers could see the pillboxes, machine guns, mortars, and artillery facing them. A pair of 20mm guns stared down at them from the bridge itself.

The men would be crossing in canvas assault boats—overloaded, nineteen-foot-long, clumsy boats with canvas sides and plywood bottoms.

"We were all amazed at the flimsy assault boats, which had folding canvas sides and wooden bottoms," Second Lieutenant Edward

J. Sims of H Company said later. "Each boat had a capacity for sixteen and each had eight paddles. It took us a few minutes to adjust and secure the canvas sides and then move to the river's edge for launching."[22]

Each boat weighed about two hundred pounds, perhaps twice that fully loaded. The teams of thirteen paratroopers and three engineers raced them to the water and climbed aboard. As they did, Major Edward G. Tyler of the Irish Guards looked on, aghast. He asked Lieutenant Colonel Reuben Tucker, the 504th's commander, if his men had ever trained for such a thing.

"No," Tucker replied, "they're getting on-the-job training."[23]

Delbert Kuehl, the 504th's chaplain, joined the men in the assault boats. He volunteered.

"The plan seemed absolutely impossible," he said, "and I felt if ever the men needed me it would be on this operation."[24]

As the first wave paddled frantically to get across the four-hundred-yard-wide river, the Germans sprayed them with such intense fire that the Third Battalion's S-1, Thomas Pitt, said, "It looked like rain in the water."[25]

Company F took a position on the riverbank to provide cover for the men in the boats. They came under intense fire from multiple directions. But at least they could take cover and shoot back.

Twenty-six assault boats went into the river for the first wave. Only thirteen made it back. Of the 260 men in the first assault, half were killed or wounded.

"I don't think that any man that went across that river that day in a boat and were fortunate enough to make the other side will ever in his life forget it," Pitt later told his son. "There is no way you can visualize what the devil it was like. I will never forget it and I have had dreams that I am back in the boat and I am paddling like mad."[26]

Witnessing the crossing, the commander of the British Second Army, General Miles Dempsey, just shook his head and said, "Unbelievable."[27]

In the end, the Americans pushed the Germans back. But not far. Almost three weeks into the fighting, the paratroopers remained pinned within sight of the Waal, with the Germans pouring reinforcements in against them.

The British Red Devils, the 1st Airborne Division, took the brunt of it. Directed to take the Arnhem Road Bridge north of Nijmegen, they ran into seasoned SS and SS Panzer divisions on the outskirts of the city.

Only one small band of British paratroopers got through to their goal. They would go no farther.

With the rest of the British division trapped in a pocket north of their target, Lieutenant Colonel John Frost's force held out at the bridge for four days. The Germans shelled them mercilessly. Their casualties mounted. Their medical supplies, food, and ammunition dwindled. Finally, with some men fighting with only their knives, the Nazis swarmed in. The British got out one last radio message: "Out of ammo, God save the King."

Eight days after the lofty start of Operation Market Garden, the ragged remnants of the British force withdrew.

"Hungry, thirsty, heavy-eyed, utterly fatigued, and reduced to a shell of a division after nine days of fighting, the Red Devils wrapped their muddy boots in rags to muffle the sound of their footsteps and began at 2145 on 25 September to run a gantlet of German patrols to the water's edge. The night was mercifully dark. A heavy rain fell. Thundering almost constantly, guns of the 30 Corps lowered a protective curtain about the periphery of the British position. In groups of fourteen to match capacity of the boats, the men inched toward the river. They had to leave their wounded behind."[28]

Nearly 10,000 had gone in; fewer than 2,400 came out. The Germans lost about 3,300.

The carnage was inescapable. As Johanna Mason, a Dutch nurse who went on to marry one of the paratroopers, remembered, the people of Nijmegen lived in a gruesome cemetery of a city, where the dead lay unburied.

"German soldiers lay everywhere; they had fallen right where they were shot," she said. "On one street, there were small 9' by 12' lawns, with iron fences around them and I remember seeing German soldiers slumped against them with their rifles sticking out between the bars. One soldier was leaning against the fence with his helmet down over his eyes and his finger still on the trigger of his rifle. Another, a young boy who looked no older than 15 or 16, was slumped back against a wall of one of the houses. His helmet had fallen off and he looked like he was taking a nap."[29]

Within the month, Gavin counted 2,490 German dead and 2,977 prisoners. The 82nd Airborne's losses included 640 missing, 1,933 wounded, and 469 killed.

One of them was Willie.

On October 6, in a forest just beyond the bridge they had risked so much to take, the 504th skirmished with the Nazis. Lieutenant William Watson led Willie and his platoon to clear out some German machine gun nests in the woods by the Dutch-German border. They crossed just inside Germany to a town called Zyfflich, about six miles from Nijmegen. They started out under a waxing moon at about 10 P.M., moving single file along a road leading to the woods.

Just before they got there, artillery shells started exploding around them. A chunk of shrapnel tore into Watson's right thigh, "dead center," and shattered his femur.

"When it hit me, it just took me off my feet and I was on my back on the ground," Watson said. "I was in severe pain. The medic gave me a shot of morphine and that eased it off. Anyway I was loaded up on a jeep. I turned the platoon over to my second in command. And they went on."[30]

As Watson was being hit on the road, Hart was on top of a stone outcropping a short distance away, getting shelled by the Germans, as well.

"We just got down between these two rocks, and I don't know how many shells those German shot at us. They just kept firing those 88s. Firing those 88s."[31]

Artillery fire set the forest ablaze. Moving through a cloak of thick smoke, Willie was climbing over a fence when he was cut down by German gunfire. A sergeant scurried to his side, but it was already too late.

It took two-and-a-half years for the War Department to piece together some idea of what happened. In April 1947, Willie's father got a letter. It said a former member of Company F, Sergeant Arthur Williamson, was with Willie when he died.

"The third platoon of the above company made an attack on a wooded area held by the Germans. As they went over a fence into the woods, Pvt. Sandoval was hit. He was examined by his squad leader and was reported dead."[32]

And the Western Union man returned to Hero Street, yet again.

CHAPTER ELEVEN

CHRISTMAS, BOMBS, AND BULLETS

Winter came early to Europe in 1944. Willie was dead, Peter still in England. But Claro, Joe, and Slugger huddled with the American forces spread over the long front, facing the deepening snow of Europe's worst winter in forty years from frost-lined foxholes in the steep, forested valleys along Germany's border.

It was bitterly cold, so cold that the oil in engines froze. Weapons froze. Men urinated on them to get them unstuck. Soldiers stomped their feet through the night, or were found frozen in their foxholes in the morning. More than one was seen pressing against the side of a burning building in the midst of battle, for no other reason than to steal a few moments of warmth.

Ask anyone who was there about the fighting, or the historic battle they went through as the year came to a close, and their first words are invariably the same: "Man, it was cold."

Slugger put on every piece of clothing he had. He wore his dress uniform under his fatigues, a sweatshirt over that. It did little good. He curled in a hole covered with branches and shivered from cold and fear as German V-2s roared overhead. Worse, Slugger knew, was when the rockets fell silent: "Boy, you'd better watch out, because it was coming down. When you heard it, it was still going somewhere."

All three Second Streeters had come across Belgium in the mad rush of men and armor that brought huge Allied advances, but stretched supply lines dangerously thin. Lack of fuel had already brought the Third Army to a halt during the summer, and Eisenhower remained acutely aware of the voracious thirst of his armored units. An Army may run on its belly, but its tanks need fuel.

They moved so fast, the press gave them the nickname the "Galloping Ghost" and raved about the unit's exploits.

"Covering sixty miles in three days," one United Press report gushed, "the division took Beauvais and Montdidier in northern France, smashing enemy armor, infantry, and motor transport that ran unexpectedly into its steel fist."[1]

The frantic pace took them to the Belgian border by September 2 and over the Albert Canal on September 8.

They didn't have much, but the Belgians found ways to show the Americans their gratitude.

After taking the airport in Liege to keep German planes from using it, Slugger said his firing team dug in by the side of an adjacent road. The summer had not technically ended yet, but the chill had already begun.

As they settled in, shivering and stomping their feet against the cold, Slugger said they saw two people coming down the road toward them. They had a kettle. It was soup they had made to give the GIs.

"We had never seen them before or nothing," he said. "That was the first cooked meal we'd had since we left England."

Before the firing team pushed on, he said, "I met some young ladies that came and took me to their house and fed me. It was just one day. After that we took off."

With Patton at the reins, the relentless Allied drive continued. The Third Army, and Slugger and Joe, rolled into Maastricht, then Heerlen. And there, a trace of home found Slugger again.

"I was sitting there drinking coffee when someone patted me on the back and said, 'Hi, Slugger!'" he said. "When I heard him say Slugger, I knew it was somebody from back home."

As it turned out, it was someone he knew from Davenport, Timothy Reyes. He was dating Slugger's cousin.

Timothy made it home, and married her. But some of the worst, and deadliest, fighting of the European Theater still lay ahead. Some was just beginning, to their north.

As Slugger sipped his coffee and chatted with Timothy, Willie jumped into Holland with Operation Market Garden.

Worse was still ahead.

As October opened, the 2nd Armored attacked the famed Siegfried Line. Built on Hitler's orders at the start of the war, Germany's defensive Westwall formed a defensive barrier nearly four hundred miles long, from Switzerland to Holland. In all, it had more than eighteen thousand bunkers, pillboxes, tunnels, and concrete tank traps known as "Dragon's Teeth."

They had no way of knowing it at the time, but the assault brought Claro, Slugger, and Joe together again. As the 30th Infantry Division struck at the German forces next to the line, Claro and the 120th attacked the bridgehead at Kerkrade, the Dutch half of a divided city straddling the border with Germany.

When the Nazis sent their Luftwaffe to stall the attack, Slugger was there, firing the mercilessly accurate Bofors and shredding German Messerschmitts as they came in for their strafing runs.

Joe rode in atop a Sherman tank, then charged forward with the 41st Armored Infantry to hold the northeastern edge of the zone. The assault freed Claro and the 120th to race to the Wurm River and dislodge the German defenders there.

The Siegfried Line's psychological significance—the last line guarding the homeland—provoked a fierce Nazi response. They unleashed an arsenal of artillery against the Allies that included at least two railroad guns, forty 105mm and forty-seven 150mm Howitzers, nearly three dozen 88mm guns, and almost one hundred anti-tank and assault guns.

It didn't matter.

Five days after the Americans began the attack, on October 7, the 30th Division's commander reported that the goal had been achieved. The battle was over.

"We have a hole in this thing big enough to drive two divisions through," he said. "I entertain no doubts that this line is cracked wide open."[2]

It had cost the 30th and the 2d Armored more than eighteen hundred killed, wounded, or missing, and fifty-two medium tanks, but they had punched a hole six miles long and four-and-a-half miles deep in the line—and rent an even bigger hole in the German military psyche.

Four days later, the 120th took Brandenburg; by the 21st, after nearly ten days of ferocious defense, Aachen capitulated. That same day, General Bradley told the commanders of the Ninth, First, and Third armies to prepare for the push to the Rhine in November.

The noose was tightening for the Germans, but the war was far from over. The Nazis may have been thoroughly demoralized by this point—their losses mounting, their supplies dwindling, their Luftwaffe nearly nonexistent—but the closer the Allies got to Berlin, the more fiercely the Germans fought.

The second week of November, Joe found himself in the midst of the biggest tank battle of the war up to that point, and about to earn a Purple Heart.

Joe's armored unit had crossed the border into Germany and faced the Nazis in the dramatic tank battle, which lasted six full days. By early December, they had faced the desperate Germans in hand-to-hand fighting for more than a week straight, earning their third Presidential Unit Citation as they pushed the Nazis back to the banks of the Roer River.

Then came the tank-against-tank showdown between the new German seventy-ton King Tiger, with its powerful high-velocity 88mm gun, and the dated American Shermans that had remained tragically prone to burst into flames.

Knowing the American tanks stood little chance in a face-to-face battle in the open, that's exactly what the German 9th Panzer Division sought. The Panzers, fresh from the Russian front and back with 150 Tigers, rolled out against the 2nd Armored with their guns blazing near the village of Puffendorf. It was no match. The Sherman shells barely put a dent in the heavy German tanks, while the Nazi rounds ripped through the American tanks with ease.

The battle began, an official Army historian noted, as the Americans watched as "out of the heavy morning mist came a German tank; two Tigers and four Panthers moved out of the woods on the western fringe of Gereonsweiler. There was a hit; one of the Shermans went up in flames, then another and another and another, as the Germans got the range. Soon the tanks of the 2d Battalion were also being thinned by murderous fire from the big tanks."[3]

The American tanks, he continued, were caught between a slope and the Nazis.

"The Shermans fought back desperately, stepping up to attempt to slug it out with their 75-mm. and 76-mm. guns, but the tanks that got close enough for their guns to be effective were quickly cut down by enemy fire. And when the American tankers did score direct hits on the German tanks, their shells ricocheted off the thick armor and went screaming into the air. One Sherman fired fourteen rounds of 76-mm. ammunition at a Tiger before it had any success at all—and the next moment was destroyed by another Tiger."[4]

They finally called up their "can openers," the 90mm tank destroyers, and beat back the attack. The losses, though, were staggering. In that single day, the 2nd Armored Division lost 38 medium tanks and 19 light tanks; 56 men killed, 281 wounded, and 26 missing.

Nonetheless, the lighter Shermans dodged and parried day after day, and the sides pounded each other with artillery through the night.

In the end, though, the brute strength of the German tanks was no match for the sheer will of the Americans.

"We won because of sheer numbers," a tank officer said. "Our men had too much will-to-win for Jerry to stomach. We knew we were licked, tank for tank, but the boys went in for a free-for-all, ganging on the Tiger until they knocked them out."[5]

Infantrymen, including Joe, turned the tide. They pounced on the Panzers and Tigers in ways their tanks couldn't, surprising the Nazis with close-range bazooka blasts. They exploited the blind spots and weaknesses of the heavily armored machines, clambering aboard to push grenades into their turrets.

In return, Joe and the other infantrymen came under a brutal shelling as they moved through the village itself, and as the Germans poured an entire battalion of Panzer Grenadiers into the battle zone, the American foot soldiers met what First Lieutenant Joseph D. Blalock, of the Ninth Army, called "the most intense and accurate small arms fire . . . I have ever encountered."[6]

The fight quickly evolved into tank-to-tank and hand-to-hand fighting of the most primitive sort. Too close to shoot, the men fought with knives and, if they had no other resort, their bare hands.

As the 115th Infantry charged into the fight, Blalock reported, they dodged the rifle and machine gun fire by "hugging the earth between rows of beets . . . only to be subjected to round after round of mortar and artillery fire."[7]

The Americans were sitting ducks. As Blalock described in vivid detail, a BAR man who ran out of ammo tried crawling to his dead ammunition bearer. "He was hit, tore off his pack and rolled over to get at his canteen and sulfa pills," Blalock said. "The Germans saw him move and shot him again and again as he struggled."[8]

The men's combat packs jutted above the leafy beet tops and gave their position away. After they saw the first few of their buddies picked off, many of the others peeled off their packs and pressed into the muddy furrows between the rows of beets, to avoid being spotted.

Eventually, the 2nd Armored's Bofors and 81mm mortars gave the men some cover, and some of them succeeded in falling back behind a low rise. But the bulk of Company C remained pinned through the afternoon and into the evening. Finally, nightfall gave the survivors the camouflage they needed to escape. Of more than one hundred who went into the beet field, only about twenty got out.

The tank battle raged for six days. When it was over, some eighty German tanks had been knocked out, along with seventy or eighty of the American tanks. American losses were heavy, but the Americans had repulsed the Nazi attack, breached a fifteen-foot-wide, ten-mile-long antitank trench, and catapulted forward to the banks of the Roer River.

The Germans made them fight for every inch. As a *Time* magazine piece on December 11, 1944, pointed out: "Near Hürtgen, the U.S. artillery fire was so heavy that houses near the guns were lifted off their foundations, fell back in ruins. The Germans answered shell for shell. . . .

"The Germans had dug elaborate trench systems in and around the villages, where ordinary-looking houses covered 5-ft. concrete outer walls, 2-ft. partitions, deep cellars. Sometimes, when the trenches were under U.S. shell fire, the Germans ran into the cellars, then back into the trenches when the firing stopped. The Yanks had to clean out every village with bayonets and grenades."[9]

Along the way, Joe was wounded.

He wrote home on the last day of November from a hospital in England.

"Well I suppose by now you've heard that I got hit in the leg, well tell my mom and dad that it's nothing in a few days I'll be walking around again, so tell them not to worry."[10]

It was much worse than he let on. His leg wound kept him in the hospital for more than three months.

As he lay there, the families back home readied for Christmas, lighting trees behind the blackout curtains, planning holiday dinners with black market sugar and ration book substitutes for ham, waiting for the war to end.

Thanksgiving had come and gone. Peter and the men of the 17th Airborne had enjoyed a distinctly American turkey dinner in the English countryside. While they waited for their summons into battle, the 139th Airborne Engineer Battalion bounced from one idyllic rural English village to another, from Ashton Keynes near the head-waters of the mighty Thames to Aldbourne, and finishing in Barton Stacey, about an hour's drive north of Porstmouth. They got to visit London. As the only jump-trained group in the airborne engineer battalion, Peter and the men of Company C made a practice jump. Two parachutes malfunctioned; two men died.

Now, with Christmas just over a week away, all but Joe were about to be caught up in the biggest land battle of the war—the Battle of the Bulge. More than a million would fight, and 160,000 would end up dead, wounded, or missing.

The night of December 15 was eerily quiet all along the snow-covered front. All movement had stopped. Over the preceding days, Hitler had surreptitiously shifted nearly half of all of his forces into place along a sixty-mile line near the Belgian-German-Luxembourg border. And on that moonless night they sat motionless, silent, and ready.

Slugger waited by the Roer with his 40mm gun. Claro's 120th Regiment camped just northeast of a Belgian city that would soon be infamous among the Americans for the atrocities witnessed there—Malmédy, where the German occupiers gunned down more than a hundred civilian men, women, and children; executed eighty-eight unarmed U.S. POWs for no reason; and left their frozen bodies in the snow to be found by the advancing Allies.

At 5:30 A.M. on December 16, the Germans opened up with nearly two thousand big guns, unleashing an artillery barrage that lit up the night sky as bright as day for ninety unrelenting minutes. Then, hidden under the thick fog blanketing the forest, German tanks and infantry streamed forward by the thousands.

"By that night, Germans were all over us, within 10, 15 yards right in front of us," Roger Rutland, first sergeant, 106th Infantry, said. "If you could see a bunch of wild cattle running wild, that's what it reminds you of. I believe they were doped. I believe that the German soldiers were doped to a certain extent, because they were— they were acting as if, 'I don't care if I get killed or not.' They were like wild men."[11]

Whole units of U.S. soldiers fled in panic. Seventy-five hundred surrendered in a single day, the worst defeat for the Americans in Europe. One of the ones who ran was a fresh replacement named Kurt Vonnegut Jr., who threw down his rifle and ran into the woods as a line of Tiger tanks charged in and his unit surrendered.[12]

German commandos, wearing American uniforms and speaking perfect English, slipped through the lines. They changed road signs, cut telephone lines, gave tanks and troops wrong directions. Once the GIs realized what was happening, they began stopping everyone at gunpoint, challenging them with tests of trivia and popular culture they figured only an American would know—who won the World Series, what was Mickey Mouse's girlfriend's name, or who was pinup girl Betty Grable's husband.

MPs even stopped General Bradley, repeatedly. At one stop, the exasperated general reportedly rolled down his staff car window and started talking before the guard even asked a question.

"I'm Gen. Bradley," he said, "and I'm getting tired of these road-blocks every half mile. At the last one they wanted me to give the position of a guard in football; at the one before that they wanted to know the capital of Illinois. What do YOU want?"[13]

At another checkpoint, Lieutenant Leonard Fox was held because he couldn't answer the sports or Hollywood questions. The infantry platoon leader had grown up in Cuba. It took six hours to confirm his identity. Then he was released.

Not all the Germans wore U.S. uniforms, of course. Regular infantrymen wore standard issue white uniforms, making them practically invisible against the snow. The Americans, in their dark uniforms, made easy targets. Soon, their commanders requisitioned every white sheet, tablecloth, or anything else for the soldiers to wrap themselves in for camouflage.

The German assault relied on a stunningly fast break through the American line, seizing U.S. fuel depots to power the Nazi tanks as they went. It also depended on bad weather to prevent the Allies from employing their superior airpower.

The Nazis had launched the attack with more than two hundred thousand men and nearly five hundred medium tanks along the sixty-mile front. They outnumbered the Americans at least three-to-one, six-to-one in some areas of concentration.

But the terrain and weather that they counted on to shield them from aerial attacks also wound up working against them on the ground. It cut the mileage of their tanks by half. And, anticipating their targets, the Americans successfully evacuated nearly 3 million gallons before the Germans could seize them.

Three days into the offensive, Nazi commanders already complained about fuel shortages. By the 20th, the 12th SS Panzer Division had ground to a standstill for lack of fuel. The next day, the 2nd SS Panzer Division stopped, too.

The Germans grew so desperate they resorted to horse-drawn wagons to transport fuel to the front. It wasn't enough.

By the end of December three of the five divisions in the Panzer Corps could barely move.

The Germans had miscalculated. The determined resistance of the American soldiers who held their ground allowed Eisenhower to use the attack to advantage. He let the Nazis come forward, let their lines stretch, then swept in to hold and pinch them off. The result: a sixty-mile bubble in the front—the "Bulge."

"Our orders were to hold or die. Somehow we held," Richard F. Proulx recalled.[14]

Inspiration came from an unlikely source: Malmédy.

The day after the counterattack began, December 17, SS-*Oberstrumbannführer* Joachim Peiper's soldiers marched 160 American POWs into a field outside of town. The first warning of what was to come came when the Americans heard the bolts cocking on the Nazi machine guns. As they opened up, a handful of survivors ran into some nearby woods. They didn't stop. They kept running until they reached the safety of townspeople who helped them reach Allied doctors and soldiers. Then they told of how the gunshots echoed behind them as they ran. First came the ugly staccato chatter of the machine guns. Then, as the Nazis walked coolly among the scattered bodies, the crack of a pistol as they shot anyone still breathing, once, behind the ear. It was a sound that cut across the snowy plain and into the woods where the survivors ran, a noise covered only by the huffing of their scorching breath.

According to a *Time* magazine article that appeared later:

By the testimony of one survivor (who escaped by feigning death after he was shot in the foot), some 160 U.S. soldiers were lined up in a snow-covered field, eight deep and 20 abreast, and raked by machine-gun fire for three minutes.

The survivor heard the "agonized screams" of wounded and dying comrades, and single pistol shots—coups de grace administered by Germans who walked among the fallen victims after the machine-gunning stopped.[15]

The story spread like lightning across the front.

"The word was out," said Robert D. Georgen, who had arrived in Europe as winter was settling in and been moved immediately to the front lines of the 28th Infantry. "Fight to the death or run like hell, but don't surrender."[16]

Still, it would take weeks of brutal, nose-to-nose fighting under arctic conditions before it was over. Claro wouldn't see it end.

He may have sensed what was coming. Before he left home, he wrote a will. He bequeathed his beloved typewriter and a bicycle to his brother's sons.

Despite his premonition, if that's what it was, Peter seemed much more likely to be the one to die. Thick cloud cover kept him and the 17th Airborne stuck in England for more than a week as the Battle of the Bulge raged. They finally landed in Reims, France, on Christmas Eve, and loaded quickly into trucks headed for Mourmelon.

As the families on Second Street opened their presents the next morning, the "Thunder from Heaven" arrived at the front.

Peter, the quiet boy with the hard home life, was among the first members of the 139th Airborne Engineer Battalion, and one of the only ones to see battle. His mother's drunken husband may have berated him mercilessly at home, made him feel worthless, but he found a mission and a home in the newly formed unit.

He had trained to jump, but his first experience in battle came as a ground soldier, assigned to Patton's Third Army. The paratroopers were raw and unproven, facing battle-hardened German fighters in fierce cold, but they were needed. And they quickly proved themselves.

The same change in the weather that allowed the planes carrying the 17th to finally make the crossing from England to France brought cold, dry winds and clear skies. More planes, Allied bombers and attack fighters, followed. The brief protection from air attack the Germans had enjoyed disappeared with the clouds.

Then, snow began to drift on the roads, impeding even further the paltry German supply efforts. By the time the Germans could bring in snowplows, the American fighters and bombers were wreaking havoc on anything that moved.

Three days after Christmas, though, the weather changed again. Blizzards driven by arctic winds cut through the men like icy knives and blinded them to everything more than a few feet ahead. Foot soldiers struggled through drifts as much as three feet tall, and the wounded in shock froze to death if they lay on the ground more than a half hour.

Soon, the cold became as deadly an enemy as the Nazis. Feet and fingers froze. They turned black as coal. If not tended to early enough, the cold could cripple a man for life.

"I had many men that I had to send back and that had feet amputated at the ankles," First Sergeant Rutland said.[17]

By New Year's, Eisenhower was ready to spring the trap. The German advance had stalled. The Allies had them nearly completely ringed.

The 17th came in from the south, outside a small Belgian village called Renaumont.

Attacking in a heavy snowstorm three days after New Year's, they came upon the quarter-mile stretch of road that would later be known as "Dead Man's Ridge." A barrage of Nazi tank and artillery shells came screaming out of the sky. Machine gun and rifle fire tore through their ranks. In seventy-two hours of fighting, the 17th lost a thousand men—killed, wounded, or missing.

Peter and the other engineers of C Company moved into an eight-hundred-yard gap in the American infantry line between the 513th Parachute Infantry and the 194th Glider Infantry. It was their first taste of combat and their introduction to the reality of war.

"People didn't crumple and fall like they did in the Hollywood movies," Bart Hagerman, private, 17th Airborne, said. "They were tossed in the air. They were whipped around. They was hit to the ground hard and their blood splattered everywhere. And a lot of people were standing close to people and found themself covered in blood and flesh of their friends, and that's a pretty tough thing for anybody to handle, and we were no exception to that."[18]

As Peter's company moved into position, with the battalion following, it was dark and snowing heavily. With the snowdrifts up to their chests in places, the men made makeshift sleds to haul their ammunition. They moved single file, holding on to the man in front of them to keep from getting lost in the blinding snow.

In his analysis of the assault, Captain Ralph Kinnes detailed the odds: "The Germans were strong in armor and in combat experience. Their morale was high due to the high degree of success gained in their initial Ardennes attack. The enemy was better equipped for winter fighting. . . . In general, the situation was that of a light infantry unit without offensive antitank weapons attacking a combat wise infantry tank team."[19]

Life, the unit history explained, "was an unending effort to keep warm."

It sapped the men's strength and jammed their weapons.

"The men by this time were very sluggish and slow to respond to anything, due to the intense cold and the light clothing they had on for this type of weather," a battalion liaison officer, Major Murray L. Harvey, remarked. "Squad leaders were told to go from foxhole to foxhole and make their men stand up, swing their arms and stamp their feet to keep them from freezing."[20]

The Germans attacked in wave after wave. They rained barrages of mortar and artillery fire on the Americans every ten or fifteen minutes. The temperature continued to drop. The wind howled so loudly they couldn't hear the artillery shells coming in.

The Nazis brought in tanks, three Mark IVs. The Americans pushed them back with 81mm mortars. The Germans responded by firing rockets at their positions.

The last attack came at around 8 P.M. on January 8. Two Mark IV tanks joined in an artillery, mortar, and rocket bombardment that lasted fifteen minutes. Grenadiers, hidden under a cloak of falling snow and darkness, the sound of their movement swallowed by the wind, came to within twenty yards of the Americans before they were spotted.

The paratroopers opened up with everything they had. At least forty Germans died there, before the rest of the attackers withdrew.

Four hours later, after three days under nearly unceasing attack and having lost close to 40 percent of their men, the paratroopers were ordered to fall back, as well.

The fighting, and the deaths, had been for nothing.

Murray could barely contain his anger.

"If this objective was worth taking, it certainly should have been worth holding," he complained.[21]

Shortly after pulling back from the ridge, Peter and the engineers returned to their primary mission, clearing minefields. As they removed them, they sent them back to be kept until they were needed again. On January 13, as they unloaded a truckload, a mine went off. It started a chain reaction. The load of mines exploded, taking the truck in a huge fireball. Five men died. Eleven were wounded.

Another reminder of the dangerousness of their work came just days later. A lieutenant checking the road through the forest near Houffalize tripped over a wire. The exploding "S" mine sent shrapnel tearing through him. The concussion flattened him. If not for the bravery of a medic, who ran through the booby-trapped woods to tend to him, the lieutenant surely would have died on the spot. Instead, the medic and a sergeant carried him carefully out of the woods to a waiting ambulance.

On January 16, as Peter cleared mines outside Houffalize, Slugger and his gun crew stood a short distance away, aiming their Bofors 40mm down on the Belgian village.

The town was crucial. It was where Patton had pinched off the bulge, and sealed the fate of Hitler's desperate Operation Nordwind.

On that frigid January day, once again, the Silvis Mexicans stood within a few miles of each other, so very far from home, at a turning point in the war.

Slugger had gone through his own hell to get there.

As the Battle of the Bulge began, he had huddled in a shallow hole in the hard, frozen ground—waiting, under orders, as the Germans showered shells on the Americans. Then, on the fourth day after the Nazis launched their surprise attack and the bulge swelled, his artillery team rushed south to pound the Germans' flank.

"We knew they were coming because they bombed us," he said. "They bombed us to distract from down there, because they didn't want us to know where they were attacking."

Once the Americans understood what the Germans were doing, and where, Slugger and the 2nd Armored joined a counterattack force that became famous for the "Miracle at Celles."

Told to get to a position on the north flank of the bulge, Slugger traveled through the night with the entire 2nd Armored, nearly one hundred miles. By eleven-thirty the next morning they had taken their position, just in time to fend off a Panzer attack at Celles.

The speed of their advance led one German commander to demand, "How many 2nd Armored Divisions do the Americans have?"

In the fighting that followed, the Americans captured or destroyed 81 of the German division's 100 tanks and seized 7 heavy guns, 405 vehicles, and another 74 artillery pieces.

As the townspeople huddled in the village, the 2nd kept the fight in the countryside, repelled the attack, and saved Celles with minimal damage.

By Christmas Day, the gun crew stood practically nose-to-nose with the Nazis, on the outskirts of a small town named Humain, firing a "serenade" of shells on the Panzer tanks blocking the entrance to the town. The barrage lasted all through the next day and night. The Germans held fast against the onslaught for two more days, and it wasn't until New Year's Eve, after the remaining Nazis pulled back and British reinforcements moved in to replace the exhausted 2nd Armored troops, that Slugger and the rest of the Americans sat down to a belated Christmas dinner.

Then, while Peter was fighting for his life on Dead Man's Ridge, Slugger was stumbling toward a trap outside the Belgian village of Samrée. German tanks, hidden among the trees and camouflaged by snow, let loose a deadly volley that destroyed three of the lead American tanks. The battle lasted three days.

By then, Slugger had gotten used to the incoming shells.

"You've got to get used to it or you don't get no sleep," he said. "Anyway, they wouldn't bomb continuously. They would surprise you. So we'd get to sleep, and when they would come they'd wake us all up."

In the end, the Americans opened up on the town from two sides and shelled it unceasingly, with more than two thousand rounds, until the flames made the hillside glow. As they came into town, seven German tanks were still smoking.

From there, Slugger and his crew crossed the snow-covered Belgian hills through a string of German-held towns until they reached Houffalize.

Claro didn't join them. As they arrived at Houffalize, the 120th was locked in one of the fiercest battles it had ever encountered.

They had been fighting almost nonstop for nearly a month straight, at Stavelot, Ster, and Parfondruy, and done so much damage that the Germans started calling them "Roosevelt's SS Troops."[22]

This time, the bloody toll began as they were caught by artillery fire crossing an open field in foot-deep snow. They were on the north side of the bulge, trying to take out a German roadblock on the Malmdy-St. Vith road. As they scrambled for cover, the elite German paratroopers holding the area opened up with such a vicious onslaught of sniper and machine gun fire that the Americans could barely lift their heads without getting hit. The fighting was intense, the casualties high.

The 120th lost 450 men. "At dusk on the 15th the third Battalion had a fighting strength of only 150 men—less than that of a single full strength company—in its three rifle regiments. The second Battalion which had taken the brunt of the first day's action was only slightly better off: G Company had only 53 men left."[23]

On January 16, the Germans attacked with six tanks and about one hundred infantry. Artillery fire sent the German foot soldiers running, but the Panzers kept coming. They raced straight into the middle of the 120th, firing as they went. Men fell, ripped apart by the German machine guns, but Claro and the rest of the 120th stood their ground. They hammered the tanks with bazookas, knocked out two of the Mark IVs and a half-track, and forced the Germans to retreat.

The Nazis fell back, but not far. They reestablished their road-block some three hundred yards farther up the road. They used the surrounding trees and firebreaks for cover and lined the approach with a series of light and heavy machine guns.

"The resistance," an after action report noted, "if anything, increased and a number of assault guns and automatic weapons delivered an extremely punishing fire on the attackers."[24]

Over the next two days, the vicious skirmishes continued in freezing sleet and snow. Thick undergrowth kept the 120th from bringing in any supporting armor or heavy weapons.

On the 18th, Claro wrote home. "I can see the Germans, but I am not afraid. I can see the eyes of death in front of me, but still I am not afraid."[25]

The next day, the 120th pressed the attack. They pushed south, past the woods of Wolfsbusch and Rotenfurt. They took the little town of Nieder Emmels, "chasing a company of enemy infantry, three assault guns and battery of horse-drawn artillery out into the open for the artillery to work over. St. Vith, only 3½ miles away, was in sight."[26]

Claro never got there. He was mortally wounded. He was rushed to a field hospital, but it was too late.

CHAPTER TWELVE

A Smile No More

As January came to a close, the outcome in Europe seemed inevitable. The Battle of the Bulge was over. The Germans were on the run. And there was hope on Second Street that the war would soon be over.

It would be, but not soon enough.

The bitter winter still kept its icy grip on the German borderlands, but Eisenhower's plan had worked. The Allies encircled the German forces that had pushed ahead, and cinched the end like a knot in a balloon. The cost to Hitler was insurmountable. The desperate push cost him an estimated 100,000 dead, wounded, or missing. Another 27,000 surrendered.

The weather, however, remained Hitler's ally. The spring thaws waterlogged the terrain and swelled the rivers, bogging down the advancing Allies. With the Germans in full retreat, the Americans took the time to refresh the troops.

Slugger camped far from the fighting, in Luxembourg, for a much needed rest. Peter and the 17th Airborne pulled back to Châlons-sur-Marne, outside Paris. They got a little rest, followed by lots of training. It was bearable though, because the work kept them away from the front line and afforded them more than ample opportunities for visits to the City of Light. The French capital was still a city mostly without electricity, and gas shortages forced most people to walk, ride bicycles, or hail one of the horse-drawn taxis that the French cabbies had improvised. But passes came frequently, and more than a hundred thousand soldiers a week spent their nights striking up conversations with Parisian girls in dance halls and drinking at bars and restaurants the Red Cross and the military set up for their pleasure.

Of course, seeing the sights of Paris frequently included nonmilitary establishments. They included Les Folies Bergère, which, as 40mm gun crewman Bob Gallagher recalled, "was the number one item on the must-see list from every GI we knew who had visited Paris before us. The beautiful showgirls who came out undressed from the waist up and stayed that way throughout the show were obviously the main attraction."[1]

Those seeking a more adventurous, or sordid, outing in Paris—and a possible bout of gonorrhea or syphilis—headed to the Place Pigale.

"It was the red-light district of Paris," Gallagher explained, "and after seeing it we all concluded it had been properly nicknamed Pig Alley. . . . There were street hawkers selling trinkets that could easily be defined as junk. Women of varying ages who all had one common denominator—they looked hard and tough—moved through the mix of GIs and civilian men. Many of the shop windows were decorated with obscene pictures. Doormen in front of some bars offered promises of exotic behavior within and those who were not involved in selling sex were yelling at the GIs, 'Cigarettes? Ciga-rettes?'"[2]

The Army warned the soldiers in no uncertain terms. It showed them movies that gruesomely depicted the dangers of venereal dis-eases. They were given pamphlets that said, flatly, "ALL PROSTI-TUTES & PICKUPS ARE probably INFECTED."[3]

Nonetheless, for men returning from weeks or months in the field, the temptation was often difficult to resist. Not all would do as Gallagher did and turn away. The Army knew it.

Recognizing the risks of losing able-bodied personnel to a social disease or worse in one of the seamier establishments, the military ran its own clubs. Fourteen opened between the liberation of Paris and the end of the war a year later. They had full-blown stage shows that competed with anything the GIs would find in the city, with singers, jugglers, trained animals, and, naturally, dancing girls. But those, too, were powder kegs—given the mix of sultry women, big band music, and battle-hardened soldiers fueled with equal parts of high-octane alcohol and testosterone.

On his visit, Gallagher watched an argument between an obvi-ously drunken paratrooper and his equally drunken date explode into a club-wide brawl in a matter of moments.

The paratrooper wanted to dance. The girl didn't. He slapped her. She swung a champagne bottle at his head.

As Gallagher described it: "Several GIs who had observed what had happened came to the aid of the damsel in distress, even though it was a great stretch of the imagination to call her a damsel. This might have been a gallant thing to do, but it was also the wrong thing because in just a minute, a fight had begun. It mushroomed into half a dozen fights and soon, people were throwing punches at everyone within reach for no obvious reason. One of the paratroopers yelled 'Geronimo!' the paratroopers' battle cry. The place must have been filled with them because they started to come from all directions, some of them swinging down onto the dance floor from the balcony. Everyone was headed for the melee, and the place was in pandemonium. We were at the epicenter of the fight, and it was hard to stay out of it because we were being pounded with blows from people we had never seen before. The paratrooper who had started the fight was standing up on his table dropkicking empty champagne bottles into the crowd. The four MPs near the front door stepped in to stop the action, but they were too outnumbered to make any difference."[4]

Gallagher and his buddies slipped out as the fight continued, and saw jeep- and truckloads of MPs heading for the club as they disappeared into the night.

It was a not irregular occurrence in Paris when Peter got there in mid-February 1945.

The 17th arrived by convoy and train and found themselves stationed at a camp a few miles from Chalons. The spring thaw made the ground muddy, and they slept in tents, but even that small bit of canvas cover felt good compared to the ice-cold nights in the Ardennes still fresh in their minds.

They called it a rest camp, but the days were filled with rigorous training, including practice jumps and a night problem involving the entire battalion.

While Peter and the rest of the 17th recuperated and trained, Joe returned to the front. In another time, or another war, he might have been sent home. But now every man was needed, especially experienced fighters. The Allied commanders could taste victory, but they knew it would only come if they continued to batter the Germans mercilessly. On the ground and from the air.

So, as Peter and Joe readied for what lay ahead, Allied warplanes continued the unrelenting bombing raids on German targets. Meeting virtually no resistance in the air and barely any ground fire, the massive flights of American and British bombers and fighters— hundreds of planes at a time—virtually blotted out the sun as they roared overhead and punished the Germans with incalculable damage. Hoping to bring a quick end to the war, they attacked both military and civilian targets.

One of the most devastating bombing runs came from February 13 to 15, when wave after wave hit Dresden. The assault included phosphorous incendiary bombs that looked like shooting stars as they fell, and were almost impossible to put out. They set off a firestorm with winds as strong as a hurricane that sucked the air from its victims' lungs and pulled them into the swirling flames. The blaze charred the city to cinders and killed more than thirty-five thousand men, women, and children. Many were found looking like the victims of Pompeii—ashen statues that crumbled to the touch.

Edda West grew up knowing the story.

"My grandmother would always begin the story of Dresden by describing the clusters of red candle flares dropped by the first bombers, which like hundreds of Christmas trees, lit up the night sky—a sure sign it would be a big air raid. Then came the first wave of hundreds of British bombers that hit a little after 10 p.m. the night of February 13–14, 1945, followed by two more intense bombing raids by the British and Americans over the next 14 hours. History records it as the deadliest air attack of all time, delivering a death toll that exceeded the atomic blasts on Hiroshima and Nagasaki. . . .

"My grandmother described the horrific firestorm that raged like a hurricane and consumed the city," she continued. "It seemed as if the very air was on fire."[5]

After the bombs stopped, the city burned for seven days.

Kurt Vonnegut Jr. was a prisoner of war there when the air raid sirens sounded. Barely two months after his capture in the Battle of the Bulge, he ended up in Dresden working on a hog farm. There were no shelters for the prisoners, so he and some others went into an underground slaughterhouse, "Slaughterhouse Five," which became the name of the novel he wrote about his experience.

"It was cool there, with cadavers hanging all around," he told an interviewer from the *Paris Review*. "When we came up the city was gone."[6]

The guards put the prisoners to work in the aftermath, cleaning up bodies.

"Every day we walked into the city and dug into basements and shelters to get the corpses out, as a sanitary measure. When we went into them, a typical shelter, an ordinary basement usually, looked like a streetcar full of people who'd simultaneously had heart failure. Just people sitting there in their chairs, all dead," he said. "We brought the dead out. They were loaded on wagons and taken to parks, large, open areas in the city which weren't filled with rubble. The Germans got funeral pyres going, burning the bodies to keep them from stinking and from spreading disease. One hundred thirty thousand corpses were hidden underground. It was a terribly elaborate Easter-egg hunt."[7]

Later, when they realized there were too many bodies to remove, they sent the prisoners in to recover their valuables. Then soldiers with flamethrowers cremated the remains where they lay.

Death toll estimates have run as high as five hundred thousand men, women, and children. In fourteen hours.

Dresden was not a military target. It was a psychological target. To demoralize the Germans.

But Hitler fought on.

So the Allies again turned to Bernard Montgomery, the British commander behind the Operation Market Garden debacle. That had been the biggest airborne assault of the war up to that time. His new plan was even bigger.

They called it Operation Varsity. It involved nearly twenty-two thousand men—including Peter and the 17th Airborne, along with the British 6th Airborne—and more than seven thousand planes. The goal: to breach the Rhine and gain a foothold in Germany, for the final march toward Berlin.

The men of the 17th Airborne boarded trains on March 20 and moved to a marshaling yard near Orléans. D-Day was set for March 24. The paratroopers spent the night before praying, fidgeting, and studying sandbox maps of the drop zone. A bunch shaved the sides of their heads into Mohawks.

At 5:30 A.M. the next morning, sergeants rousted the men. The ones who weren't too nervous to eat downed breakfast. They had steak and eggs. Chaplains led last-minute services.

Then, at 7 A.M., they boarded the waiting planes.

Curiously, for all his training parachuting, Peter never got the chance to jump into battle. None of the engineers did. They boarded gliders, jumpers and all.

The rest of the 17th boarded transport planes, 836 C-47 Dakotas and 72 of a new breed of deployment aircraft, the C-46 Commando. The C-46 could carry twice as many paratroopers as the C-47.

It was the first time the Commandos were headed into battle. No one knew yet that the new planes had a fatal flaw.

Peter and the men of the 139th Engineers climbed into the gliders connected to the transports by tow ropes. There were 902 in all, typically 2 per plane. They lifted off at 8:19 A.M., a total of 9,387 men, and rendezvoused with their British counterparts—another 8,000 soldiers in 800 planes—an hour later.

The flight took just over three hours, and it was particularly rough. Buffeted by turbulent winds and the prop wash from nearly 1,800 giant transports, they bounced and rocked cruelly. Nervous pilots fought to keep them from slamming into one another, or from tangling in a tow rope that could easily rip off a wing.

It was too noisy to talk. The engineers smoked, vomited, and looked out through the tiny portholes at the people waving up at them from below.

One of the waving men was Slugger. "I didn't know Peter was in one of those planes," he said.

There were so many planes that it took more than a half hour for the flight to pass overhead.

Churchill, smoking one of his customary Romeo y Julieta cigars, stood dangerously close to the Rhine, excitedly watching the planes fly over. He had insisted. With him stood the upper echelon of the British battle command—Field Marshals Montgomery and Alan Brooke, and General Henry Crerar.

The first planes reached the landing area at 9:53 A.M. The Germans were waiting. As the planes came over Wesel, black puffs of exploding flak filled the sky. Shrapnel ripped through the fabric-and-plywood gliders.

"Bullets zipped through one side of the flimsy plywood fuselage and out the other as we approached our landing zone, and as we came in to land part of one wing, an aileron, and the tail section were shot to pieces by shell fire," Private Denis Edwards, flying with the British, remembered. "Listening to the bullets ripping through woodwork around us was none too pleasant, but amazingly none of us was hit by them."[8]

Not all were so lucky. The gliders carrying Peter and the engineers came into a flak field so thick one officer growled, "You can walk down from here."

As the 139th's history described it: "Flak tore through gliders sometimes harmlessly and sometimes not. Many men were hit. One glider, carrying a load of demolitions was struck in mid-air and exploded. All personnel in the glider were lost."[9]

The glider pilots shouted to the men, "Get ready!" and yanked the handle releasing the tow lines.

German automatic weapons and rifle fire raked many of the gliders once they were on the ground. Unlike previous air assaults, Varsity marked the first time gliders came down in landing zones not already secured by paratroopers. Eighteen glider pilots were killed and another eighty were wounded or injured in crashes.

One of the engineer gliders carrying medics and supplies was hit by a mortar shell right after it landed. The blast killed a medic and destroyed all of the medical supplies.

Above them, the paratroopers stepping into the open doorways of the transport planes to jump were low enough to make out the individual German soldiers firing from their foxholes. The bullets thudded against the planes. They shouted "Umbriago!"—Jimmy Durante's comic curse—and plunged into the sky.

The famed *Life* photographer Robert Capa was with them. "We dropped at 10:25, four miles north of the Rhine," he said. "Our plane was a hell of a lot hit before we got out of it."[10]

The fate for the 17th was devastating. The transports lumbered into a lethal barrage of antiaircraft fire that damaged or downed more than half of the planes.

That's also when they discovered the deadly weakness of the new C-46s: They lacked self-sealing fuel tanks. Once a bullet or piece of shrapnel punctured a tank, the high-octane fuel spilled across the wing to the fuselage. German 20mm incendiary rounds provided the spark. The planes spun sickeningly in flames. Nineteen were lost, fourteen ablaze. Thirty-eight returned, severely damaged. The survivors spilled through the open bay doors just a few hundred feet from the ground. Their chutes seemed barely to open before they landed.

"The most amazing thing I ever saw is the way everybody just lays on the ground when they get down," Capa said. "It seemed like two minutes and everybody was just laying there. The first thing is a certain relief. You are down, you are not hurt. You are reluctant to start the next phase."[11]

Then the real fighting started. Capa's pictures show the soldiers scattered across open fields of flat farmland. The paratroopers had to crawl on their bellies. The Germans picked off anyone who dared to kneel or stand up. Deadly mortar fire rained on the rest. The ones who sought cover along the tree line soon found that that was worse: Artillery shells splintered the trees, turning the shards into lethal shrapnel that speared the men cowering around them.

Worse still was what happened to the unfortunate paratroopers who drifted into those trees.

"There were some paratroopers hanging in the trees and they were murdered by the Germans," Capa said. "They were shot twenty times."[12]

For the first two hours, there was little they could do but try to stay alive. Capa didn't even get to take a swig from the canteen of whiskey he carried. Then, the men of the 17th began to regroup. Within hours, they took more than three thousand German prisoners.

Peter and the engineers played a vital role. Their bazooka men took out an ack-ack gun firing on the planes overhead. They seized a house for a command post, taking thirty prisoners. And, as the unit history noted: "One squad, a glider load of 9 men, came down about three miles from the designated position. They landed in a nest of German 88's and took cover. Immediately, one of the men was killed, two were seriously wounded, two more sent on a short patrol never returned, but nevertheless, after about three hours of fierce fighting and maneuvering into position, this squad of engineers killed 20 Germans, captured and wounded about 60, and knocked out five 88 guns. Then, in a captured German command car, they rode up the road, herding their prisoners before them to the CP."[13]

The battle would be regarded as a great success. But in that first day alone, the 17th suffered more than 1,400 dead or wounded, with another 164 missing in action.

One of the dead was from Hero Street. Peter never made it out of the landing zone. The smiling ladies' man with the memorable baritone would smile no more.

CHAPTER THIRTEEN

FIVE DEATHS IN APRIL

Two days after Peter died, Iwo Jima finally fell.

Americans back home had become captivated by the weeks of savage fighting on the tiny spit of volcanic rock, between the nearly invisible Japanese defenders dug into a network of underground tunnels and the valiant Marines dying by the thousands—especially after a photograph of a group of men raising a flag there had splashed on newspaper front pages across the country.

It was a world away, and completely different from the fighting in Europe. The Pacific islands were a place of sweat, snakes, and salt water, pitted against an enemy determined to fight to the death, and to kill as many Americans as possible in the process.

But while the Allies fought inch by brutal inch across the Pacific toward Japan, the gains in Europe quickened. They swarmed over the Rhineland, taking the vital bridge at Remagen and the ancient German city of Cologne, and over Düsseldorf and Worms. By the time Peter died, the Allies had 4.5 million men poised along the Rhine, and the final push to take Germany had begun.

Joe had rejoined the fight by then. His leg wound healed, he wrote his father on March 6 in halting Spanish.

"Well, papa," he penned, "I am in France once again, and in a few days I think I'll be on the move. I hope God will help me and that nothing will happen to me."[1]

A little later, he continued, "How is my mom? Tell her not to worry about me, that I good."

He signed it, "Jose Sandoval."

The censor's note on the front said simply, "Wrote in Mexican. Base Censor."

As he sent it, the 41st Armored Infantry was spearheading the rush to the Elbe River, on the road to Berlin. Slugger raced just behind as the 41st reached the crossing at Remagen. The Ninth Army had beaten them there, and found the Ludendorff Bridge still intact. It was a welcome, and stunning, surprise.

The Rhine was Germany's last natural line of defense. The river, especially swollen with spring runoff, widened to a quarter mile and more along its more than 750-mile length. It's more than seven stories deep at its deepest point. That posed, at the very least, a significant impediment to the passage of tanks and heavy weapons, as well as to the rapid advance of any sizeable number of troops.

Knowing that, the Germans had methodically destroyed every bridge along the river before the Allies got to them. But not the Ludendorff. The newly appointed commandant in the city delayed its destruction to give German soldiers and tanks fleeing ahead of the Allies a chance to get across. The Germans still placed demolition charges to blow the bridge before the U.S. Ninth Army arrived, but they had to make do with weak mining explosive.

When the Americans attacked at 1:40 that afternoon, the Germans were only able to set off two of the charges. One blew a thirty-foot hole in the ramp on the left bank. The second blast lifted the bridge up, but then it dropped back onto its foundation.

The Americans had their bridge, and their gateway to Berlin.

The press called it the "Miracle at Remagen." Eisenhower called it, "worth its weight in gold."

Eight thousand men crossed the first day. Then came the Sherman tanks. And, a short time later, Slugger and his gun crew.

Joe joined them on the other side.

Mostly, they faced ragged ranks of untrained grandfathers and children pressed into service by the desperate Nazis, or battle-hardened and fanatical Waffen SS troops who fought fiercely rather than surrender. The rabid, unthinking fervor of the *Hitlerjugend* (Hitler Youth) and *Volkssturm* (literally, "People's Storm," mostly elderly volunteers and veterans of World War I) left a scar on Slugger's memory: "Old men and kids came at us. We had to kill them. One was just a kid—sixteen, seventeen years old."

Nothing stopped the Allies. Pressing toward Berlin, the U.S. First Army raced northeast with Joe and the 41st Armored Infantry in the lead, and Slugger close behind, until they met the 3d Armored at Lippstadt, encircling the heavily populated Ruhr industrial zone and sealing Germany's fate.

Both sides called the Ruhr the "armory of the German Reich," and both knew its value. Dresden may have been a psychological target, but taking the Ruhr area was a mortal wound.

"Rich and extensive coal and iron ore deposits in this area furnish the life blood for armament, steel, synthetic oil plants and chemical factories which are located conveniently nearby," Lieutenant Colonel John Beckner said in an analysis after the war. "The

Ruhr, within its 6,000 square miles, contained the body and soul of the German material war effort."[2]

As proof of its value, the Ruhr held the "largest concentration of anti-aircraft guns in Germany," Beckner noted, along with an estimated twenty-one Army divisions and an additional hundred thousand antiaircraft troops.

It also held close to 4 million civilians caught up in a net of their führer's making, with no way to escape. Allied planes, unable to target the factories accurately because of the low-lying haze and smoke cover belching from smokestacks, instead bombarded the civilians with leaflets. They urged the military to surrender and the civilians to flee the "Death Zone of the Ruhr." They couldn't. They had no way to run.

Slugger and Joe helped complete the circle around them on April Fool's Day. The fighting continued for three more weeks. The last pocket near Düsseldorf fought through the 21st, until Field Marshal Model put a gun to his head and committed suicide.

"Field marshals don't become prisoners," he said. Then he pulled the trigger.[3]

The assault trapped about 430,000 German soldiers and millions of civilians. Some fought bitterly, even preferring to commit suicide in plain view of the advancing Americans over capture. It took twenty-two days in all, but in the end 325,000 Nazi fighters capitulated—the largest mass surrender of German troops in the war.

By then the Americans were already pushing east, in a headlong dash for the banks of the Elbe. Joe and the 41st led the way again, plunging through the Teutoburg Forest, where German tribesmen had once destroyed the Roman legions sent to crush their revolt, and opening the way through the last mountain obstacle to the central German plain. Then, in one of the heaviest engagements east of the Rhine, they battled their way through intense artillery shelling—

from sixty-seven antiaircraft guns—to seize the Hermann Göring Steel Works in Wolfenbuttel.

Hitler's war machine was disintegrating. His army was in tatters. His air force all but nonexistent. And now the heart of his military-industrial complex, run by the Führer's second in command, had fallen.

On April 11, the 2nd Armored became the first American division to reach the Elbe, barely fifty-six miles from Berlin. They got there just as General Patton's Third Army arrived at Buchenwald. The crematorium furnace was still burning. Black smoke and the stench of incinerating bodies hung over the concentration camp.

Legendary CBS reporter Edward R. Murrow described what they found: "There surged around me an evil-smelling stink, men and boys reached out to touch me. They were in rags and the remnants of uniforms. Death already had marked many of them, but they were smiling with their eyes. I looked out over the mass of men to the green fields beyond, where well-fed Germans were ploughing."[4]

He went into a prisoner barracks that had once housed eighty horses. The Germans had herded twelve hundred men into it, "five to a bunk."

Then he examined the camp doctor's roster. "Behind the names of those who had died, there was a cross. I counted them. They totaled 242—242 out of 1200, in one month.

"As we walked out into the courtyard, a man fell dead. Two others, they must have been over 60, were crawling toward the latrine. I saw it, but will not describe it."[5]

Realizing the end was near, and realizing how the world would react to the horrors of the concentration camps, the Nazis scrambled to destroy the evidence—including the prisoners themselves.

They did it again as Joe readied to head out on patrol across the Elbe on April 13. At around 4 P.M., concentration camp guards rounded up a little more than a thousand of their prisoners and herded them into a barn about an hour north of Joe. The barn smelled of fuel, but it wasn't until the guards locked the doors and set the straw on fire that the prisoners realized what was happening. When they tried to put the flames out, the guards threw hand grenades into the burning piles and sprayed machine pistol and rifle fire at anyone who got near the fires.

Some broke through a door and ran, only to be mowed down by the guards outside. Others clawed at the dirt under the doors trying desperately to tunnel their way out. American soldiers of the 102nd Infantry found them there the next day—heads and a shoulder jutting out into the open, their charred bodies inside.

The barn, and the bodies, were still smoking when the GIs arrived.

A handful did escape, crawling out after darkness fell and hiding in the woodlands nearby. They told the Americans how they could hear the agonized screams of the men burning inside. They told how the German guards had waited for hours as the flames lit the night, then had called out, promising any survivors medical attention. Miraculously, a few had survived, shielded from the flames by the piles of bodies on top of them. When they answered, the Germans shot them.

Then they called for local townspeople—members of the fire brigade and the *Volkssturm*, the volunteer defense force—to dig mass graves to hide any traces of what they had done.

The Americans got there before they could finish.

In all, 1,016 men died.

"I never was so sure before of exactly what I was fighting for," a sergeant on the scene told the Associated Press. "Before this you would have said those stories were propaganda, but now you know they weren't. There are the bodies and all those guys are dead."[6]

Slugger and his artillery crew rolled into another camp at Langenstein, filled with prisoners of war.

As Captain Frederic Pamp Jr. described it: "South of Halberstadt they found it, another one of the Concentration Camps we'd never believed the stories of in the States for all the years we'd heard about them. This was called Langenstein, and it was a small one, only 1500 or so, although ten times that number had died. When first found it, the parade ground was piled high with bodies of the dead. In the huts the dead lay in the same bunks with the living, and they both rotted. And all that green countryside stank from the death that Nazism had put there."[7]

Two of the prisoners, a Russian nurse and a sergeant, spoke some English. When Slugger told them the Russian troops were just across the river and they could reunite the two of them with their comrades, they both said, "No. They'll kill us," Slugger remembered. "They'll shoot us because we surrendered."

By then, both the Americans and the Russians were less than forty-eight hours from Berlin.

On April 12, the Berlin Philharmonic gave its last concert of the war. The bombed-out city in ruins around them, the tuxedoed players began with Wagner's *Götterdämmerung*, "Twilight of the Gods." On the way out, guests would help themselves to cyanide pills.

As the orchestra played, three companies of the 41st loaded into assault boats and headed across the Elbe near Schonebeck. Not a shot was fired. Around 10:30 P.M. Joe and his company crossed. They assembled on the far bank to stand guard through the night as engineers hastily built a pontoon bridge over the river, barely fifty-six miles from the German capital.

Across the ocean, President Roosevelt posed for a painting at the presidential retreat in Warm Springs, Georgia. At 1:15 P.M., he suddenly stiffened, raised his hand to his forehead, and said, "I have a terrific headache." Then he collapsed, unconscious. Just over two hours later, he was pronounced dead.

The doctor traveling with him called it a "massive cerebral hemorrhage." Nothing could be done.

The day before, the only president ever elected to more than two terms had worked on a speech to be delivered on Jefferson Day. "The only limit to our realization of tomorrow, will be our doubts of today," it said. "Let us move forward with strong and active faith."

The word reached the soldiers in Europe the next day, as Joe and the rest of Company I seized the town of Randau. They were down to four officers and sixty men, but they took the town without any trouble, accepting the surrender of 250 prisoners who seemed happy to be captured.

Joe's company was supporting a group of engineers trying to complete a bridge across the river when the Germans counterattacked with a blistering barrage of artillery.

"They just continued to throw heavy concentrations all over the bridge site," Lieutenant Colonel Louis W. Correll, the division engineer, said. "So much was coming in, the Forward Observers just couldn't locate it."[8]

At one point, an analysis of the mission reported, "A man walked out on the bridge to check the damage and immediately 22 rounds of artillery were fired in on him."[9]

The Americans pulled back from the city just as they spotted "six or seven" tanks in the woods north of them. The 41st was ordered to establish a bridgehead farther south. The order came at 7 P.M. They didn't get there until nine hours later, at 4 A.M.

"This march was very uneventful except the men were out on their feet, and if they sat down for a moment they were snoring." The analysis quoted a commander identified only as Lieutenant Fitzhugh. [10]

Then the Germans hit them with "a mighty assault"—at least six tanks, two 20mm flak wagons, and about a battalion of infantry.

They forced the 2d Armored back across the river and sent the 41st Armored Infantry scrambling for cover.

Lieutenant Colonel Carlton E. Stewart ordered them to fall back. It was too late. L Company was cut off and couldn't; I Company—Joe's company—was scattered.

"The majority of our men hid in the cellars which the Jerries did not search," said Captain Stamford. "I destroyed all my maps and prepared to wreck the radio. We remained in the cellar and occasionally we could see the feet of the Jerries as they passed by the windows." [11]

The rest of the 3d Battalion gathered up in the woods, but a battalion of German infantrymen and at least eight Mark V tanks rolled over their position in the dark before dawn, guns blazing. The company dropped back to a line by a levee next to the river. The attackers kept coming. When they got about 150 yards away, I Company "opened up with every available weapon."

Their commander, a young lieutenant, described it later: "I saw two bazookas each fire three rounds of American bazooka ammunition at the Mark V tanks. Of the six fired, I personally saw four hits merely ricochet off. We had no way to stop them, for they had American prisoners of war marching in front of the tanks and they were firing machine guns and tank guns right through them." [12]

Facing certain death or capture, the lieutenant ordered his men to retreat across an antitank ditch.

"By 1130," the analysis noted dryly, "the Armored Infantry, fighting without anti-tank weapons, other than bazookas, disintegrated into isolated groups and were no longer an effective fighting force."[13]

The official tally counted 1 killed, 9 wounded, and 90 missing from the 30th Infantry Division. The 2d Armored Division lost 6 killed, 23 wounded, 147 missing.

That included Joe. The Army record is even more dry.

"Circumstances of disappearance: The subject enlisted man was cut off from possible withdrawal by an enemy attack near Schonebeck, Germany."[14]

The date: April 14. As the men of I Company fought off the Germans at the edge of the Elbe, five hundred thousand people lined the streets of Washington, D.C., for President Roosevelt's funeral. His coffin, draped in the flag taken down from the pole at the Little White House, in Warm Springs, left Georgia in the last car of the presidential train. Thousands, tens of thousands, gathered mutely along the tracks to watch it pass. In Washington, the masses crowded into the two-mile stretch from Union Station to the White House to watch in silence as the coffin rolled past on a caisson of honor drawn by six white horses.

Four days later, the nation was shocked again. Ernie Pyle, the great war correspondent who had been at Anzio with Willie, was cut down by a Japanese sniper's bullet on the island of Ie Shima, west of Okinawa. He died instantly when a bullet hit him in the left temple.

In his pocket he had the draft of a column.

"Here are many of the living who have had burned into their brains forever the unnatural sight of cold dead men scattered over the hillsides and in the ditches along the high rows of hedge through-out the world," he wrote.[15]

"Dead men by mass production—in one country after another—month after month and year after year. Dead men in winter and dead men in summer.

"Dead men in such familiar promiscuity that they become monotonous.

"Dead men in such monstrous infinity that you come almost to hate them.

"These are the things that you at home need not even try to understand."

Before April ended, news of two more deaths would rock the world.

Partisans caught the ousted fascist leader Benito Mussolini as he tried to escape the advancing Allies. They executed him and his mistress on April 28 and hung their bodies in a town square to be defiled by an angry mob. One woman fired five shots into his body, scream-ing: "Five shots! Five shots for my five murdered sons!" Others spit on him. Still others shouted, "He died too quickly! He should have suffered!"[16]

Two days later, his world and his Reich disintegrating around him, Adolf Hitler and his wife of forty hours, Eva Braun, went into a study in the Führer's bunker complex beneath Berlin and commit-ted suicide. They both took cyanide. Hitler made doubly sure. After swallowing his capsule, he shot himself in the head.

His valet and Martin Bormann, Hitler's confidant, found them. The bodies were seated on a small sofa. The room had the telltale smell of burned almonds, a common sign of cyanide. Hitler had a small wound in his right temple and a Walther PPK lying at his feet.

Eight days later, the war in Europe ended. Americans from Times Square to the Golden Gate hugged, cheered, and kissed total strangers in the streets.

But not Angelina Sandoval. The word that Joe was missing had just arrived.

CHAPTER FOURTEEN

BEER AND SAWDUST

When Harry S. Truman took the oath of office at 7:09 P.M. on April 12, he had never heard of the Manhattan Project or the weapon it was building, the atomic bomb. He had never even been in the War Room. Vice president for just eighty-three days, he was considered ill-prepared and ill-suited to be president. And he knew it.

At the swearing-in ceremony, he told reporters, "Boys, if you ever pray, pray for me now."

Prepared or not, Truman and all America now turned their attention to the war in the Pacific. Germany had fallen. The Americans and the British had begun carving up Berlin with the Russians, splitting the country, and Europe, in two.

But, half a world away, the Japanese fought on. Obstinately. Pitilessly. To the death.

They had proven it on Saipan, where soldiers refused to surrender and women threw their children off cliffs, then jumped after them onto the jagged rocks below, rather than be captured by the invading Marines.

They had proven it on Iwo Jima, where they scurried through a vast warren of carefully constructed tunnels and caves that allowed them to remain almost invisible as they poured a vicious rain of machine gun and rifle fire on the American Marines. Then, when the Marines turned their fire on one spot, the Japanese scampered away unseen, only to pop up and surprise the Americans from another spot behind, above, or beside the one where they had been.

Artillery seemed useless against them. The Japanese defenders merely hid deep in the interconnected tunnels and waited as barrage after barrage of bombardment from the battleships off shore pounded the rocks above. When the American ground troops returned, the Japanese were there, waiting in ambush yet again.

Japanese artillery was much more effective. Terrifyingly so.

The Americans came ashore on Iwo Jima at 9 A.M. on February 19, expecting the worst. They encountered nothing. The biggest obstacle was the soft powder of volcanic ash on the beaches that made each step feel like they were trapped in an hourglass. Especially with sixty pounds of gear on their backs.

"The island," as Don L. Miller and Henry Commager described it, "looked abandoned."[1]

Two hours later, they found out different.

By then, men and equipment crowded the beach. That's when they met the massive mortars, the "flying ashcans" as the Marines nicknamed them, that the Japanese threw at them.

The frighteningly powerful blasts "blew parts of men and machines as high as a hundred feet in the air."[2]

They tore off legs, ripped men open, left them screaming in horror and pain, with their guts spilling out beside them.

There was no place to run, no place to dig in. Try as the Marines might, the fine volcanic sands only sifted back in to refill the shovelfuls they had just scooped out.

The Japanese deliberately targeted medics and doctors.

"Our medical team had landed with two doctors and forty corpsmen," squad leader Albert J. Ouellette said. "Before the day was out, one doctor was killed when he lost both legs, and only two corpsmen were left. All the rest were dead or wounded."[3]

The fighting lasted thirty-four days. It ended March 25.

Of 70,000 Marines who landed, 6,821 died. Another 19,000 were wounded. The Japanese, however, had been given orders to fight to the death. They did. Of an estimated 22,000 Imperial Army soldiers on Iwo Jima when the Marines attacked, only 216 surrendered.

The Americans knew: This was a battle of the bloodiest—island by island, all the way to Japan.

From Europe, the victorious troops watched developments in the Pacific warily. They suspected, correctly, that the war planners were considering shifting the battle-ready fighters from the fields of Europe to the jungle islands leading to Tokyo.

Slugger had made it through the Bulge, and through the fall of Berlin. His artillery was quiet. But he was still a long way from Hero Street.

So was Frank Soliz. The oldest of Claro's nephews sat aboard a ship off a place called Okinawa, the last major island between the Allies and Japan, watching as an increasingly weak Japanese empire threw the last remnants of its battle forces against the Americans, like the final vicious lashing out of a mortally wounded beast.

Attacks on civilian targets meant to weaken the will of the Japanese seemed to have no effect. They withstood the firebombing of Tokyo, which killed more than eighty-eight thousand people in a single night. They withstood the slow starvation decimating Japan's populace. They withstood the increasingly frequent air raids on their homeland, the swarms of B-29s thick as locusts, virtually unopposed.

Instead of yielding, the Japanese responded with a new, desperate weapon: kamikaze.

The Americans had massed sixteen hundred ships and half a million men in preparation for the attack on Okinawa. Including Frank Soliz.

The island was a vital outpost en route to Japan, destined to be the staging point for the final assault on Japan itself. Taking it would prove to be the bloodiest battle of the Pacific.

It was held by some 110,000 Japanese fighters and 24,000 Okinawan conscripts, dug into an underground labyrinth of tunnels, caves, and—gruesome as it seems—crypts. Almost 107,000 of them would die, along with an estimated 100,000 civilians. Nearly 50,000 Americans would fall fighting, including more than 12,000 dead.

On April 1, the Americans attacked. It was Easter Sunday, and April Fool's Day. They unleashed the heaviest concentration of naval gunfire in the history of the war—more than 3,800 tons of artillery, what the Okinawans came to call the *tetsu no bow*—the "storm of steel"—as sixty thousand Marines and soldiers landed.

The Japanese were nowhere to be seen.

For five days, the invaders met no resistance. Then, on April 6, the Japanese sprang the trap. On land, sea, and air.

As the Marines moved between limestone cliffs near the island's southern third, the Japanese opened up. Firing from nearly invisible fortified positions carved in the rock wall, they caught the Americans in a lethal cross fire.

At almost the same moment, the Japanese unleashed an unprecedented kamikaze air assault—355 planes came out of the sky at once, hurtling down to crash into the American ships in exploding fireballs. The wooden decks of the aircraft carriers were particularly prized targets, especially ones with airplanes lined up for takeoff, fully loaded with volatile high-octane fuel.

They called the attack *Kikusui*—"floating chrysanthemum." And they came, day after day, in wave after wave. By the end of the Battle of Okinawa, 1,465 kamikazes had sunk 30 American ships and damaged 164 more.

"They would come at you in such numbers and so low that you could see the expressions on the faces of the pilots from the deck of the ship," signalman Mort Zimmerman said. "It was awful to see the guys who got burnt in the fires these planes set off. They looked like mummies with the wraps off. They looked like charcoal logs."[4]

On that first morning, as the Japanese planes scored devastating hits on the American fleet, the *Yamato,* the largest battleship ever built, steamed toward Okinawa along with eight destroyers and a light cruiser. It was a suicide mission. They only had enough fuel for a one-way trip. Their aim: to beach themselves on the island, turn their cannons on the invaders, and fight until their last man was dead.

They never made it. The Americans saw them coming and, at 10 A.M. on April 7, struck. U.S. planes and submarines pounded the ships for two solid hours. Twelve bombs and seven torpedoes hit the *Yamato*. Of its crew of 2,747, only 23 officers and 246 enlisted men survived.

Within three hours, all the Japanese ships were scuttled or dead in the water. It was Japan's last naval action of the war.

But the land and air battle continued—for weeks and then months—with the Americans fighting for inch by painstaking inch. As the monsoons of summer swept in, they turned the battlefield into a muddy morass. Rotting dead bodies littered the combat zone, so thick with fat maggots that the ground seemed to move.

"There were body parts lying all over the place," said Marine Eugene B. Sledge, a twenty-year-old from Mobile, Alabama. "We called it 'Maggot Ridge.' If we went down the ridge and slipped and fell, we slid all the way to the bottom. When we came to our feet, the maggots were falling out of our dungaree pockets, our cartridge belts and everything else."[5]

As the Battle of Okinawa raged, the Americans began planning what it would take to defeat Japan. Operation Downfall, the final invasion of the home islands, would involve the entire Pacific Fleet, over five thousand airplanes and 1.7 million men—almost double the size of the invasion force at Normandy on D-Day. The cold calculations anticipated that as many as a million of them would die.

In preparation, the Americans made 500,000 Purple Hearts. For starters.

The attack was set for November 1. They expected to face as many as 800,000 Japanese military in total, and "a fanatically hostile population." They were wrong by almost a million on the military. But not on the civilians. The Japanese equipped them with whatever could be used as a weapon and trained them for fighting. One high school girl later remembered being given an awl and told to go for the abdomen.

Faced with such staggering possibilities, Truman struggled over his decision.

On July 16, another option presented itself. The first nuclear explosion in the world lit the early morning sky at Alamagordo Air Force Base in New Mexico. The "awesome roar" of the blast could be heard for 100 miles; the "searing light" was seen 180 miles away. As the lead scientist, J. Robert Oppenheimer, watched, he thought of the Bhagavad-Gita: "Now I am become death, destroyer of worlds."[6]

Oppenheimer's team of scientists included a multinational mélange of the world's leading physicists, "experts" in what until now had been a theoretical conjecture about the means of splitting the atom and what would happen when they did. Enrico Fermi. Niels Bohr. Luis Alvarez.

Prevented from participating because of his perceived pacifist leanings was the man whose ideas and gentle insistence gave birth to the project in the first place—Albert Einstein.

The team had labored there for two years, in a secrecy so complete that babies born during the project's development had birth certificates listing their birthplace only as P.O. Box 1663, Santa Fe.

Just before 2 A.M. on August 6, the engines of a B-29 named the "Enola Gay" sputtered to life. Then it lifted off toward a Japanese city few in the United States had ever heard of before, but one they would never forget: Hiroshima. At 8:16 A.M., the plane released its payload, an atomic bomb nicknamed "Little Boy." It's impossible to know how many died. Some simply incinerated. One left a shadow burned permanently into the courthouse steps. The body vanished.

Three days later, they dropped a second one on Nagasaki.

Japan surrendered.

It was still August 14 in the United States, August 15 in the Pacific, when it was announced. People in the United States went wild. Some 2 million revelers poured into the streets around Times Square. In Europe, as American soldiers got the word and realized that the war was really over and they had survived, they broke down and cried.

The front page headline on the *New York Times* screamed: "Japan Surrenders, End of War."

The celebration gave birth to what may be the most famous photograph from the war: Alfred Eisenstaedt's *The Kiss*. It showed a sailor dipping a nurse to kiss her amid the crowd in Times Square, with confetti and paper strewn all around them.

Similar celebrations, and kisses, broke out across the country, and around the world.

In the Pacific, the first American reaction seemed to be stunned silence. Men walked around like zombies, or sat dazed. Then came wild cheering, and guns fired in celebration into the air.

Aboard Frank Soliz's ship, they pulled out boxes of beers packed in sawdust and passed the bottles out. The beer was warm, but it didn't matter. The war was finally over.

"Man, it tasted good," Frank said.

CHAPTER FIFTEEN

A Hearse in the Mud

They waited more than three years for the dead to come home to Hero Street.

The survivors started arriving right away. A rush of discharged men flooded back to the States to pick up lives where they had left off or to begin new ones.

They came home ready to work and ready to start families. The demand for houses gave rise to Levittown—and knockoffs just like it thrown up around the country. Detroit turned from putting out tanks and bombers to making cars again—large, comfortable, and powerful machines with luxuries like automatic transmissions and power steering—to carry these new workers and their families to and from these far-flung "suburbs."

Nine months later another phenomenon that would reshape the country began: the baby boom.

Some of the men, though, returned damaged in terrible ways,

even when the wounds were not always obvious. Louis Ramirez moved back into the house at the end of Second Street, shaken and plagued by memories of Guadalcanal. In World War II they called it "battle fatigue" or "shell shock," but that came nowhere near describing the terrible waking nightmares that left its victims trembling uncontrollably and screaming at ghosts.

Some found they couldn't handle city noises anymore. A car backfiring sounded too much like a gunshot.

"The clank of a starting tank, the scream of the shell through the air, the ever-rising whine of fiendishness as a bomber dives—these sounds have their counterparts in normal life, and you would be hard put to distinguish them in a blindfold test. But once heard in war, they remain with you forever," Pyle explained, or tried to.[1]

"Their nervous memories come back to you in a thousand ways—in the grind of a truck starting in low gear, in high wind around the eaves, in somebody merely whistling a tune. Even the sound of a shoe, dropped to the floor in a hotel room above you, becomes indistinguishable from the faint boom of a big gun far away. A mere rustling curtain can paralyze a man with memories."[2]

After he'd been in the Battle of the Bulge, sunset in the Maine forests made Richard Proulx shake.

"There was something ominous about the evening in the country. It echoed of faint screams and the crash of shell fire. I just had to get inside and with someone or I would tremble."[3]

Even the ones who weren't broken that way came home changed. Boys had become men. The things they had seen in the war made them see things at home differently.

Some had new ideas. Blacks who had fought the same enemy, and won, returned with a sense that they should be treated differently now—equally. Such radical thinking laid the groundwork for the Civil Rights Movement. The GI Bill fueled a record level of college enrollments, as men who otherwise might never have considered the possibility took advantage of the government's tuition assistance.

Soon blacks would be asking to attend traditionally white universities, even in places like Alabama.

But not on Hero Street. The Mexican-Americans found jobs at International Harvester and John Deere. They married. Settled down. Raised families.

Slugger was like that. He got home in December of 1945, just in time for Christmas. He didn't want to have anything more to do with the military, and he didn't want to think about the war. He wanted to forget about the dying and get on with living. And he did.

He met Lupe Savala at a "Mexican dance" in Davenport, just one week after he got home. The Griff Williams Orchestra was in town, at Danceland. Her brother Sam introduced her. "I almost flipped over," Slugger said. "Because Mexican guys didn't do that. My sister? My dad always told me, 'Your sister, she goes out with a guy, you watch her. She fools around with a guy, you bring her home and you tell me.'"

Lupe was pretty, and she dressed nice. She acted much more like the *güeras* she grew up with in her neighborhood than any of the Mexicans Slugger knew. He fell for her fast, and hard. Soon enough, they were married and buying furniture for their brand-new house, custom-built to match the plan Lupe sketched out. He adored her, and stayed with her, close to the street where he had grown up, for more than fifty years.

A few of the younger men, though, drafted late in the war or just after, served with the U.S. occupation forces in the tense but relative calm of postwar Germany or Japan. Two of Joe and Frank Sandoval's brothers went to Europe. A second of Claro Soliz's nephews joined the Navy. And a kid named Joe Gomez headed off for a tour in Germany.

"Cheppe," as everyone who knew Joe called him, was an amateur boxer with an odd, hunched over style. He had quick fists and a quick temper, and never hesitated to wade into a fight to defend a friend. His willingness to put up his fists got him stabbed one night, after a dance at the Eagle Club, where Hero Street girls under the watchful eyes of chaperones traded glances with young men until one worked up the courage to ask for a dance. Cheppe wore his blood-soaked shirt as a badge of honor and refused to go to the hospital.

"He was macho," the girl who would one day be his wife, Terry Garza, recalled, years later. "I remember at the dances whenever anybody wanted to fight he'd be right in the middle. The men would always fight at the dances. The Davenporters against the East Molines."[4]

"He was kind of a quiet tough guy," his buddy and, later, brother-in-law Phil Garza said. He didn't go out looking for trouble, but he wouldn't back away from trouble. And he was very well qualified to take care of himself."

One day, one of the older Second Streeters, Ray Alonzo, came home on furlough from Fort Sheridan. He ran into Cheppe as he stepped off the bus at Second Street. Cheppe looked Ray's uniform up and down and asked what it was like to be in the Army. "Heck," Ray told him, "it's like going on vacation."

That was the way much of the country felt then. After years of ration books and war bond drives, the postwar years arrived full of peace and prosperity. Supplying the hordes of young husbands and wives with everything from houses and cars to suits and cigarettes brought an avalanche of jobs. Jobs brought money. Money brought demand for more—of everything: bigger houses, better cars.

Electricity arrived on Second Street, along with indoor plumbing. No more running to the outhouse in the snow or waiting for morning to empty the pot.

Times were good, filled with hope and happiness.

Then, across America, the bodies started coming home. On Second Street, Peter's mother retreated into herself and, some said, the bottle. Angelina still cried, every day.

Frank came first. The Army removed his body from the grave in India where he was buried, and shipped it to the Schroeder Mortuary up the street from the house where he grew up. It rained the day it arrived, and his sister Georgia watched the men track mud into the family home as they carried it inside. Second Street remained unpaved, just a dirt street that turned to mud, as Claro had said.

For the military, delivering the body—one of more than 170,000 shipped home after the war's end—was a matter of crisp efficiency, and costs.

A telegram sent a month earlier said:

RECORDS OF THIS OFFICE INDICATE YOU WISH REMAINS DELIVERED TO SCHROEDER MORTUARY 701 FIRST AVE. SILVIS. PLEASE CONFIRM. . . . THIS IS YOUR FINAL OPPORTUNITY TO CHANGE DELIVERY INSTRUCTIONS AT GOVERNMENT EXPENSE.

Frank's family held a traditional Mexican wake. The men drank; the women cried. They set the casket in the home's front room and watched it for three days. On September 14, 1948, they carried it back out to the hearse and drove it to the new National Cemetery at the Rock Island Arsenal.

They buried Frank in grave No. 21, in the shade of a rough-barked pine. They saved No. 22 for his brother Joe.

. . .

After they buried Frank, the funerals came too fast to dry the tears.

They buried Joe, then Claro. They held memorial services for the rest, with markers over their empty graves. The bodies were never found.

Every year after, on Memorial Day, Angelina put fresh flowers on her sons' graves. For the most part, though, the war faded into the past, and life went on.

It was a story playing out across America. The men who had come home from the fighting settled into their jobs and new lives; the younger crowd looked to the future. On Hero Street, Cheppe's buddies Phil Garza and Johnny Muños hung out together. They went to the Mexican dances at the Eagle Club, and they dated the girls they met there.

That's where Johnny met Mary Beserra. It was, literally, love at first sight. His friend John Puebla said he could tell when they went to the dances and Johnny would see Mary sitting by the wall with her mother. He could see it in his eyes: "I knew I lost a good buddy there."[5]

They met at a park, on a Fourth of July. She was picnicking with her family. Everyone had come to Lake Storey for a baseball game.

"He came up and started talking to me," she said. "And from then on, we saw each other."[6]

If he had a wild side, she never saw it.

After Johnny met Mary, Phil said, he settled down. He stopped drinking. She sang with a Mexican band in Galesburg, and Johnny went to every one of her shows, wearing a suit and tie. He waited patiently until the band took a break, then danced with her between sets. By day he worked with Phil in the machine shop at International Harvester. To get there, Phil hopped on the morning train as it passed near his house in Davenport, and caught a ride over the Mississippi to the plant or continued on into the rail yard in Silvis.

"I could get up in the morning," Phil said, "and jump on the Silvis shop train and hitch a ride for a nickel from Davenport to East Moline. They would drop me off at International Harvester. Then they'd go on to the Silvis shops. Then at four o'clock they'd come back, about five or ten after. I'd jump back on for a nickel and come back on home to Davenport.

"It was pretty good transportation for a nickel. Of course, I was only making a buck-thirteen an hour."[7]

Life was good: They had money in their pockets and high hopes. All across America, homes were going up. Industry was growing. Babies were being born.

The prosperity sweeping the nation touched Hero Street, too, in its own way. Second Street remained an unpaved dirt strip stretching up the rise at the foot of Billy Goat Hill, but the hill itself began to change. The demand for housing brought on by the soldiers returning from World War II brought a demand for foundation dirt, and Billy Goat Hill contributed to the growth of nearby Moline one dump truck load at a time.

Still, a divide remained between America's lighter and darker skinned citizens, and now the feelings of discontent became palpable. Simmering tensions over discrimination bubbled to the surface like water in a pot coming to a boil.

The signs had begun as early as 1943, while the war was still going on, with lunch counter sit-ins by blacks demanding service at Jack Spratt's coffee shop in nearby Chicago.

That same year, L.A.'s "Zoot Suit Riots" pitted pachucos against busloads of sailors and soldiers who came into the Mexican neighborhood to beat the distinctively dressed Hispanics. Police sided with the military. The United States Attorney's office in Los Angeles announced it was checking federal laws to see whether action could be taken against anyone assaulting men in uniform, the *L.A. Examiner* reported, even though multiple reports agreed it was the men in uniform who were the aggressors.

A "Special to the *New York Times*" report written on the second day of the clashes commented: "LOS ANGELES, June 6—Subdued and no longer ready to do battle, twenty-eight zoot-suiters, stripped of their garish clothing and with county jail barbers hopefully eying their flowing ducktail haircuts, languished behind bars today after a second night of battle with officers and servicemen.

"The arrests came after a 'war' declared by servicemen, mostly sailors, on zoot-suit gangs which have been preying on the East Side as well as molesting civilians."[8]

Part of the problem, apparently, was the zoot suits themselves. The pants were pegged, high-wasted; the legs, wide at the top and tight at the bottom. The coats were extra-long, like Rhett Butler's in *Gone with the Wind*, but tight in the waist and wide at the shoulders, with wide lapels. They were luxuries and, considering the wartime limits on wool, possibly illegal.

Another part of the problem was the youths who wore them. They were Mexicans. Or Mexican-Americans, but the hyphenation was a fine point easy to ignore in 1943.

When the riots ended, the tensions remained. So did the segregation.

By 1946, full-blown race riots had erupted in Athens, Alabama, and Philadelphia. Before the end of the decade, an astoundingly capable black baseball player named Jackie Robinson had broken the color lines and joined the Brooklyn Dodgers; the first "Freedom

Riders" had tested the limits of interracial mixing; and a presidential panel that would give a name to a movement—the Committee on Civil Rights—had issued a report condemning racial injustice in America.

Still, the differences would not be swept away with the stroke of a pen or well-intentioned gestures. Second Street remained a narrow, rutted stretch that turned into a muddy mire whenever it rained.

In their own way, though, the Mexicans on the street enjoyed the fresh wind of hopefulness blowing across the country.

Cheppe came home from occupation duty in Germany and signed up with the Army Reserves. He got a job at John Deere and kept boxing on the side. He was a natural, even with his odd, stoop-shouldered style. He made it all the way to the regional Golden Gloves, but he didn't like training. He liked chasing girls better. That is, until he met Phil Garza's sister Terry. Soon enough, the muscular boxer and the pretty convent school grad had fallen for each other.

"He would take me out to teach me to drive," Terry said. "And one thing just led to another."

They didn't wait for a big wedding. They couldn't. Terry discovered she was pregnant. One April night they slipped off to Chicago with another young couple and got a preacher to marry them for $10. They came back to Silvis as husband and wife, the Second Street boy and the Davenport girl.

They moved into Cheppe's house on Second Street and dreamt of having a house of their own. Two weeks before Christmas, 1949, their daughter Linda was born.

Six months later, in June of 1950, North Korea invaded South Korea, and the United States found itself swept into a war it didn't want. Soon enough, men across the country would be summoned to leave their civilian lives and take up their weapons again, and Cheppe would be a part of it.

No one thought it would last three years.

The country went into Korea naively thinking it could flex its military muscle and quickly convince the North Koreans to back down. Instead, it found itself mired in a viciously bloody conflict in brutal conditions it was grossly unprepared for.

Three years later, more than 36,000 Americans would be dead, another 100,000 wounded or missing.

Within weeks of the start, the South Korean and U.S. forces had been driven back nearly the length of the Korean peninsula. They clung to a tiny sliver of land in the southeast corner of the country. The emboldened North Koreans pressed the attack relentlessly, determined to push the Occidentals into the sea.

At Truman's urging, the United Nations Security Council issued a resolution condemning the attack and demanding North Korea's withdrawal.

A day later, the president issued a statement that made clear the government's intentions.

"Those responsible for this act of aggression must realize how seriously the Government of the United States views such threats to the peace of the world," it said. "Willful disregard of the obligation to keep the peace cannot be tolerated."[9]

Truman would later call the military response a "police action," but the country—and the world—knew that was just semantics. America was at war again.

It was far from ready.

The war-weary United States had sent its troops home after World War II and now found itself desperately short of men and equipment. Facing imminent defeat, America rushed to shore up its forces. It quickly summoned its reservists and stepped up the draft. Men who had grown accustomed to workdays in hard hats or suits dug out their dusty helmets and uniforms and said good-bye to their families.

The draft letters started arriving on Hero Street within weeks. Johnny Puebla got one and decided to join the Marines. Tony Soliz, yet another of Claro's nephews, joined his brother in the Navy. Cheppe knew it was only a matter of time. With baby Linda still in diapers, he waited to be called.

While he did, the United States struck back in Korea. General Douglas MacArthur hit the North Koreans far behind their lines, at Inchon, in September. He attacked with seventy thousand men, Johnny Puebla with them. The success of the invasion sent the North Koreans into full retreat; the Americans chased them back to the line they had first crossed in June, and pressed the attack deep into North Korea.

In November, the war escalated. With the North Korean Army close to collapse, the Chinese got nervous that the American thrust wouldn't stop at the Yalu River dividing China from North Korea. Combining stealth and sheer mass, the Red Chinese Army swarmed in. It quickly overwhelmed the U.S. and South Korean forces.

Now it was the Americans' turn to retreat hastily—and so began the bloody back-and-forth that would drag on into 1953 and require the United States to race a continuing supply of ill-trained replacements into battle.

Cheppe was among them. On a cold October morning, as their daughter Linda slept at home, Terry waved good-bye at the bus station in Moline. Cheppe headed off to training in California.

They didn't get much preparation in boot camp. The country needed men on the front lines with guns, even if they couldn't use them very well.

"They needed bodies," Phil Garza said. "In the worst way."

They were so ill-prepared, in fact, Captain Patrick Donahue insisted, "Korea was America's only 'come as you are' war."[10]

In his classic look at the on-the-ground reality of the Korean War, T. R. Fahrenbach gave an example of what happened when a green unit came under attack and their commander ordered them to withdraw: "The withdrawal immediately became ragged and chaotic. The men got out of their holes, leaving their crew-served weapons. . . . They left their dead where they lay, and abandoned the 30 or so wounded who were too hurt to walk."

Instead of a withdrawal, he continued, it became a rout.

"Covered with slime and running, these men tossed aside their steel helmets. Some had dropped their shoes and many had lost their shirts. None of them had weapons, other than a few rifles."[11]

"However," Donahue noted, "this poor performance was the high point for the regiment." The 3rd Battalion retreated twenty miles "without even making contact with the enemy."

When Cheppe got his summons, basic training took a mere eight weeks. Men got to the front lines not knowing how to assemble their weapons or how to keep them clean so they wouldn't jam.

The timing was good for Cheppe, though. He got to come home again after basic, in December.

With Christmas just around the corner, the family planned a visit to see Cheppe's brother Bob, who had landed in prison for stealing a car. Cheppe, Terry, baby Linda, and Cheppe's mom, Amanda, all piled into Cheppe's brother Buddy's 1941 Plymouth convertible and drove north to Pontiac. Buddy drove. On the way back that night, it was snowing. They met an oncoming car on a narrow road. Buddy tried to move over, but there wasn't room. They crashed. The

Plymouth slipped off the icy road and rolled into a ditch. The door came open. Amanda flew out of the car.

Miraculously, the baby was okay.

"My mother-in-law had been holding her, but I said, 'No, she's tired,'" Terry said.[12]

She fixed a blanket in the rear deck by the back window and laid her daughter there to sleep as they glided home through the night. Somehow, as the car hit and slid off the road, Linda stayed bundled snugly and safe.

Not Amanda. The ambulance was too late. She died before she reached the hospital.

In pictures at the funeral, a grim-faced Cheppe stands next to the casket, surrounded by his younger brothers and sisters, wearing his uniform. He still has a white bandage on his forehead.

Much later, Buddy said it might have been for the best.

"My mother was very emotional," he said. "We always talked about what it would have done to her if she had been alive when Cheppe was killed."[13]

No one could know it then, but that wasn't too far off.

After the funeral, Cheppe went back to his unit, the 38th Infantry Regiment, Company K. They were moving out. Just weeks after they said good-bye, Terry got to see Cheppe one more time before he boarded a ship for Korea.

As his train came back through on its way east, Cheppe had a stopover in Chicago. He invited Terry up.

It's funny the things people remember, later.

Terry took Linda, on the train. The three of them stayed at a friend's house, and they went to an Italian restaurant. Cheppe's friend ordered a dish Terry had never heard of, and Terry wasn't quite sure what to think. It was something they didn't have in Silvis yet, a gooey mess with tomato sauce and melted cheese spread out on a round, thin crust.

"I had never heard of pizza. This was 1951, remember. They brought it out and it was all this—it looked like somebody had thrown up on it. I went, 'Ugh, ew!' I didn't know what that was. I didn't want to eat it."[14]

Finally, Cheppe took a bite.

"It's good," he told her. "You'll like it."

She did.

It was the first time she ever ate pizza, and the last time she ever saw Cheppe.

CHAPTER SIXTEEN

May Massacre, Bloody Ridge

Korea was cold. Bitter cold.

The freezing winter winds whipped over the hillsides, and the soldiers huddled cursing against the frigid chill. Temperatures dropped to thirty below at night and barely rose above zero through the day.

Nearly a quarter million Americans were on the ground in Korea, all grossly unequipped for the Korean winter. No one had expected the fighting to last that long.

The Army had sent them with lightly insulated jackets and thin leather boots. The Marines got "shoe-pacs" with removable felt liners, which were only slightly better. But it was enough of a difference to make the shoes coveted. At night, soldiers slipped into the Marine camp to try to steal them. The ones who succeeded smiled a little more and cursed a little less the next day.

Even with those, recalled Marine second lieutenant James W.

Stemple, whenever they stopped moving they "could actually feel the inserts freezing in the boots."[1]

Frostbite ate away at their fingers and toes, and their chests rattled with pneumonia. The difference between being kept at the front to fight or being sent to a hospital to recover depended on how high a fever they ran.

"God couldn't have made a worse place to fight than Korea," Preston Solomon, a member of Cheppe's platoon, said. "You'd get so cold you'd say, 'I wish God would just let me die.' Of course, then they'd start shooting and you'd change your mind."[2]

Staying warm, though, came at a price.

"When I first got over they had some of what they called mountain sleeping bags," Solomon said. "It was fur-lined inside. You'd get in that thing and zip yourself up and just leave your nose sticking out. You'd be just as warm as you could be.

"But a bunch of them got killed in sleeping bags before they could get out and fight," he said, "and they took all that away from us. They give us one blanket and one shelter half and one poncho."

It was a brutal war, for both sides.

Richard Bohart, then a twenty-two-year-old Marine from Chicago, described a sad encounter when his platoon was on the move and they came across three Chinese soldiers stumbling through the brush. The first held a branch that the second clung to, and the second held one for the third.

"It appeared that they had been bombed by napalm. Their eyes were sightless. Their whole bodies were covered with blackened skin with red, open sores. They had maggots eating the raw flesh. I can't imagine how they were still alive," Bohart said. "They were taken a few yards away, out of sight, and disposed of. This, of course, was the only humane thing to do."[3]

Cheppe was sent quickly to the front, as a rifle-toting infantry grunt, to join the American troops holding the icy ground against the North Koreans.

On January 27, he sent a telegram. "ALL WELL AND SAFE," it shouted in all capital letters. "WISH I COULD BE WITH YOU. BEST LOVE FROM DADDY."

He was in Japan when he sent it, still en route. He arrived in Korea four days later and "well and safe" were quickly forgotten.

"I'd like to get out of here because they're killing a lot of guys over here," he wrote to a friend from Silvis. "I hope I make it out."[4]

For all the front-line Americans, the fighting was close, and fierce. In a letter in May, Cheppe referred to one bloody encounter with the Chinese that nearly wiped out his company. "We ran a road block at Hongsang and out of our company of 205, 80 of us came out safe," he wrote. "Boy, if I go through another one like that, I hope I make it."[5]

That came nowhere near describing the real brutality they were facing. There was no mention of the harrowing, desperate scramble to escape that Cheppe and the men of Company K had gone through.

The Chinese lay hidden in the sparse brush as night covered the Korean mountainsides and the temperature plummeted. They used the dark to slink silently across the snow to encircle the GIs. When the sun rose again, they seemed to spring out of nowhere, screaming and with bugles blaring, firing away at Cheppe and Preston Solomon and the rest of the raw recruits of the 38th.

"They could have overrun us I think, but they didn't," Solomon said. "I think the reason they didn't overrun us is because they knew they'd pay a lot for it. We'd kill a lot of them."[6]

The firefight lasted all day. The GIs lay in the open, pressed against the side of a hill, shooting at anything that moved, and watching their buddies die.

"Just as night was approaching they passed the word up the line to come on down to the road and try to fight our way out," Solomon said. "I was glad to get a chance to try to run."

It was a trap.

The Chinese assault cleverly funneled the Americans toward a narrow icy road. The U.S. soldiers piled onto trucks like a ghastly layer cake: first the dead, then the wounded, then those still able to fight. But before they could pull away, the Chinese opened up with deadly accurate mortar fire.

"They waited until we tried to get out," Solomon continued. "They already had the road zeroed in and they just shot us down like . . ."

It took him a moment to continue. When he did, he said, "I got out of there. I don't really know how I got out of there."

Cheppe was right, Solomon said. Out of almost two hundred men, only thirty-eight survived.

When they went back, Solomon said, they found the dead frozen where they had died. They were naked. The Chinese had stolen their clothes, their boots. And more.

"If one of them had a ring, they cut his finger off so they could take the ring," Solomon said. "If one of them had a little gold in his teeth, a filling or something, then they had their teeth knocked out. To get that little bit of metal."[7]

Cheppe was one of the survivors, miraculously unharmed. But just over a month later, while he was out on patrol, he wasn't so lucky. They ran into a regiment of Chinese. A grenade exploded. The shrapnel hit Cheppe. "We lost a few," he wrote to Tony Soliz, with his boxer's bravado showing. "I got a rest at the hospital."[8]

The letter ended hopefully: "From what they tell me I will get to go home sometime in July. That's when I complete 6 months over here."

The letter was dated May 1. It arrived after Cheppe was already dead.

Cheppe got out of the hospital and returned to the front April 8, just in time for what is known as the Chinese Spring Offensive. It remains one of the biggest battles of the war, in which the Red Army threw a "human wave" of close to 700,000 men against the Americans.

When Cheppe arrived, the temperatures were warming. During the steamy days, it was almost like being back at the onion fields on the Mississippi. The men pulled off their sweaty shirts and pants and dove into the rivers swelling with the snowmelt off the mountains.

The U.N. forces skirmished with the Chinese sporadically. Then, as May began, the front went quiet, and the Americans braced for a new assault.

It came on May 17, at 10 P.M. Cheppe and Company K sat on the bald top of a sixteen-hundred-foot rise they nicknamed Bunker Hill, at the peak and very center of the American defensive front. Even from that vantage point, they had only hints that the Chinese were massing for attack, slithering almost imperceptibly into the low shrubs and weeds behind a hill facing the American line.

The Americans were well prepared. Anticipating the attack, they had dug reinforced earthen bunkers lined with logs and sandbags, strung barbed wire, and set fifty-five-gallon drums filled with napalm along the line, ready to explode into a hundred-foot-long wall of flame when detonated.

The battalion commander wanted them ready for a worst-case possibility: "If it is necessary," he said, "I don't want you to worry about calling in the fire. I'll do that. All you have to do is fix up your bunkers so that you will have a clear field of fire to your front and to your neighbors' bunkers and won't get hit by your own shell fragments when I call down the fire."⁹

Seven hundred civilians helped. They brought 237,000 sandbags, 385 rolls of barbed wire, and 39 of the fifty-five-gallon fougasse drums up the hill. Thirty-two oxen brought up 4.2-inch mortars and shells.

It made no difference. The Americans could see nothing as the Chinese swarmed toward them invisibly in the dark. Then, the GI's communications went dead. Someone on the American side had forgotten to bury the telephone line. The Chinese quickly cut the exposed cable. Minutes later, an artillery blast destroyed the Americans' radio.

With no means of communicating, and Chinese seemingly everywhere, the American line crumbled into chaos. Men scrambled frantically down the hill, fleeing the rapidly advancing Chinese.

Refusing to be beaten, the 2nd Platoon's lieutenant gathered up the tattered remnants of his broken troops, about thirty-five men, including Cheppe, and attacked.

"To hell with it!" he said. "We can take the damned hill ourselves."¹⁰

They walked upright, a skirmish line of insanely determined men eerily lit by the flashes of exploding phosphorous grenades and the fire from their own guns as they marched back up the hill.

By midnight, they had closed in on the top of the hill. The Chinese opened up on them from two machine guns—"one of their own and one Company K had abandoned on the top of the hill."¹¹

One man took a bullet in the neck and dropped dead.

Cheppe did what he had always done back in Silvis—he hadn't started this fight, but he was determined to end it. He charged alone, firing as he ran toward one of the machine guns, ignoring the hail of bullets coming at him. The Chinese fell. Then Cheppe did, too, riddled with shots.

At 1:30 A.M. on May 18, Company K retook Bunker Hill. The battle had lasted five-and-a-half hours. One man died. Eight were wounded.

Cheppe was one of them. He hovered near death, bleeding badly as medics raced him to a field hospital. For nine days, he refused to die. On May 28, his fight ended. His death made Terry part of a rapidly growing group of Americans—the thousands of war widows with newborns, with dreams of a house and a husband suddenly snuffed.

"I remember when that telegram came," Terry said.

She was living with her mother again, in Davenport, working as a waitress at the Knights of Columbus. She was just getting ready for work when the knock came at the door.

"The word 'killed' just jumped out immediately," she said.

Her membership in the widows' club came with a special distinction: The Army gave Cheppe a Silver Star for his bravery. Terry held baby Linda in her arms when it arrived.

When her brother Phil heard, he took it hard.

He had joined the Marines by then and was in Korea himself, part of a highly trained "recon" unit.

"You go behind enemy lines and you bring back prisoners," he said.

Despite the deadly nature of his work, and seeing others die around him, Cheppe's death struck home.

"I was devastated. I really couldn't believe it," Phil said. "You never really believe that somebody that you know is going to die and not come back."

Harsher, still, was how he found out.

"We used to write," he said. "And I got a letter back. And on the front of it, it said, 'Deceased.' That's the way they let you know somebody had died."

Phil's other good friend expected to die.

Johnny Muños had had a premonition. He told Phil about it as they drove the dark road back to Silvis after a weekend visiting Mary Beserra and her family in Galesburg. Mary and Johnny had talked again about their upcoming wedding. Phil was to be one of the ushers.

But Johnny was worried. With draft letters arriving in homes across America nearly every day and the war filling the papers and—for the first time in U.S. history—playing out on television sets during the nightly network news, Johnny felt a chill. Everyone in the country could see that things were bogging down and the death toll was rising. Johnny had just gotten his draft letter.

Besides, he had dodged a bullet in the previous war. He got his draft letter then just as World War II was coming to an end.

"He got a letter, then he got another letter saying disregard that one," his sister Mary Ramirez said.[12]

So Johnny may have felt his luck running out. He didn't say. But that Sunday night on the way home from Galesburg, Johnny told Phil he didn't think he was coming back from Korea.

"Why are you going to get married, then?" Phil demanded.

Johnny looked troubled as he answered, "I just think it's something I have to do."

He talked with Phil several other times about that sick feeling inside, always on the long drives back in the late dark of Sunday night. But he never told his fiancée.

In fact, she resists the idea.

"He said, 'It won't be long, it's just for a year,'" she said. "He took it good like, you know, he was going to be all right. So I took it good, too. I said, 'Well, in a year he'll be home.' But it wasn't like that."

In the wedding pictures, she smiles blissfully—a beautiful young bride in a shimmering white gown, unaware of the dark worry Phil said her groom hid behind his own broad smile.

Johnny kept it hidden as they enjoyed their newlywed life, as the holidays came and went. Then, with 1951 barely begun, he left for basic training at Fort Leonard Wood, in Kansas. His newlywed bride Mary went with him to the train station in Galesburg to say good-bye.

"It was cold. And damp. And sad," she said.

By then, the Chinese Communist forces had taken back nearly every inch of the U.N. forces' gains, along with the South Korean capital of Seoul. General MacArthur wanted to use the atomic bomb, but Truman chose instead to continue sending more men and to press for peace. On April 11, the president went on the radio to tell the American people he was replacing MacArthur and continuing the war. More men would be needed.

"In the simplest terms, what we are doing in Korea is this: We are trying to prevent a third world war," he said. He went on. "The dangers are great. Make no mistake about it. Behind the North Koreans and Chinese Communists in the front lines stand additional millions of Chinese soldiers. And behind the Chinese stand the tanks, the planes, the submarines, the soldiers, and the scheming rulers of the Soviet Union."[13]

The speech fit perfectly into the Cold War fears gripping the nation. The "Red Scare" promoted by Senator Joe McCarthy had neighbors and coworkers eyeing each other warily, wondering who among them might be a Communist or, perhaps even more frightening, who might accuse them of being one.

Spring approached amid that spreading atmosphere of mistrust, as Johnny trudged through long marches and practiced on the firing range. Instead of shipping out as soon as they finished training, though, Johnny's unit got held back. As Cheppe slogged through his short, bloody tour in Korea, Johnny waited at Fort Leonard Wood. That put him close enough to Galesburg that he could go home for the weekends to visit Mary and enjoy at least a portion of his new married life.

Then, as Cheppe lay dying, the orders came sending Johnny's unit overseas.

He begged for one last leave before he sailed. He got it, a seventeen-day furlough. It cost him his life.

As Johnny spent the end of May and beginning of June with Mary, the rest of the men in his unit headed to Germany. When he reported back to duty, Johnny didn't. He went to Korea.

By June he was on the front lines, high in the Korean mountains, and none too happy.

"These bastards didn't waste much time getting me to this lousy hole," he wrote in a letter to a friend. "Boy! I'd give my right nut to be back in the states. This place isn't fit for a dog."[14]

As cold as the winter was, the summer was its opposite. It began with heavy rains that washed over the mountainsides in sheets, soaking the men in their holes. Then the sun baked the ground, turning the terrain into a sticky steam bath as the temperatures soared into the nineties.

By the time Johnny arrived, the war had ground down into a sullen, bloody back-and-forth where neither side seemed capable of winning, but neither was willing to lose. As one soldier grumbled, "We can't win. We can't lose. We can't quit."[15]

Back home, support for the war was plummeting, even as the number of draftees went up. Ultimately, the fight would involve 5.7 million U.S. troops—roughly one out of every five fighting-age men in the country. The United Nations and the Communists pursued halfhearted peace talks in Kaesong, while the troops continued to die. They traded mortar fire and air strikes, artillery shelling and napalm until they had laid the hilltops bare.

As the shells rained down, Johnny huddled in a bunker he had helped carve out with his own hands—"just a hole in the ground with logs on top and sand lays on top of that," he wrote. "We're way up here on top of a big hill and if we need water or anything we have to go way down to the bottom. Down there they have a little creek that runs by and that's where we get our water. The same clothes I've got on right now are the same ones I came up here with, 31 days with the same clothes."[16]

To make matters worse, the soggy start of August brought extensive downpours. Rivers swelled. Bridges gave way. Roads were washed out. And the Chinese called down increasing amounts of artillery fire.

In mid-August, South Korean forces supported by U.N. troops launched an attack against the Communists. They ran into two North Korean battalions, dug into a system of bunkers and tunnels, who "rose from their holes and battled hand-to-hand with the attackers, using bayonets and grenades," according to an after action report.[17]

They called in Johnny's unit to help.

That was the start of what came to be known as the Battle of Bloody Ridge, one of the biggest combat actions of the war, when the Chinese and North Koreans threw some 850,000 men against the U.N. forces and turned the bare hilltop—a ragged line as sharp as a knife's edge—into a slaughtering field. It lasted three murderous weeks and left more than 46,000 dead or wounded.

With Johnny and the 38th pulled into the fray, the battle locked into an ugly stalemate with each side raining artillery and mortar fire on the other.

As one lieutenant described it: "Minutes seemed like hours, hours like days, and days like one long, terrible, dusty, blood-swirled nightmare."[18]

Then, on the 26th of August, the Communists came swarming over the hilltops on several sides, with their battle bugles blaring. By noon, they had completely surrounded the South Korean forces and were focusing on Johnny and the men of Company F.

The battle raged into the night, the Communists unrelenting. They showered the Americans with lethal mortar fire and picked off stragglers with a steady stream of rifle and machine gun fire.

At ten minutes to eleven that night, Johnny and the men were ordered to move to the next hilltop to help a group of South Korean soldiers who were near exhaustion from repelling attacks. The next day he was dead.

A mortar shell had exploded nearly on top of Johnny. Shell fragments ripped him apart.

The formal language of the casualty report put it delicately, compared to the reality. "Killed in action by shell fragment wound penetrating throughout body," it read.

But back on Second Street they say there were too many pieces to bring home.

CHAPTER SEVENTEEN

HERO STREET

The weather was mercifully dry the December day Cheppe's body arrived home in Silvis. Rain had not fallen for seven full days, and Second Street sat dusty and cold as the Rock Island Railroad train carrying his coffin pulled into the station just after 1 A.M. that Saturday morning.

The war still had two years left to go. More men from Silvis remained in Korea. But Second Street would give no more lives.

The men came home to lives and wives they had left behind. They went back to their jobs at International Harvester and John Deere. They had babies, and bought cars and televisions and houses, and looked forward to at least a few years of peace and prosperity.

Still, these were tense times, and not just because of the war. McCarthyism bred mistrust; racism bred prejudice. Hatred and fear festered openly, and lynchings, beatings and murders occurred with a sickening frequency.

Virulently prejudiced whites, including members of the Ku Klux Klan, often acted with impunity.

The year that Cheppe and Johnny died was, in many ways, pivotal for the Civil Rights Movement. It saw some of the last major efforts by the movement's torchbearers of prior decades and the emergence of a new generation of civil rights leaders. And, underscoring the viciousness they were combatting, the year began and ended with killings that further fueled the fight for equality.

In February, three months before Cheppe died, the Commonwealth of Virginia carried out the executions of seven black men convicted of raping a white woman. The night before the first execution, hundreds of protesters, about half of them white and half black, turned out in defense of the "Martinsville Seven." They held a prayer vigil at the state capitol and called on the governor to stay the executions. The demonstrators insisted that the executions were little more than legal lynchings—all forty-five men sent to the electric chair for rape up until that time were blacks accused of attacking white women.

The governor refused to block the executions.

Two months later, the students of Moton High in Virginia staged a student strike to protest school conditions. Built for 180 students, enrollment had swollen to more than 450. The school had become so crowded that teachers held three classes simultaneously in the auditorium. School buses had been converted into classrooms.

Still, when nearly the entire student body walked out to demand better conditions, the school superintendent refused to meet with them. On the third day of the strike, the students and their adult supporters decided to go beyond demands for improvements. Instead, they sued for desegregation. The lawsuit became one of the five cases consolidated into the landmark *Brown v. Board of Education* decision.

Then, on December 17, Civil Rights leaders presented a book-length petition, "We Charge Genocide: The Crime of Government Against the Negro People," to the United Nations. It documented hundreds of lynching cases and laid the blame squarely on the government.

"We maintain, therefore, that the oppressed Negro citizens of the United States, segregated, discriminated against and long the target of violence, suffer from genocide as the result of the consistent, conscious, unified policies of every branch of government."[1]

And even though they were calling on the U.N. to condemn the United States, the document's authors insisted their motives came from love for their country, not hate.

"And now we ask that world opinion, that the conscience of mankind as symbolized by the General Assembly of the United Nations, turn not a deaf ear to our entreaty," they wrote.

"We plead as patriotic Americans, knowing that any act that can aid in removing the incubus of United States oppression of the American Negro people from our country is the highest patriotism. The American Dream was for justice, justice for all men, regardless of race, creed, or color."

Instead of hearing their pleas, the U.N. ignored them. Its authors found themselves harassed by the FBI and other government agencies throughout the fifties.

A week later, on Christmas Eve, 1951, a bomb went off under the bedroom of Harry and Harriette Moore in Mims, Florida. Both died—Harry immediately, Harriette nine days later. Harry, a pioneer of the Civil Rights Movement in Florida, had helped register more than 100,000 black voters to challenge the all-white elections dominating state politics at the time.

No one was ever charged with the crime.

Like the blacks, Mexican-Americans came home from the war as decorated veterans and thought they had earned the right to share equally in the American Dream. Instead, they were barred from certain restaurants and whites-only bathrooms and sent to the "coloreds" section in movie theater balconies. Discrimination shaped their lives, and after—even if they had died fighting for the United States.

The year before the bomb exploded under Harry and Harriette Moore's bedroom, the body of a young Mexican-American infantryman finally made its way back from the Philippine jungle to Three Rivers, Texas.

Felix Longoria had grown up there. In November 1944 he enlisted. The Army sent him to the Philippines to fight the Japanese. Two weeks after he got there, he died.

When his body was finally on its way home in 1949, his widow tried to make arrangements at the local funeral home. The funeral director refused. The town's whites, he said, "might object." After the *New York Times* wrote about it, then–U.S. senator Lyndon Johnson stepped in. He arranged for Longoria's burial at Arlington National Cemetery, with full military honors.

"I deeply regret to learn that the prejudice of some individuals extends even beyond this life," Johnson said.

But, as Johnson demonstrated, change was in the air. Barely three months before Cheppe's body came home, a black man named Oliver Brown tried to enroll his daughter Linda in the elementary school seven blocks from their house in Topeka, Kansas. The incident became the basis for the landmark Supreme Court decision that would make segregation illegal in 1954.

It made little difference. Segregation may have been illegal, but it wasn't gone.

A year after the decision came down, a fourteen-year-old black boy named Emmett Till accepted a dare from some friends and, after he bought two cents' worth of bubblegum at a Mississippi store, asked the white owner's young wife, "How about a date, baby?"

A few days later, her husband and another man took Emmett from his uncle's house. Three days later, Emmett's body turned up in the Tallahatchie River. He had been shot in the head. One eye was gouged out. His skull was crushed.

An all-white jury found the two men who took him not guilty. Till's mother left the courtroom before the verdict was read.

"I was expecting an acquittal," she said, "and I didn't want to be there when it happened."

After the trial, the two men accused of the murder confessed to *Look* magazine for $4,000. The men were never retried.

Things were never that bad in Silvis, but all the Mexican-Americans knew how a lot of the other townsfolk felt about them. The others didn't exactly keep it a secret.

Even before the *Brown v. Board of Education* ruling, Ray Alonzo and some of the other Mexican-American vets in Silvis bristled against the discrimination. The last straw was when a few of the men who had come back from the fighting in Korea walked into the VFW in Moline one afternoon and asked to join.

The Mexican-Americans had a sandlot baseball team that played on the diamond next to the VFW. That day, as they sipped on beers after practice, they asked the VFW bartender about joining. The bartender gave them applications and they filled them out. Then came the surprise.

A couple of weeks later, when they went to find out what the

VFW members had decided, the bartender told them, "'I'm sorry, but you guys are blackballed. The membership was afraid there are so many of you guys that you would take over the post,'" Ray recalled. "It pissed me off."

The bartender, though, had a suggestion. "He said, 'Don't take this wrong, but there's enough of you guys; why don't you form your own post?'"

They found out they needed twenty-five eligible members to start a post. They got sixty. They got their charter, Ray said, the same month the Supreme Court issued its *Brown v. Board* ruling.

They named the post for Cheppe and Mike Ybarra, an Army sergeant from Moline killed in action in Korea.

All it needed was a home. Al Sandoval, Willie's kid brother, found a place—an abandoned church at the edge of the city. He was in real estate, so he helped negotiate the deal with the church and the bank.

Sale price: $52,000.

They hosted bingo nights and raffles and sold tacos and tamales to raise money to come up with the down payment, and held some more when proceeds from the VFW's bar and dues wouldn't cover all the expenses.

As time went by, membership at the whites' VFW shrank. The remaining members joined with another predominantly white post, even though it was farther away. The move reflected the turbulence still wracking the country. As the push for civil rights spread steadily, extended hands reached out to bring people together, but many still extended fists instead.

The year after the Mexican-Americans opened their post, a mild-mannered seamstress named Rosa Parks refused to give up her seat to a white man on a bus in Montgomery, Alabama.

When the white bus driver told her she'd have to get up or he'd call the police and have her arrested, she told him, "You may do that."

The incident wound up sparking the Montgomery bus boycott, led by a young and largely unknown minister named Martin Luther King Jr. From there would come marches and protests, beatings and bombings.

Change was coming, but slowly. Second Street remained a rutted dirt track that ran past Billy Goat Hill.

Then, as the fifties came to a close, a young man named Joe Terronez began his own civil rights fight, in Silvis.

When he began, the Little Rock Nine were making headlines, and he had seen the angry faces of white men and women on the evening news, contorted monstrously in their rage as they screamed invectives at the group of black kids trying to integrate a high school in Arkansas. He also realized there were lessons in the methods of the blacks. The NAACP's voter registration drives, in particular, caught his attention. He recognized the power of votes, and he knew that for the Mexican-born residents of Silvis to become voters, they first needed help to become citizens.

So that's what he and a group of friends, did. They helped folks get naturalized; then they helped them register to vote.

Then he ran for office. It took two tries, but in 1963 Terronez became the first Hispanic on the city council.

Soon, Terronez was making a motion to get Second Street paved. Then, when John and Joe Ponciano came up with the idea to call it "Hero Street U.S.A.," Terronez pushed for that, too. And, to complete the vision, he said Billy Goat Hill, where his heroes used to play, should be turned into a park in their memory.

So he launched his own battle, to win them—and the little street—the recognition he thought it deserved. And he refused to quit.

In his mind, the sacrifice of the families on Second Street was similar to the story of the five Sullivan brothers from nearby Waterloo, Iowa. When World War II broke out, the five joined the Navy and insisted on serving together. During the sea battle of Guadalcanal (in fact, just two days after Luis Ramirez reunited with U.S. troops on the island), a torpedo hit the Sullivans' ship. All five died. The family's tragic loss quickly became a symbol of heroic determination and the fighting spirit that would lead America to victory.

"The most from one family to be killed in World War II were the five Sullivan brothers, and there's a destroyer named after them," Joe reminded the council. "And the eight guys from Second Street who were killed were like brothers, because they were all raised together. We want their street named after them."

Terronez's fight for Hero Street finally caught the attention of the U.S. Department of Defense, which looked into the matter. The department's director of military equal opportunity made it official: Fifty-seven men from Second Street fought in both World War II and Korea. As far as he could determine, this was the largest number of servicemen of the same ethnic background to come from any area of comparable size during those conflicts.

Finally, on Memorial Day, 1968, Second Street officially became Hero Street, U.S.A. A red-white-and-blue sign was unveiled at the corner of Second Street and First Avenue to proclaim it. It had taken a decade to get here, but as the Los Amigos marching band played "America," Joe Terronez could afford to smile.

Three years later, he won another victory.

Congressman Thomas Railsback helped obtain a federal grant to make the Billy Goat Hill park possible. Finally, the Department of

Housing and Urban Development agreed to pay half the $88,000 cost if the town would match the funds.

Volunteers swung into action. Local 1304 of the United Auto Workers collected money at factory gates all over the area. Other local Mexican-American communities raised money with fiestas. The John Deere and International Harvester companies contributed machinery, as did the city of Silvis.

Gradually, a third of Billy Goat Hill was cut away, and a concrete monument shaped like an Aztec temple was fashioned into it. Where the heroes once dropped a rubber ball into a hoop nailed to a tree, they built a full basketball court. And where they once played in the mud, they put up a playground with a jungle gym.

Hero Street Park was dedicated October 30, 1971.

Four years later, the little street that gave so much was finally paved. Claro Soliz's family could at last ride their bicycles in all seasons and little Second Streeters would be able to practice their basketball shots at the hoops in the park.

More than twenty more years went by before some of the people on that tiny street decided the men who had died deserved more. The Hero Street Monument Committee was born in a meeting at the Ybarra-Gomez VFW post, with the vision that a permanent memorial honoring the men and their sacrifices belonged on the street.

The design came to one of Claro Soliz's nephews in a dream. Guadalupe "Sonny" Soliz had been tremendously influenced by his artistic uncle. He grabbed a pencil and started sketching what had come to him in his sleep.

It would soar toward the sky, but stand solidly on the ground of Hero Street—an imposing structure of marble and bronze, with artistic touches hinting at both their Mexican roots and their American pride. It had a spread-winged eagle on top, clutching an M1 rifle in one set of talons, a flag in the other. The eagle flew above a helmet, which sat, meaningfully, atop a base shaped like a Mayan temple. All of that sat on a concrete and marble base bearing reliefs of the Hero Street Eight.

In all, it rose seventeen-and-a-half feet and weighed thirty-five tons.

It took the committee fourteen years to raise the money, have it built, and transport it from the Mexican artist's home to Silvis. But on October 6, 2007, it was finished and ready for the dedication ceremony. It stood proudly at the very end of Hero Street, where passersby on First Avenue, the main road through town, could see it and, if they stop, can read the inscription on its base:

Hero Street USA Monument

This monument represents the ideals of duty, honor and country as exemplified by military service rendered to our nation by all American veterans during all wars to preserve freedom for the United States of America.

A special tribute is mentioned here to honor the eight men from Hero Street USA who gave the supreme sacrifice during World War II and the Korean War.

** We remember them **

Standing next to the monument on a crisp October morning and speaking of the local war heroes, Joe Terronez reflected back on the basketball coach who inspired the kids on Second Street to surprise the world with what they could achieve.

"Coach Gauley used to say the problem was that most people wouldn't give us a chance to show what we're made of," Terronez said. "They showed what we're made of."

CHAPTER EIGHTEEN

THE BOMBARDIER'S WIFE

The hearses would no longer get stuck in the mud, but the men and women of Hero Street would continue to give. More than 110 from Second Street served in World War II, Korea, and Vietnam. Whole new generations went to the Gulf War and Iraq.

Today, the memorial still stands at the end of Second Street, the screaming eagle's wings permanently outstretched. It was built so that the Hero Street Eight would not be forgotten, but it is not just for them. It is a reminder of wars past and present and the true meaning of sacrifice. These were not just their wars. America fought. They were part of it.

Piecing together complete pictures of the men was difficult. Like all the others who lived through those times, the ones who fought and the ones who waited are disappearing. Memories are fading. Those who knew the eight men are dying. Almost all their personnel records were lost in a fire that swept through the archives in St. Louis.

Nonetheless, the goal of this book is to let them live on in all of our memories, and to make sure that the significance of their actions lives on. Not just the men of Hero Street, but the entire generation that answered the call.

They came together, regardless of the color of their skin, to fight against those who would aim their hatred and their might against those of another race or another religion, and they brought those ideals back home to make them the standard for our nation to uphold. We may not always achieve it, but we can never forget what we stand for—at home and across the globe.

This book is a tribute to all of the men and women who stood up when they were needed, to do what needed to be done. It is a reminder also of the true price of war and why it must be avoided.

Nearly seven decades have passed since World War II came to a close. Yet, for those who were a part of it, the war lives on.

Until his death in 2012, one member of Tony Pompa's crew still woke up screaming from nightmares about the day the plane went down. He remembered the bombardier bleeding to death in the Plexiglas nose of the plane as they hurtled down in flames.

His wife grows grim as she speaks of those times. "They call it a Good War," she told me. "They're wrong. It was a terrible war. . . . There was a time when it seemed like everyone you knew had someone close to them who had died."

"Tell it," Helen Gordon said, "so that people can learn from it. It can never happen again."

ACKNOWLEDGMENTS

The journey to complete this book stretched, for a variety of reasons, over seven years. It would have been impossible without the help of some truly wonderful people who believed in the story. They opened their hearts, their homes, and their lives to me in ways and with a warmth I never would have expected. Some of them didn't make it to see its end. I am sorry for that, and all the more thankful for the time I was able to spend with them and the memories they shared.

There are so many to thank that I cannot possibly name them all. There are some, however, I must.

I am eternally in debt and forever grateful for the patience and support of my wonderful editors, Natalee Rosenstein and Robin Barletta, who stuck with me long after most others would have given up. Also, to the world's best agent, Greg Aunapu, who, even after all these years, continues to amaze and inspire me with how talented, how funny, and how kind he is.

ACKNOWLEDGMENTS

Special thanks go to the people of Hero Street and their relatives. They gave of themselves willingly and unselfishly time and again. They taught me not just about life on Second Street and the men who had lived there, but about the value and importance of family.

Al Sandoval, Luz "Slugger" Segura and Terry Garza didn't get to see the finished product, but I hope they continue to live on in these pages.

My thanks, too, to Ruben and Rufina Sandoval, and Phil and Mary Garza, for making me feel so much like a part of their family. And Emma Sandoval, who fattened me up with enchiladas and never complained about sharing Al with me.

Joe and Frank Sandoval's family took me under their wings from the very beginning. I don't think this book ever would have been written without the help of Tanilo Sandoval and Georgia Herrera. They were my guides and my guiding lights.

Thanks, also, to Mary Ramirez and her sister Sara Fields; to Mary Beserra and her wonderful husband, Joe; to Buddy Gomez; to Slugger's son, Bob; to Ray Alonzo; to Dan Knox; and to Claro's nephews, who struggled so hard to see that the Hero Street Monument would be completed, Sonny, Tony and Frank Soliz.

And, of course, there might not have been a Hero Street, or this book, without the help of the former mayor who fought so hard to get it named, Joe Terronez.

Last, but hardly least, my thanks to the men who fought side by side with the Hero Street Eight. They gave so much for their country, and shared so much with me. Elliott "Tommy" Thompson and George Gordon survived the plane crash that killed Tony Pompa, but they didn't get to see themselves remembered in this book. Leo Hart, William Watson, Preston Solomon—you are all heroes to me, and we are all in your debt. Thank you.

BIBLIOGRAPHY

(n.d.). Retrieved from http://content.time.com/time/magazine/article/ 0,9171,780092,00.html#ixzz2i5qclHhV

(n.d.). Retrieved from http://www.ibiblio.org/hyperwar/USA/USA-E-Breakout/ USA-E-Breakout-27.html.

(n.d.). Retrieved from http://www.pbs.org/wgbh/amex/macarthur/filmmore/ reference/primary/officialdocs03.html.

(n.d.). Retrieved from http://www.pbs.org/wgbh/americanexperience/features/ transcript/bulge-transcript/?flavour=mobile.

(1941, Dec. 8). *Pittsburgh Post-Gazette*.

(1941, Dec. 15). *Time* magazine.

(1941, Dec. 9). *St. Petersburg Times*.

(1941, Dec. 8). *New York Times*.

2d Lt. David Garth, w. a. (1946). *ST-LO (7 July–19 July 1944)*. War Department, Historical Division. Washington, D.C.: Center of Military History.

Adams, J. (n.d.). *6 August 1944 to 13 August 1944: letter to Chad Collins, 16 April 2001* . Retrieved from The World War II Experiences of John M. Adams, Jr.: http://donchesnut.com/johnadamswwii/index.htm.

Anderson, C. R. (1991). The U.S. Army Campaigns of World War II. *Tunisia*. U.S. Army Center of Military History.

Anonymous. (n.d.). *Ledo Diary, Excerpts from a road builder's diary.* Retrieved 2013, from THE LEDO ROAD, China-Burma-India Theater of World War II : http://home.comcast.net/~ledoroad/Story_diary.html.

Axelrod, A. (2009). *Patton's Drive: The Making of America's Greatest General.* Guilford, Connecticutt: The Lyons Press.

Basden, B., & Scheffel, C. (2007). *Crack! and Thump: With a Combat Infantry Officer in World War II* . Llano, Texas: Camroc Press.

Beckner, L. C. (n.d.). Military Monograph/analysis.

Bjorge, G. J. (1996). *Merrill's Marauders: Combined Operations in Northern Burma in 1944.* Washington, D.C.: U.S. Army Center of Military History.

Blumenson, M. (1960). The Liberation of Paris. In M. Blumenson, *Breakout and Pursuit.* Washington, D.C.: Center of Military History, U.S. Army.

Blumenson, M. (1986). *America's First Battles, 1776-1965.* Lawrence, Kansas: University Press of Kansas.

Bohart, R. i. (2000). *Veterans' Memoirs: Richard Bohart.* Retrieved from Korean War Educator: http://www.koreanwar-educator.org/memoirs/bohart_richard/index.htm#SpringOffensive.

Bradley, O. N. (1983). *A General's Life: An Autobiography.* New York: Simon and Schuster.

Camp Davis Public Relations Office Brochure. (n.d.). *Introducing Camp Davis.* Retrieved June 24, 2013, from Skylighters: http://www.skylighters.org/places/intro.html.

Churchill, W. S. (1943). A Speech at the Lord Mayor's Day Luncheon at the Mansion House, London, 9 November 1942. In W. S. Churchill, *The End of the Beginning* (pp. 265-). London: Cassell.

Clem, R. (2011, August 1). PHENIX CITY The Tyranny of the Mob. *Longleaf Style.*

Collins, L., & Lapierre, D. (1965). *Is Paris Burning?* New York: Warner Books.

Cushman, M. A. (1943). *Observer Report, March 29, 1943.* Washington, D.C.: Army War College.

Dansette, A. (1994). *Histoire de la libération de Paris (1946). Réédition.* Paris: Perrin.

D'Este, C. (2002). *Eisenhower: A Soldier's Life.* New York: Henry Holt and Company, LLC.

Donahue, C. P. (1986). *The Danger of Poor Training Management: The Us Army in Korea–July, 1959.* Military Analysis, U.S. Army Maneuver Center of Excellence , Ft. Benning, GA.

Doolittle, J. H., & Glines, C. V. (1991.). *I Could Never Be So Lucky Again: An Autobiography.* New York: Bantam Books.

Durdin, T. (1945, Feb 11). "General Pick Of 'Pick's Pike'; The builder of Stilwell Road is more like a country doctor than a hard-driving engineer." *New York Times*, p. SM7.

Eisenhower, G. D. (n.d.). *Report of the Commander-in-Chief Allied Forces to the Combined Chiefs of Staff on Operations in North West Africa.* Retrieved June 30, 2013, from hyperwar: http://www.ibiblio.org/hyperwar/USA/rep/TORCH/DDE-Torch.html#race.

Fehrenbach, T. (1963). *This Kind of War.* New York: MacMillan.

Frank, A. (1996). *The Diary of a Young Girl, the Definitive Edition.* (S. Massotty, Trans.) New York: Anchor Books.

Gallagher, R. F. (n.d.). *World War II Story by Robert F. Gallagher.* Retrieved from http://www.gallagher.com/ww2/index.html.

Gugeler, R. A. (1984). *Combat Actions in Korea (CMH Publication 30-2).* Washington, D.C.: Center for Military History.

Hansen, C. B. (n.d.). War Diaries, Chester B. Hansen Collection. Carlisle, Pa.: U.S. Army Heritage and Education Center.

Harris, M. J. (1984). *The Homefront, America During World War II.* New York: Putnam Books.

Hatfield, E. C. (2003). Personal diary, February 14, 1943. In Vincent M. Carr Jr., *The Battle Of Kasserine Pass: An Examination Of Allied Operational Failings.*

Hogan, D. W. (n.d.). *India-Burma, 2 April 1942-28 January 1945.* U.S. Army. Center of Military History.

Holabird, L. J. (n.d.). Cornelius Ryan collection. Alden Library, Ohio University.

House Naval Affairs Subcommittee to Investigate Congested Areas, Part 3. (1943, April 13). Testimony of John L. DeWitt. 739-740.

Howe, G. F. (1957). *Northwest Africa: Seizing the Initiative in the West.* Washington, D.C.: Office of the Chief of Military History, Department of the Army.

Information Section. (1947). *Army Ground Forces Fact Sheets.* U.S. Army.

Ingraham, R. (1945, May 7). "Death in Milan." *Time.*

Jost, H. F. (July). *Airborne Operations in Sicily, July 1943.* After Action Report.

Kappel. (n.d.).

Kerley, M. R. (n.d.). *Operations of the 2nd Battalion, 120th Infantry (30th Infantry Division) at Morain, France 6–12 August 1944.* U.S. Army.

Kessler, L. W. (1999). *Never in Doubt: Remembering Iwo Jima.* Annapolis Naval Institute Press.

Kluckhohn, F. L. (1941, December 12). "U.S. Now at War with Germany And Italy." *New York Times*, p. 1A.

Komosa, C. A. (1943). *Airborne Operation, 504th Parachute Infantry Regiment C/T, 82nd Airborne Division, Sicily, 9 July–19 August 1943.*

Lyons, C. F. (1991, July). *Merrill's Marauders in Burma.* Retrieved 2013, from Ex-CBI Roundup: http://cbi-theater-10.home.comcast.net/~cbi-theater-10/marauders/marauders.html.

Lyons, F. O. (n.d.). *Merrill's Marauders in Burma.* Retrieved 2013, from Ex-CBI Roundup: http://cbi-theater-10.home.comcast.net/~cbi-theater-10/marauders/marauders.html.

MacDonald, C. B. (1963). *The Siegfried Line Campaign.* Washington, D.C.: Office of the Chief of Military History, Department of the Army.

Marsh, D. R. (n.d.). *Diary of Don R. Marsh.* Retrieved from http://www.2nda moredhellonwheels.com/Don_R_Marsh_Diary/diary_entry_4.html.

Mason, J. (n.d.). Johanna Mason, Nee Bremen. (C. Ryan, Interviewer) Adler Library, Ohio University.

Massin, M. A. (1995). *209th Engineer Combat Battalion Unit History.* Retrieved 2013, from Ex-CBI Roundup: http://www.cbi-history.com/part_vi_209th _eng_combat_bn.html.

McCutcheon, M. (1995). *The Writer's Guide to Everyday Life from Prohibition through World War II.* Cincinnatti, Ohio: Writer's Digest Books.

McIntosh, E. P. (2012, Dec. 6). "Honolulu after Pearl Harbor: A report published for the first time, 71 years later." *Washington Post.*

Merriam, R. E. (2007). *World War II Journal: Battle of the Bulge.* Bennington, Vt.: Merriam Press.

Miller, D. L., & Commager, H. S. (1945). *The Story of World War II.* New York: Touchstone.

Moore, Robert R. C. 2. (n.d.). 2d and 3d battalions, 168 infantry, History (extract), 3 – 19 February 1943. In U. S. history, *Kasserine Pass Battles, readings volume 1, part one.*

Munroe, L. C. (1952). *The Second Infantry Division in Korea 1950-1951.* Tokyo: Toppan Printing.

New York Times. (2004, May 22). Gen. Robert F. Seedlock, 91; Oversaw Building of Burma Road.

Nichols, D. (1987). *Ernie's War: The Best of Ernie Pyle's World War II Dispatches.* New York: Simon & Schuster.

Nin, A. (1971). *The Diary of Anais Nin, Vol. 4: 1944-1947.* Orlando, FL: Harcourt, Brace, Jovanovich.

Nordyke, P. (2005). *All American All the Way.* St. Paul, Minnesota: Zenith Press books.

North Carolina Historic Sites. (n.d.). *Fort Fisher: Fort Fisher During World War II*. Retrieved June 23, 2013, from http://www.nchistoricsites.org/fisher/ww2/ww2.htm.

Pitt, T. J. (n.d.). *The Waal River Crossing, An interview with Thomas Pitt*. Retrieved 2006, from The Drop Zone: An interview with Thomas Pitt.

Pyle, E. (1986). Brave Men, Brave Men! In D. Nichols, *Ernie's War: The Best of Ernie Pyle's World War II Dispatches* (pp. 103-105). New York: Random House.

Pyle, E. (n.d.). *On Victory in Europe*. Retrieved from Indiana University School of Journalism: Ernie Pyle: http://journalism.indiana.edu/resources/erniepyle/wartime-columns/on-victory-in-europe/.

Rohter, L. (1989, December 10). A Mexican Relic Is Buried at Last. *New York Times*.

Russell, I. L. (n.d.). *Into the Wildest Blue Yonder*. Retrieved from ex-CBI: http://cbi-theater-6.home.comcast.net/~cbi-theater-6/blueyonder/blueyonder.html#TOP.

Ryan, C. (1974). *A Bridge Too Far*. New York: Simon & Schuster.

Sims, L. (n.d.). *Sicily and Holland with the 504th parachute infantry Regiment, 82nd Airborne Division*. Retrieved from Brookdale Community College Center for World War II Studies and Conflict Resolution: http://www.brookdalecc.edu/pages/960.asp.

Solomon, P. (2008, Dec 6). (C. Harrison, Interviewer).

Southern Poverty Law Center. (1997), *A Hundred Years of Terror*.

Stemple, J. W. (n.d.). *James Stemple, Korean War Veteran of the United States Marine Corps*. Retrieved from Korean War Educator: http://www.thekwe.org/memoirs/stemple_james/index.htm.

Sullivan, J. (1988). The Botched Air Support of Operation Cobra. *Parameters*, 97–110.

Takei, G. (n.d.). TED Talk.

The Paris Review. (1977). Kurt Vonnegut, The Art of Fiction No. 64.

Time Magazine. (1944). World Battlefronts: Battle of the Roer.

Times (June 7, 1943). Zoot Suiters Seized on Coast After Clashes With Service Men.

U.S. Army. (1944). "Fighting in Normandy". *Combat Lessons—Rank and file in combat: What they're doing; How they do it*.

U.S. Army. (1946). *First United States Report of Operations 20 October 1943 to 1 August 1944*.

U.S. War Production Board. (1942, April 29). Emergency Statement to the People of the United States. *Des Moines Register*.

United States. War Dept. (n.d.). *UNT Digital Library: Engineer soldier's handbook.* Retrieved June 29, 2013, from http://digital.library.unt.edu/ark:/67531/metadc28313/.

Valdés, D. N. (2000). *Barrios Norteños: St. Paul and Midwestern Mexican Communities in the Twentieth Century.* Austin, Texas: University of Texas Press.

van Lunteren, F. (2009). *Brothers in Arms, The men of A Company, 504th Parachute Infantry Regiment during WWII.* Retrieved June 25, 2013, from http://www.freewebs.com/a504/activationoverseas.htm.

Watts, J. C. (n.d.). *The Capture of the Maas River Bridge During Operation Market Garden.* Retrieved from The Drop Zone: http://thedropzone.org/europe/Holland/watts.htm.

Weber, M. D. (2013). *"Vas Du das Krieg ist über!"* Retrieved October 3, 2013, from http://freepages.family.rootsweb.ancestry.com/~webermd1/wwII.html.

Webster, D. (2003). *The Burma Road, The Epic Story of the China-Burma-India Theater in World War II.* New York: Farrar, Straus and Giroux.

West, E. (2003). The Dresden Bombing—An Eyewitness Account. *Current Concerns.*

Westrate, E. V. (1944). *Forward Observer.* Philadelphia: Blakiston.

Wetzel, N. (1979, July). *Return to Burma.* Retrieved 2013, from Ex-CBI Roundup: http://cbi-theater.home.comcast.net/~cbi-theater/menu/cbi_home.html.

Wilson, M. (2009). *Hero Street USA: The Story of Little Mexico's Fallen Soldiers.* Norman, Okla.: 2009.

WWII Diary of Chick Bruns—70 Years Ago . (n.d.). Retrieved June 30, 2013, from http://70yearsago.com/nov-8-1942-sunday.

NOTES

CHAPTER TWO

1 Álvaro Obregón, translation from memoir quoted in Rohter, Larry. "A Mexican Relic is Buried at Last." *New York Times,* December 10, 1989: World Section.

2 U.S. Bureau of Immigration, *Annual Report of the Commissioner-General of Immigration to the Secretary of Labor, 1914,* p. 458.

3 *Los Angeles Times*, September 18, 1916.

CHAPTER THREE

1 Southern Poverty Law Center, *A Hundred Years of Terror*, Montgomery, Alabama, 1997, http://vlib.iue.it/history/USA/ERAS/klukluxklan.html.

2 Southern Poverty Law Center, *A Hundred Years of Terror*, Montgomery, Alabama, 1997, http://vlib.iue.it/history/USA/ERAS/klukluxklan.html.

3 Letter to the editor, "Protecting Mexicans in the United States," *New York Times*, November 18, 1922. http://query.nytimes.com/mem/archive-free/pdf?res=F00A1FFC3D5C1A7A93CAA8178AD95F468285F9

4 Dionicio Nodín Valdés, *Barrios Norteños: St. Paul and Midwestern Mexican Communities in the Twentieth Century* (Austin, Texas: University of Texas Press, 2000).

5 Ibid.

6 Marc McCutcheon, *The Writer's Guide to Everyday Life from Prohibition through World War II* (Cincinnatti, Ohio: Writer's Digest Books, 1995).

7 Ibid.

8 Ibid.

CHAPTER FOUR

1 Elizabeth P. McIntosh, "Honolulu After Pearl Harbor: A Report Published for the First Time, 71 Years Later," *Washington Post*, December 6, 2012.

2 Ibid.

3 *Pittsburgh Post-Gazette,* December 8, 1941.

4 "The U.S. at War: National Ordeal," *Time*, December 15, 1941.

5 *St. Petersburg Times,* December 9, 1941.

6 Frank L. Kluckhohn, "U.S. Now at War with Germany and Italy . . ." *New York Times*, December 12, 1941, p. 1A.

7 Anne Frank, *The Diary of a Young Girl, the Definitive Edition,* translated by Susan Massotty (New York: Anchor Books, 1996).

8 James H. Doolittle and Carroll V. Glines, *I Could Never Be So Lucky Again: An Autobiography* (New York: Bantam Books, 1991).

9 U.S. War Production Board, "Emergency Statement to the People of the United States," *Des Moines Register*, April 29, 1942.

10 Mark Jonathan Harris, *The Homefront, America During World War II* (New York: Putnam Books, 1984).

11 Ibid.

12 George Takei, *My Broadway Debut at Age 75,* TEDxBroadway 2013. http://blog.ted.com/2013/03/28/george-takei-on-star-trek-musicals-and-japanese-american-internment/.

13 Ibid.

14 House Naval Affairs Subcommittee to Investigate Congested Areas, Part 3, "Testimony of John L. DeWitt," April 1943, pp. 739–740.

CHAPTER FIVE

1 Camp Davis Public Relations Office Brochure, "Introducing Camp Davis," *Skylighters,* http://www.skylighters.org/places/intro.html (accessed June 24, 2013).

2 North Carolina Historic Sites, *Fort Fisher: Fort Fisher During World War II,* http://www.nchistoricsites.org/fisher/ww2/ww2.htm (accessed June 23, 2013).

3 Robert Clem, "PHENIX CITY The Tyranny of the Mob," *Longleaf Style*, August 1, 2011.

4 Ibid.

5 Phil Nordyke, *All American All the Way* (St. Paul, Minnesota: Zenith Press Books, 2005).

6 Ibid.

7 United States War Dept, *UNT Digital Library: Engineer soldier's handbook*, http://digital.library.unt.edu/ark:/67531/metadc28313/ (accessed June 29, 2013).

8 *WWII Diary of Chick Bruns—70 Years Ago*, http://70yearsago.com/nov-8-1942-sunday/ (accessed June 30, 2013).

9 George F. Howe, *Northwest Africa: Seizing the Initiative in the West* (Washington, D.C.: Office of the Chief of Military History, Department of the Army, 1957).

10 General Dwight D. Eisenhower, "Report of the Commander-in-Chief Allied Forces to the Combined Chiefs of Staff on Operations in North West Africa," *hyperwar*, http://www.ibiblio.org/hyperwar/USA/rep/TORCH/DDE-Torch.html#race (accessed June 30, 2013).

11 Major Allerton Cushman, *Observer Report, March 29, 1943* (Washington, D.C.: Army War College, 1943).

12 Edwin V. Westrate, *Forward Observer* (Philadelphia: Blakiston, 1944).

13 Major Robert R. Moore, Commanding, 2nd Battalion, 168th Infantry, "2d and 3d Battalions, 168th Infantry, History (extract), 3–19 February 1943," *Kasserine Pass Battles, readings volume 1, part one* (U. S. Army Center of Military History).

14 Ernest C. Hatfield, "Personal Diary, February 14, 1943," in Vincent M. Carr Jr., *The Battle of Kasserine Pass: An Examination of Allied Operational Failings* (2003).

15 Martin Blumenson, *America's First Battles, 1776–1965* (Lawrence, Kansas: University Press of Kansas, 1986).

16 George F. Howe, *Northwest Africa: Seizing the Initiative in the West* (Washington, D.C.: Office of the Chief of Military History, Department of the Army, 1957).

17 Major Allerton Cushman, *Observer Report, March 29, 1943* (Washington, D.C.: Army War College, 1943).

18 Carlo D'Este, *Eisenhower: A Soldier's Life* (New York: Henry Holt and Company, 2002).

19 David Nichols, *Ernie's War: The Best of Ernie Pyle's World War II Dispatches* (New York: Random House, 1986).

20 Ernie Pyle, "Brave Men, Brave Men!" in David Nichols, *Ernie's War: The Best of Ernie Pyle's World War II Dispatches* (New York: Random House, 1986), pp. 103–105.

21 Ibid.

22 Charles R. Anderson, "The U.S. Army Campaigns of World War II," *Tunisia* (U.S. Army Center of Military History, 1991).

23 Ernie Pyle, "Brave Men, Brave Men!" in David Nichols, *Ernie's War: The Best of Ernie Pyle's World War II Dispatches* (New York: Random House, 1986), pp. 103–105.

24 Winston S. Churchill, "A Speech at the Lord Mayor's Day Luncheon at the Mansion House, London, 9 November 1942," in Winston S. Churchill, *In the End of the Beginning* (London: Cassell, 1943), pp. 265.

25 Charles R. Anderson, "The U.S. Army Campaigns of World War II," *Tunisia* (U.S. Army Center of Military History, 1991).

26 Harry F. Jost, "Airborne Operations in Sicily, July 1943," After Action Report, July.

27 Captain Adam A. Komosa, "Airborne Operation, 504th Parachute Infantry Regiment C/T, 82nd Airborne Division, Sicily, 9 July–19 August 1943" (1943).

28 Ibid.

29 Ibid.

CHAPTER SIX

1 Turner, 1st Lt. Damon A., War Diary: 449Th Bombardment Group (22 November 1943–30 June 1944).

2 Ibid.

3 Thompson, Elliott, Interview with author.

4 Turner.

5 Thompson.

6 Tony Pompa, letter to his sister, July, 22, 1941.

7 Tony Pompa, letter to his sister, Feb. 21, 1943.

8 Thompson, Elliott, interview with author

9 Turner.

10 Thompson.

11 Ibid.

12 Tony Pompa, letter to his sister, Jan. 2, 1944.

13 Turner.

14 Pyle, Ernie. Wartime column, Jan. 21, 1944.

15 Weber, Michael D. *"Vas Du das Krieg ist über!"* 2013. http://freepages .family.rootsweb.ancestry.com/~webermd1/wwII.html (accessed October 3, 2013).

16 Tony Pompa, letter to his sister, January 28, 1944.

17 Ibid.

18 Thompson interview.

19 Ibid.

20 Ibid.

21 Ibid.

22 Ibid.

23 Ibid.

24 Ibid.

25 Missing Air Crew Report 2403, February 5, 1944.

26 Ibid.

27 Thompson interview.

28 Ibid.

29 Gordon, George. Interview with author.

30 Ibid.

31 Thompson interview.

32 Ibid.

33 MACR 2403.

34 Ibid.

CHAPTER SEVEN

1 Matthew B. Ridgway and Harold H. Martin, *Soldier: The Memoirs of Matthew B. Ridgway* (Greenwood Press, 1956), page 65.

2 Letter from Willie to Rufina dated October 18, 1943.

3 Phil Nordyke, *All-American All the Way* (Zenith Press, 2005), p. 110.

4 Unit Journal of the 2nd Battalion, 504th Parachute Infantry Regiment, p. 22.

5 Ibid., p. 47.

6 Report of the 504th Parachute Infantry Combat Team in Operation Avalanche.

7 Ross S. Carter, *Those Devils in Baggy Pants* (Appleton-Century-Crofts, Inc., 1951), p. 128.

8 David Nichols, *Ernie's War: The Best of Ernie Pyle's World War II Dispatches* (New York: Random House, 1986), p. 172.

9 Lloyd Clark, *Anzio: Italy and the Battle for Rome—1944* (New York: Atlantic Monthly Press, 2006), pp. 40–41.

10 David Nichols, *Ernie's War: The Best of Ernie Pyle's World War II Dispatches* (New York: Random House, 1986), p. 172.

11 Unit Journal of the 2nd Battalion, 504th Parachute Infantry Regiment, p. 44.

12 Letter from Willie to Rufina dated December 13, 1943.

13 Rick Atkinson, *The Day of Battle* (New York: Henry Holt and Company, 2007), p. 291.

14 Phil Nordyke, *All-American All the Way* (Zenith Press, 2005), p. 163, quoting interview with Corporal Shelby Hord, Company H.

15 Lloyd Clark, *Anzio: Italy and the Battle for Rome—1944* (New York: Atlantic Monthly Press, 2006), p. 93.

16 James Megellas, *All the Way to Berlin: A Paratrooper at War in Europe* (New York: Presidio Press/Random House, 2003).

17 Ross S. Carter, *Those Devils in Baggy Pants* (Appleton-Century-Crofts, Inc., 1951), pp. 102–103.

18 James Megellas, *All the Way to Berlin: A Paratrooper at War in Europe* (New York: Presidio Press/Random House, 2003), p. 59.

19 Phil Nordyke, *All-American All the Way* (Zenith Press, 2005), p. 166.

20 James Megellas, *All the Way to Berlin: A Paratrooper at War in Europe* (New York: Presidio Press/Random House, 2003), p. 60.

21 Ibid.

22 Phil Nordyke, *All-American All the Way* (Zenith Press, 2005), p. 167.

23 Lloyd Clark, *Anzio: Italy and the Battle for Rome—1944* (New York: Atlantic Monthly Press, 2006), p. 115.

24 Captain William J. Sweet Jr, "Operations of the 2d Battalion, 504th Parachute Infantry Regiment (82nd Airborne Division) on the Anzio beachhead, 22 January to 23 March 1944, (Anzio campaign), (personal experience of a battalion operations officer and company commander)" (Infantry School, 1947–1948, courtesy of the Donovan Research Library, Fort Benning, Georgia), pp. 13 to 14, quoted in Phil Nordyke, *All-American All the Way* (Zenith Press, 2005), pp. 170–171.

25 Ibid.

26 Ibid.

27 Lloyd Clark, *Anzio: Italy and the Battle for Rome—1944* (New York: Atlantic Monthly Press, 2006), p. 155.

28 Ibid., pp. 227–228.

29 David Nichols, *Ernie's War: The Best of Ernie Pyle's World War II Dispatches* (New York: Random House, 1986).

30 Myers, Deb, editor, *Yank, the G.I. story of the war* (New York: Deull, Sloan & Pearce, 1947) p. 22.

31 Clark, p. 236

32 David Nichols, *Ernie's War: The Best of Ernie Pyle's World War II Dispatches* (New York: Random House, 1986), p. 248.

33 Lloyd Clark, *Anzio: Italy and the Battle for Rome—1944* (New York: Atlantic Monthly Press, 2006), pp. 259–260.

34 Ibid.

35 Phil Nordyke, *All-American All the Way* (Zenith Press, 2005), p. 182.

36 James Megellas, *All the Way to Berlin: A Paratrooper at War in Europe* (New York: Presidio Press/Random House, 2003), p. 68.

37 Letter from Father E. J. Kozak to Joseph Sandoval, March 4, 1944.

38 Ross S. Carter, *Those Devils in Baggy Pants* (Appleton-Century-Crofts, Inc., 1951), p. 179.

39 Interview, Joachim Liebschner, Sound Archive, Imperial War Museum, London, quoted in Lloyd Clark, *Anzio: Italy and the Battle for Rome—1944* (New York: Atlantic Monthly Press, 2006), p. 247.

40 David Nichols, *Ernie's War: The Best of Ernie Pyle's World War II Dispatches* (New York: Random House, 1986), pp. 258–259.

41 Ibid, p. 249.

42 Ibid.

43 Lloyd Clark, *Anzio: Italy and the Battle for Rome—1944* (New York: Atlantic Monthly Press, 2006), p. 260.

44 Lieutenant William D. Mandle and Private First Class David H. Whittier, "The Devils in Baggy Pants, Combat Record of the 504th Parachute Infantry Regiment, April 1943–July 1945" (Paris: Draeger Freres, 1945).

CHAPTER EIGHT

1 *New York Times* Staff. "Gen. Robert F. Seedlock, 91; Oversaw Building of Burma Road." *New York Times*, May 22, 2004.

2 Dod, Karl C., The Corps of Engineers: The War Against Japan. Washington, D.C.: Center of Military History, CMH Pub 10-6, 1966.

3 Durdin, Tillman. "General Pick Of 'Pick's Pike'; The builder of Stilwell Road is more like a country doctor than a hard-driving engineer." *New York Times*, Feb 11, 1945: SM7.

4 Monroe, Letter to Angelina Sandoval.

5 Wynter, Philip, "Life Reports: Elephants at War, In Burma, Big Beasts Work for Allied Army." *Life* magazine, April 10, 1944.

6   Nevin Wetzel, "Return to Burma," *Ex-CBI Roundup,* July 1979, http://cbi
-theater.home.comcast.net/~cbi-theater/menu/cbi_home.html (accessed
2013).

7   Captain Fred O. Lyons, as told to Paul Wilder in 1945, in "Merrill's Marauders in Burma," *Ex-CBI Roundup,* July 1991, http://cbi-theater-10.home.com
-cast.net/~cbi-theater-10/marauders/marauders.html (accessed 2013).

8   Ibid.

9   David W. Hogan, *India-Burma, 2 April 1942–28 January 1945,* CMH Pub
72-5 (U.S. Army, Center of Military History).

10 Frank, letter to brother Joe, Oct. 17, 1943.

11 Kessler, Lloyd, with Bart, Edmond B. *Never in Doubt: Remembering Iwo
Jima.* Annapolis Naval Institute Press, 1999.

12 Anonymous, "Ledo Diary, Excerpts from a road builder's diary," *THE
LEDO ROAD, China-Burma-India Theater of World War II,* http://home
.comcast.net/~ledoroad/Story_diary.html (accessed 2013).

13 Donovan Webster, *The Burma Road: The Epic Story of the China-Burma-
India Theater in World War II* (New York: Farrar, Straus and Giroux, 2003).

14 Ibid.

15 Ibid.

16 Ibid.

17 First Lieutenant John Walker Russell, "Into the Wildest Blue Yonder,"
Ex-CBI Roundup, http://cbi-theater-6.home.comcast.net/~cbi-theater-6/
blueyonder/blueyonder.html#TOP.

18 Ibid.

19 United States Army Air Forces Office of Flying Safety, Safety Education
Division. "Jungle Desert Arctic Ocean Survival Handbook." Washington,
D.C., 1943.

20 Gary J. Bjorge, *Merrill's Marauders: Combined Operations in Northen Burma
in 1944* (Washington, D.C.: U.S. Army Center of Military History, 1996).

21 Captain Fred O. Lyons, as told to Paul Wilder in 1945, in "Merrill's
Marauders in Burma," *Ex-CBI Roundup,* July 1991, http://cbi-theater-10
.home.comcast.net/~cbi-theater-10/marauders/marauders.html (accessed
2013).

22 David W. Hogan, *India-Burma, 2 April 1942–28 January 1945,* CMH Pub
72-5 (U.S. Army, Center of Military History).

23 Letter to Colonel Kai Rassmussen, June 14, 1944.

24 Kessler.

25 Ibid.

26 Ibid.

27 Monroe.

28 Ibid.

29 Ibid.

30 Murray A. Massin, "209th Engineer Combat Battalion Unit History," *Ex-CBI Roundup,* 1995, http://www.cbi-history.com/part_vi_209th_eng _combat_bn.html (accessed 2013).

CHAPTER NINE

1 John Adams, "6 August 1944 to 13 August 1944: letter to Chad Collins, 16 April 2001 " in *The World War II Experiences of John M. Adams, Jr.,* http:// donchesnut.com/johnadamswwii/index.htm.

2 Don R. Marsh, *Diary of Don R. Marsh,* http://www.2ndarmoredhellonwheels .com/Don_R_Marsh_Diary/diary_entry_4.html.

3 Omar N. Bradley, *A General's Life: An Autobiography* (New York: Simon and Schuster, 1983).

4 Ernie Pyle, "A Slow Cautious Business." August 11, 1944.

5 U.S. Army, ""Fighting in Normandy," in *Combat Lessons—Rank and file in combat: What they're doing; How they do it,* NO. 4 (Washington, D.C.: War Department, 1944).

6 Second Lieutenant David Garth, with additional documentation by Colonel Charles H. Taylor, *ST-LO (7 July–19 July 1944),* American Forces in Action Series, Historical Division, War Department (Washington, D.C.: Center of Military History, 1946).

7 Ibid.

8 Omar N. Bradley, *A General's Life: An Autobiography* (New York: Simon and Schuster, 1983).

9 Chester B. Hansen, War Diaries, Chester B. Hansen Collection, U.S. Army Military History Institute, http://cdm16635.contentdm.oclc.org/ cdm/ref/collection/p16635coll16/id/3658.

10 Sullivan, J. J. "The Botched Air Support of Operation Cobra." *Parameters,* 1988: 97-110.

11 Barry Basden and Charles Scheffel, *Crack! and Thump: With a Combat Infantry Officer in World War II* (Llano, Texas: Camroc Press, 2007).

12 Omar N. Bradley, *A General's Life: An Autobiography* (New York: Simon and Schuster, 1983).

13 U.S. Army, "First United States Report of Operations 20 October 1943 to 1 August 1944" (1946).

14 Martin Blumenson, "Closing the Pocket," in Martin Bluemenson, *Breakout and Pursuit* (Washington, D.C.: Center of Military History, U.S. Army, 1960).

15 Ibid.

16 Ibid.

17 Major Robert Kerley, *Operations of the 2nd Battalion, 120th Infantry (30th Infantry Division) at Morain, France 6–12 August 1944* (Monograph, U.S. Army).

18 Ibid.

19 Ibid.

20 Ibid.

21 Ibid.

CHAPTER TEN

1 Anais Nin, *The Diary of Anais Nin, Vol. 4: 1944–1947* (Orlando, FL: Harcourt, Brace, Jovanovich, 1971).

2 Martin Blumenson, "Closing the Pocket," in Martin Bluemenson, *Breakout and Pursuit* (Washington, D.C.: Center of Military History, U.S. Army, 1960).

3 http://www.ibiblio.org/hyperwar/USA/USA-E-Breakout/USA -E-Breakout-27.html.

4 Letter, Kluge to Hitler, August 18, translated by MIRS London, May 28, 1945, CRS Files, EAP 21-X/15; Kluge's Farewell to Hitler, August 18, M.I.-14/7, OCMH Files; see Hodgson's translation in R-58; see also Bormann File on Kluge in OCMH Files. Eberbach believed later that Kluge might have averted the defeat in August by disobeying Hitler and withdrawing to the Seine at the beginning of the month, but Eberbach conceded that Kluge was being watched so closely after the July 20 putsch that a false step would have resulted in his immediate relief and the substitution of a more manageable commander. MS # A-922 (Eberbach).

5 Ibid.

6 12th AGp WD Observers Bd Ltr, AGF Bd Rpt, ETO, No. 208, Visit to Falaise Pocket, 31 Aug.

7 Hitler Msg, quoted in full in Msg, OB WEST to AGp B, 1100, 23 Aug, AGp B Fuehrerbefehle. Choltitz (Soldat unter Soldaten, pp. 255-59) and Schramm (MS # B-034) date Hitler's order as August 22, and it is pos-

sible that some commanders received the substance of the message before the official reception and recording of it. The AGp B KTB reports the order in an entry at 1030, 23 August.

8 Martin Blumenson, "The Liberation of Paris," in Martin Bluemenson, *Breakout and Pursuit* (Washington, D.C.: Center of Military History, U.S. Army, 1960).

9 Adrien Dansette, *Histoire de la libération de Paris (1946), réédition* (Paris: Perrin, 1994).

10 Omar N. Bradley, *A General's Life: An Autobiography* (New York: Simon and Schuster, 1983), p. 391.

11 Larry Collins and Dominique Lapierre, *Is Paris Burning?* (New York: Warner Books, 1965).

12 David Nichols, *Ernie's War: The Best of Ernie Pyle's World War II Dispatches* (New York: Random House, 1986), pp. 351–354.

13 Larry Collins and Dominique Lapierre, *Is Paris Burning?* (New York: Warner Books, 1965), p. 301.

14 Peter Chen, *Liberation of Paris, 25 Aug 1944,* World War 2 Database, http://ww2db.com/battle_spec.php?battle_id=115.

15 Leo Hart. Interview with author.

16 Captain Carl W. Kappel, *The Operations of Company "H," 504th Parachute Infantry (82nd Airborne Division) in the Invasion of Holland 17–21 September 1944 (Rhineland Campaign) (Personal Experience of a Rifle Company Commander),* Advanced Infantry Officers Course, 1948–1949, General Subjects Section, Academic Department, the Infantry School, Fort Benning, Georgia.

17 Joseph Charles Watts Jr., "The Capture of the Maas River Bridge During Operation Market Garden," The Drop Zone, http://thedropzone.org/europe/Holland/watts.htm.

18 Major General James W. Gavin, 82nd Airborne Division, Operation Market Historical Data, 1946.

19 Hart.

20 Forrest Dawson, *Saga of the All-American: History of the 82nd Airborne Division, World War II* (Nashville, Tenn.: Battery Press, new edition, March 1980).

21 Lieutenant John Holabird, 307th Engineers, 504 RCT, Interview "The Second Omaha Beach"—Crossing the Waal, the Drop Zone Virtual Museum, http://www.thedropzone.org/europe/holland/waal1.htm.

22 Second Lieutenant Eward J. Sims, Sicily and Holland with the 504th Parachute Infantry Regiment, 82nd Airborne Division, Brookdale Community

College Center for World War II Studies and Conflict Resolution, http://www.brookdalecc.edu/pages/960.asp.

23 Cornelius Ryan, *A Bridge Too Far* (New York: Simon & Schuster, 1974).

24 Ibid.

25 Thomas Pitt, S-1, 3rd Battalion, 504th Parachute Regiment, The Waal River Crossing, An Interview with Thomas Pitt, the Drop Zone Virtual Museum, http://www.thedropzone.org/europe/Holland/pitt.html.

26 Ibid.

27 82nd Airborne Unit History, the 82nd Airborne During World War II, Campaigns—Rhineland, http://www.ww2-airborne.us/division/campaigns/holland.html.

28 Charles B. MacDonald, *The Siegfried Line Campaign* (Washington, D.C.: Office of the Chief of Military History, Department of the Army, 1963).

29 Johanna Mason, interview by Cornelius Ryan, *Johanna Mason, nee Bremen*. Adler Library, Ohio University.

30 William Watson. Interview with author.

31 Ibid.

32 Letter to Joseph Sandoval from Major General Edward F. Witsell, April 11, 1947.

CHAPTER ELEVEN

1 United Press, "U.S. 2d Armored Unit in Action in Germany," *New York Times*, October 5, 1944.

2 Charles B. MacDonald, *The Siegfried Line Campaign* (Washington, D.C.: Office of the Chief Of Military History, Department Of The Army , 1963).

3 Lida Mayo, "Lessons of the Roer and the Ardennes," in *The Ordnance Department: On Beachhead and Battlefront* (Washington, D.C.: Center of Military History, United States Army, 1991).

4 Ibid.

5 Harry Yeide, *Longest Battle: September 1944 to February 1945—From Aachen to the Roer and Across (St. Paul, Minnesota:* Zenith Press, 2005) p. 151.

6 Ibid.

7 Ibid.

8 Ibid.

9 *Time*, December 11, 1944.

10 Letter from Joe Sandoval, November 30, 1944.

11 Roger Rutland, first sergeant, 106th Infantry, in PBS, *The American Experience*, "The Battle of the Bulge: World War II's Deadliest Battle," Novem-

ber 9, 1994, http://www.pbs.org/wgbh/americanexperience/features/transcript/bulge-transcript/?flavour=mobile.

12 Donald L. Miller and Henry Steele Commager, *The Story of World War II* (New York: Touchstone, 1945).

13 Ibid.

14 Ibid.

15 *Time*, "War Crimes: Clemency," January 17, 1949, http://content.time.com/time/magazine/article/0,9171,780092,00.html#ixzz2i5qclHhV.

16 Donald L. Miller and Henry Steele Commager, *The Story of World War II* (New York: Touchstone, 1945).

17 Roger Rutland, first sergeant, 106th Infantry, in PBS, *The American Experience*, "The Battle of the Bulge: World War II's Deadliest Battle," November 9, 1994.

18 Bart Hagerman, private, 17th Airborne, in PBS, *The American Experience*, "The Battle of the Bulge: World War II's Deadliest Battle," November 9, 1994, http://www.pbs.org/wgbh/americanexperience/features/transcript/bulge-transcript/?flavour=mobile.

19 Captain Ralph Kinnes, "The Operations of Company C, 513th PIR (17th Airborne Division), in the Attack on Flamierge, Belgium, 4 January 1945 (Ardennes Campaign)."

20 Major Murray L. Harvey, "Operations of the 3d Battalion, 507th Parachute Infantry (17th Airborne Division) 'The Battle of Dead Man's Ridge,' Vicinity of Laval-Chisogne, Belgium, 7 1945 (Ardennes Campaign)" (Infantry School, Fort Benning, Georgia).

21 Ibid.

22 Information Section, Army Ground Forces Fact Sheets, U.S. Army, 1947.

23 Robert E. Merriam, *World War II Journal: Battle of the Bulge* (Bennington, Vermont: Merriam Press, 2007).

24 St. Vith Offensive After Action Report, January 16–20, 1945.

25 Marc Wilson, *Hero Street USA: The Story of Little Mexico's Fallen Soldiers* (Norman, Oklahoma: 2009).

26 Robert E. Merriam, *World War II Journal: Battle of the Bulge* (Bennington, Vermont: Merriam Press, 2007).

CHAPTER TWELVE

1 Robert F. Gallagher, "World War II Story by Robert F. Gallagher," http://www.gallagher.com/ww2/index.html.

2 Ibid.

3 Ibid.

4 Ibid.

5 Edda West, "The Dresden Bombing—An Eyewitness Account," *Current Concerns*, 2003.

6 Kurt Vonnegut, "The Art of Fiction No. 64," *Paris Review*, 1977.

7 Ibid.

8 Lloyd Clark, *Crossing the Rhine: Breaking into Nazi Germany, 1944 and 1945—the Greatest Airborne Battles in History (New York:* Atlantic Monthly Press, 2008), p. 315.

9 Source: Pavel Bergmann. He says it's a copy of a 139th AEB Pamphlet printed after the war. Printed by Alfred Selb Muelheim, Rhur, and signed by Lt. Col. S.T.B. Johnson. No more info about.

10 Robert Capa, "World: This Invasion Was Different," *Time*, April 2, 1945, http://content.time.com/time/magazine/article/0,9171,775473,00.html#ixzz2mvHnSEXj

11 Ibid.

12 Ibid.

13 Johnson. Unit History.

CHAPTER THIRTEEN

1 Letter from Joe Sandoval to his father, March 6, 1945.

2 Lieutenant Colonel John Beckner, Military Monograph/analysis.

3 Charles B. MacDonald, *The Last Offensive Pursuit* (Washington, D.C.: Center of Military History, U.S. Army, 1973).

4 Edward Murrow, "They Died 900 a Day in 'the Best' Nazi Death Camp," *PM*, April 16, 1945, http://www.jewishvirtuallibrary.org/jsource/Holocaust/murrow.html.

5 Ibid.

6 Associated Press, April 19, 1945.

7 Captain Fredric Pamp, "XIX Corps history, Normandy to the Elbe, 1945," http://www.scribd.com/doc/180289285/XIX-Corp-Normandy-to-the-Elba-pdf.

8 Lieutenant Colonel Louis Correll, interview in official military history "Elbe Operation," Chapter II, "Westerhausen Crossing," http://www.history.army.mil/documents/elbe-fm.htm.

9 Ibid.

10 "Elbe Operation," Chapter III, "Southern Switch," http://www.history.army.mil/documents/elbe-ch3.htm.

11 Ibid.

12 Ibid.

13 Ibid.

14 Letter to Jose Sandoval, April 1945.

15 Ernie Pyle, "On Victory in Europe," *Indiana University School of Journalism: Ernie Pyle,* http://journalism.indiana.edu/resources/erniepyle/war time-columns/on-victory-in-europe/.

16 Reg Ingraham, "Death in Milan," *Time*, May 7, 1945.

CHAPTER FOURTEEN

1 Donald L. Miller and Henry Steele Commager, *The Story of World War II* (New York: Touchstone, 1945).

2 Ibid.

3 Lloyd Kessler with Edmond B. Bart, *Never in Doubt: Remembering Iwo Jima* (Annapolis Naval Institute Press, 1999).

4 Donald L. Miller and Henry Steele Commager, *The Story of World War II* (New York: Touchstone, 1945).

5 Ibid.

6 J. Robert Oppenheimer, Interview, television documentary, "The Decision to Drop the Bomb." 1965. http://www.youtube.com/watch?v=26Y LehuMydo.

CHAPTER FIFTEEN

1 David Nichols, *Ernie's War: The Best of Ernie Pyle's World War II Dispatches* (New York: Simon & Schuster, 1st Touchstone edition, 1987).

2 Ibid.

3 Donald L. Miller and Henry Steele Commager, *The Story of World War II.* (New York: Touchstone, 1945).

4 Terry Garza. Interview with author.

5 John Puebla. Interview with author.

6 Mary Beserra. Interview with author.

7 Phil Garza. Interview with author.

8 "Zoot Suiters Seized on Coast After Clashes With Service Men," *New York Times*, June 7, 1943.

9 Harry S. Truman, "Statement by the President on the Violation of the 38th Parallel in Korea," June 26, 1950. Online by Gerhard Peters and John T. Woolley, *The American Presidency Project.* http://www.presidency.ucsb .edu/ws/?pid=13537.

10 Captain Patrick J. Donahue, "The Danger of Poor Training Management: The Us Army in Korea—July, 1959," Military Analysis, U.S. Army Maneuver Center of Excellence, Fort Benning, Georgia, 1986.

11 T. R. Fehrenbach, *This Kind of War* (New York: MacMillan, 1963).

12 Terry Garza. Interview with author.

13 Raoul "Buddy" Gomez. Interview with author.

14 Terry Garza. Interview with author.

CHAPTER SIXTEEN

1 James W. Stemple, "James Stemple, Korean War Veteran of the United States Marine Corps," *Korean War Educator,* http://www.thekwe.org/memoirs/stemple_james/index.htm.

2 Preston Solomon, interview with author., December 6, 2008.

3 Richard Bohart, interview by Lynnita Brown, "Veterans' Memoirs: Richard Bohart," *Korean War Educator,* 2000, http://www.koreanwar-educator.org/memoirs/bohart_richard/index.htm#SpringOffensive.

4 Joe Gomez. Letter to Tony Soliz, May 1, 1951.

5 Ibid.

6 Solomon.

7 Solomon.

8 Letter from Joe Gomez to Tony Soliz, May 1, 1951.

9 Russell A. Gugeler, *Combat Actions in Korea* (CMH Publication 30-2) (Washington, D.C.: Center for Military History, 1984).

10 Ibid.

11 Ibid.

12 Mary Ramirez. Interview with author.

13 President's Radio Report to the American People on Korea and on U.S. Policy in the Far East, April 11, 1951, *Public Papers of the Presidents*, p. 223. http://books.google.com/books.

14 Johnny Muños. Letter to Tony Soliz, Aug. 13, 1951.

15 Ruth Tenzer Feldman, *The Korean War: Chronicle of America's Wars* (Minneapolis: Lerner Publications Co., 2004).

16 Muños letter to Soliz, August 13, 1951.

17 Lieutenant Clark C. Munroe, *The Second Infantry Division in Korea 1950–1951* (Tokyo: Toppan Printing, 1952).

18 Ibid.

CHAPTER SEVENTEEN

1 Civil Rights Congress, We Charge Genocide: The Historic Petition to the United Nations for Relief From a Crime of The United States Government Against the Negro People (New York: Civil Rights Congress, 1951), pp. xi-xiii, 3-10. See more at: http://www.blackpast.org/we-charge-genocide -historic-petition-united-nations-relief-crime-united-states-government -against#sthash.bZkSAKmR.dpuf.

INDEX

INDEX

INDEX

INDEX